TAKE A NEW BEARING

TAKE A NEW BEARING

Skills and Sensitive Strategies for Sharing Spiders, Stars, Shelters, Safety, and Solitude

Phyllis M. Ford

American Camping Association®

Many Thanks to:

Girl Scouts of the U.S.A.
for the use of illustrations from *Outdoor Education in Girl Scouting* in chapters seven, eight and nine.

Camp Fire Inc.
for the use of illustrations from *The Outdoor Book.*

Eastern Pennsylvania Section, American Camping Association
for the financial support they provided in the development of this book and other Outdoor Living Skills materials.

American Camping Association
5000 State Road 67 North
Martinsville, IN 46151-7902
317/342-8456 American Camping Association National Office
800/428-CAMP American Camping Association Publications Office
317/342-2065 FAX

Library of Congress Cataloging-in-Publications Data
Ford, Phyllis M.
Take a new bearing : skills and sensitive strategies for sharing spiders, stars, shelters, safety, and solitude / Phyllis M. Ford.
p.cm.
Includes bibliographical references (p.) and index.
ISBN 0-87603-119-X : $17.95
1. Outdoor recreation — Study and teaching 2. Outdoor education. 3.Environmental education. I. American Camping Association. II. Title.
GV181.35.F68 1991
790'.07 — dc20   91-2007
                                                          CIP

Outdoor Living Skills Pledge

I pledge:

to be among the animals and plants,
and in providing for my comfort and safety,
to respect my natural neighbors and their homes;
to step carefully and travel gently,
finding friendship and beauty in my natural world.

Contents

Outdoor Living Skills

Take a New Bearing is the leader handbook of the American Camping Association's Outdoor Living Skills Program. This program provides the new skills we need to love and explore our world while preserving it for future generations. Each time we travel through a natural area, whether on a short hike or a week-long backpacking adventure, we make choices — choices that impact our environment. Without a set of environmental values we are apt to value only ourselves without consideration for the natural inhabitants (plants and animals).

ACA's program is divided into five levels and participants can enter at any point depending on their maturity and existing camping skills. There are no age requirements per say. Level one can be successful with participants as young as five or six.

Many materials have been published to support the OLS. Besides this leader handbook, there are brightly-colored recognition patches and tracking booklets for participants. The pocket-sized *OLS Trackers* list all of the skill requirements for each level, provide a place for the leader to initial accomplishments, room to write safety rules, outline trip responsibilities, or sketch a cloud or two. There is also a super poster and an *OLS*

Instructor Manual. All materials are available from the ACA Bookstore.

While you train as a leader you may want to refer to the information contained in each *OLS Tracker.* It is provided at the end of this book. To help you overview the skill areas in the program, a detailed skills schematic is given also.

Training for both leaders and program directors is available all across the United States. Training is offered by local offices of the American Camping Association and by other youth serving organizations. Contact the American Camping Association for more information.

American Camping Association
5000 State Road 67 North
Martinsville, IN 46151-7902
800/428-CAMP ACA Bookstore
317/342-8456 American Camping Association

1

Getting Started

Why is the outdoors such a fascinating place? How can we enjoy it fully? Can we enjoy the environment and protect it at the same time? You'll find the answers to these and many more questions in this book. You'll learn outdoor-living skills that keep people safe, comfortable, and happy in an environment that is only temporarily their home. You'll also learn minimum-impact camping skills that help people leave the outdoors just the way they found it or even better.

As you read, remember that in this book, *outdoor activities* means recreational activities that depend on natural resources (plants, animals, land, or water), and *outdoor-living skills* refers to activities using, understanding, and/or appreciating natural resources.

So . . . What's So Great About the Outdoors?

Outdoor activities are among the most popular forms of recreation for North Americans and people from many other parts of the world. Still, many people don't understand the attraction to outdoor recreation. Could you explain to them why it appeals to you?

Like many others who enjoy outdoor living, you might say that the outdoors represents a certain amount of freedom; there are no walls and no ceilings, so you don't feel hemmed in. Or perhaps you'd talk about the clean, fresh air, or the beauty and serenity of nature. You might explain that the outdoors is a place where you can have adventures, test your skills, and venture into unknown territory; Almost everyone likes to try new things, and there are many new things to try in the outdoors. You may also say that you feel at ease outdoors; for one thing, you don't have to dress up to go camping.

Whatever draws you to the outdoors, the same things might appeal to other people. Sharing your thoughts about the appeal of outdoor living will help them appreciate it too.

What Kind of People Go Outdoors Anyway?

In early human history, everyone was a camper. Camping really means housekeeping outdoors, and all primitive people made their homes outdoors; there were no houses or even tents. Gradually, humans learned to build shelters, make clothes; eventually they, developed cities and became indoor dwellers. Almost as soon as they had comfortable houses to which they could return when they became cold, wet, or tired, they returned to the outdoors for recreation.

Today, nine of every ten Americans participates in some form of outdoor recreation every year; using understanding, or simply appreciation of nature. Grandparents plant gardens to grow fresh vegetables or beautiful flowers. Parents push strollers through parks to enjoy the fresh air and well-kept landscapes. People of all ages walk, hike, boat, explore, swim, and ride bicycles. People who use wheelchairs or crutches, people who are blind or deaf, and those who have asthma, diabetes, rheumatic fever, or other conditions that may limit some of their activities also enjoy the outdoors. Big-city, small-town, and rural residents, rich and poor alike, seek the outdoors for recreation.

You may wonder, then, if people who enjoy outdoor activities have any common characteristics. They do. Following is a list of those traits. Both leaders and participants may already have some of these traits and can develop the others; both will also have many that are not listed here. The characteristics that seem to be common among most outdoor enthusiasts are as follows:

- They want to be outdoors. This is the most important trait of people who enjoy nature. They really want to see what's out there.

- They don't mind being away from home overnight. Even if they've never tried it, they're willing and are usually eager to do so.

- They are willing to be cooperative members of a group. These people can work together on such things as planning a trip, pitching tents, finding drinking water, and cooking. They're cooperative not just with their best friends or people they already know, but also with new friends with whom they may have only one thing in common — they want to be there, too.

- They have a spirit of adventure. Those who love outdoor living are comfortable with new and different things such as unfamiliar sounds at night, meals that are very different from their favorite fast-food and from Mom's good cooking. They're capable of living without electricity, indoor plumbing, and hot water, as well as living with insects and perhaps rain, clouds and wind.

- They can get along without total privacy. They can share a tent with another camper.

- They can follow instructions. Whether the instructions are written or verbal, they will follow them willingly and correctly.

- They can take care of their belongings. This means keeping their personal items organized and reasonably clean, even in a small tent or backpack.

- They enjoy housekeeping outdoors. People who like camping usually like cooking, cleaning up, getting water, and practicing other outdoor-living skills, and they want to do these things with other campers.

- They enjoy activity. These people don't want to just sit and watch; they want to be involved. However, they are also comfortable sitting quietly and observing; a very different level of activity.

Of course, not everyone is immediately enthusiastic about being outdoors. Those who are introduced to camping as part of a group situation may enjoy the outdoors but might be uncomfortable with the group. Those who attend youth camps through an organization to which they belong may like their fellow campers but might be apprehensive about being with them in a strange environment. And some people don't enjoy either the group or the outdoors — at least in the beginning. That's natural though; nearly everyone who enjoys camping today, went through a process of change. Maybe you did too. At first, you were unfamiliar with the outdoors (and perhaps a bit frightened there), but eventually you became comfortable and at home in natural surroundings.

With time and patience, even the most reluctant person may learn to like being in an outdoor setting. Much of this change may come because of the understanding and consideration of the leader and others in the group. Campers will never have equal interest in, enthusiasm for, or knowledge of the outdoors, but you can help them develop their interests and skills beyond the ones they brought to the program. In time, they may even develop the traits listed earlier in this chapter, and become enthusiastic, fun-loving group workers who want to learn and grow through an outdoor experience.

Where Is . . . *Outdoors*?

With a little imagination — and respect for private property — you'll find thousands of places to enjoy nature and use out-door-living skills. Even if you live in a city, you probably have access to parks, picnic areas, and playgrounds. You can even practice many outdoor-living skills in your own backyard or school-yard.

Among the best places to go, of course, are the thousands of youth and adult camps in the United States and Canada. Many youth agencies and churches sponsor camps of some type; as do other not-for-profit organizations and private individuals.

If you are not familiar with the camps in this country, contact the American Camping Association, 5000 State Road 67 North, Martinsville, IN 46151-7902, and ask for information. They can tell you how to find camps that specialize in outdoor-living skills.

These camps are in every state and in all kinds of settings — in the mountains, in forests, on the coast, or near rivers.

Every state and nearly every county offers public parks. Most of these parks permit people to cook outdoors, explore the grounds and camp overnight at either designated sites or in more primitive areas away from roads and formal camp-grounds. State forests are ideal places to practice camping skills farther away from the amenities of city life.

On the federal level, the U.S. Forest Service manages more than 100,000 miles of trails in 156 national forests. The Bureau of Land Management manages thousands of acres west of the Mississippi River, and many of those areas are available for camping. Also, the U.S. Army Corps of Engineers operates some camping sites and leases many others to counties.

You can enjoy an excellent outdoor-living experience at a national park. However, don't expect to be able to use all your outdoor-living skills in every national park; many parks have historical or scientific importance, and as a result, visitors' activities may be restricted. Still, you can use both simple and advanced outdoor skills at most parks, by staying in or near well-developed campgrounds, or traveling into the back-country to camp under more primitive conditions.

Finally, consider visiting a federal wildlife refuge. Most wildlife refuges do not permit camping, but you can observe wildlife, take photographs, study nature, and go hiking. You may even be allowed to go boating.

So many places offer outdoor recreation that it's impossible to list them all. At the end of this chapter is a list of agencies you may contact for more information.

How Do Campers Travel?

Getting to an outdoor-recreation area usually requires motor-ized transportation — buses, trains, automobiles, motor-homes, or camping trailers. Some people, however, travel by bicycle, by boat, on horseback, or on foot, and they continue to use these modes of transportation when they get where they're going. However you travel to your campsite, expect to travel under your own power once you arrive. Remember to take into account the physical condition of your group members when structuring your outdoor activities so that they can enjoy the experience.

One important outdoor-living skill is knowing *how* to travel, so when you walk, paddle, or ride, use good judgment about how far you can expect to go in one day. Eight miles may be enough for a hike, especially when you're carrying a pack; ten to twelve miles is probably enough when you're paddling downstream in a loaded canoe; a bicycle trip of ten to fifty miles is reasonable depending on the wind direction and the load you're carrying. As a group leader, you must know how far your group can travel (include enough time and energy to get back to base camp if that is the plan).

Travel skills require strength and energy. For many people, these skills involve some form of movement across land or water — walking, biking, horseback riding, paddling, sailing or rowing. For some, transportation may also include using a wheelchair or crutches. For others, travel skills may simply mean driving to a site and setting up camp. No matter how you travel to your site, travel skills also include packing equipment in such a way that it will arrive in good condition. If you pack carefully, you'll be able to participate in all the activities you planned, because you have everything you need.

What Next?

As many things as there are to do outdoors, the most popular activity is walking. Walking includes everything from strolling in the fresh air, to hiking miles with a pack on your back.

The second most popular activity is one that everyone enjoys — eating. Some people like to pack a cold lunch before they leave home or camp; others prefer to cook hamburgers or a one-pot meal over charcoal. Eating outdoors can even involve elaborate preparation, such as baking in a reflector oven, roasting chicken on a stick, or making ice cream in a hay hole.

Beyond walking and eating, the list of favorite outdoor activities goes on forever. While many campers want to learn all they can about the area — its rocks, plants, animals, waterfalls, land formations, weather, and so forth — others want to explore the area using a map and compass, or simply rest and look at the scenery. Outdoor activities can be sedentary, such as writing poetry or telling stories, or active, such as picking berries for making pies or pancakes.

Can you think of others? Your list may include the following: rock climbing, canoeing, hiking, cross-country skiing, snow-shoeing, fishing, beachcombing, bird-watching, taking photographs, sketching, rock hunting, singing and yodeling, catching butterflies, and searching for Native American artifacts.

Members of a group may want to vote on activities. In this way, no one does only the thing he or she selects, but is exposed to a wider variety of activities. This will also afford the group a sense of togetherness. No group can afford to disintegrate into individuals going off in different directions, which may mean chaos.

To Be Comfortable . . . or Not to Be Comfortable?

One reason why many people don't want to participate in outdoor activities is that they don't know how to be comfortable. They may have had a bad experience with mosquitoes or poison ivy, or didn't know how to dress properly, or brought too much or too little equipment. Perhaps they find the outdoors to be too hot, too cold, too dirty, too buggy, too unfamiliar, or just plain boring.

For many people, outdoor experiences are *new* experiences. These people aren't comfortable outdoors because they've never had any experience doing things in an environment where there are no telephones, stores, traffic noises and other things that make them feel at home. After all, most of us are accustomed to indoor toilets, flowing tap water, refrigerators and microwave ovens, screens on the windows, and heating and air conditioning. Why should anyone venture into the unknown, where he/she might have to cook over a smoky fire; dig a toilet; purify water for drinking; crawl into a tiny tent to stay dry on a rainy night; and worry about skunks, snakes, and who knows what else all night? No wonder many first-time campers are uncomfortable and not quite sure they want to be there.

Almost everyone can become comfortable outdoors. However, comfort comes in two forms — physical and psychological — and outdoor-living skills applies to both.

Physical comfort

The first consideration for most campers is physical comfort. No one likes to be too hot, cold or wet. How much is *too much* is often a matter of individual opinion — some people prefer cold and some prefer hot temperatures. Still, remember, a person who feels uncomfortable won't enjoy any outdoor experience.

The following factors contribute to physical comfort:

1. Dressing correctly and having adequate shelter. (See chapter 3, "On Your Way.")

2. Getting enough sleep and rest before a trip. If hikers, boaters, or even the cooks are tired, they not only won't have fun, but may present a risk themselves and to the rest of the group by not being at full energy or mental capacity.

3. Being in good physical shape. Physical conditioning helps prevent muscle cramps and the possibility of hypothermia and hyperthermia. Physical conditioning includes proper rest. (See chapter 3, "On Your Way," and chapter 4, "Being Safe.")

4. Preparing and eating enough of the right kinds of food to maintain high energy levels. The right types of food also help prevent muscle cramping, fatigue, and hyperthermia and hypothermia. (See chapter 6, "Putting It On Your Plate.")

5. Drinking adequate amounts of water. Knowing how to find it and how to ensure its purity are two of the most important outdoor-living skills. (See chapter 4, "Being Safe.")

In review, the things that make people physically comfortable are proper body temperature maintained by proper clothing and shelter, adequate safe drinking water, adequate rest and sleep, and sufficient amounts of high-energy food. As the leader of a group venturing into the outdoors, you'll have a great responsibility from the beginning. You must insist that each participant (yourself included) have proper clothing; sufficient water, food and rest; and be in the proper physical condition for the planned activities. You must consider all these things *before* anyone sets off into the outdoors.

Psychological comfort

Psychological comfort refers to how people feel mentally and emotionally.

Perhaps our greatest psychological need is the assurance that our biological needs have been met. If the members of your group are *physically comfortable* and know they have the right equipment to maintain this comfort, their biological needs will be met. They won't worry about being hot, cold, wet, hungry, or thirsty. Mentally and emotionally, they'll be more inclined to feel good about their situation and responsive to the outdoors.

Our second greatest psychological need is emotional security. Knowing that we're not going to be harassed, ridiculed or scolded, plays an integral part in our emotional security. Members of your group need to feel secure under your leadership and with the group; assured of no threat of abuse, violence, or ridicule. Certainly, emotional security, along with physical comfort, contributes to psychological comfort.

Your group members also need to feel that they understand enough about the outdoors to be competent campers; they need to know that they'll be all right outdoors and that there is safety in being part of the group.

Anyone who has had a great deal of experience outdoors may not be able to imagine what there is to worry about when participating in an outdoor experience. Of course, people worry about being physically uncomfortable and about not feeling at home with the group, but what is there in nature to worry about? Fear of the unknown, is commonly what worries people about the outdoors, or about any unfamiliar environment. The unknown may be such innocuous things as darkness, open spaces, or just being away from home. Or it may be unfamiliar plants, animals and sounds. If people don't know, for example, that animals fear humans and will run away from them, or if they believe the old stories about marauding wild beasts, they may be very frightened.

Third on the list of psychological needs is a sense of belonging. Every member of your group needs to feel that he/she is wanted, that he/she can make a contribution, that the leader accepts him/her, and that the other group members feel they can rely on him/her. It is up to you, the leader, to make sure that everyone feels that he/she belongs and is a competent member of the group. Leaders may be able to perform many tasks better than group members; however, doing so only teaches campers to be dependent on the leader. The leader should facilitate learning experiences that help campers increase their understanding and skills. As group members participate, learn, and contribute to the group, their sense of belonging, worth, and commitment to the group will increase.

Another way you can make people feel that they belong is to earn their trust. Never ridicule or undermine your group members' efforts. Never play practical jokes on the group or try to frighten them. Never do anything that would destroy the confidence that group members must have in you if they are to enjoy the experience and feel comfortable.

In summary, what makes people feel comfortable is knowing that their physical needs are met, being emotionally and physically secure, and feeling that they belong to the group.

Skills Campers Need

In order to be physically and psychologically comfortable and safe in the outdoors, campers need to know the following:

- How to take care of themselves.
- What equipment they need and why, and how to use it.
- How to keep from getting lost.
- How to find potable (safe) water.
- How to pack, prepare and store food.
- How to use a stove safely.
- How to read and follow a map.
- How to administer basic first-aid.
- How to function competently and responsibly in a natural environment.

The rest of this book discusses skills for outdoor living and how to teach others those skills. It's recommended that you read the next three chapters in order, because information on comfort and safety must come first. Then you can go on to learn about the other skills for living outdoors. At the end of the book is a list of references that may help you increase your knowledge of those skills.

For More Information On Sites

Each of the following agencies administers federal properties, and each has different policies for their recreational use. You should investigate all categories of recreational land before you select an area in which to practice your outdoor-living skills.

Bureau of Land Management
Office of the Director
U.S. Department of the Interior
Washington, DC 20240
(This agency manages lands primarily in the western states.)

Bureau of Land Reclamation
U.S. Department of the Interior
Washington, DC 20240
(This agency supervises much of the water resources in the Western states.)

U.S. Fish and Wildlife Service
Office of the Director
U.S. Department of the Interior
Washington, DC 20240
(This agency administers federal wildlife refuges and controls migratory animals and birds.)

National Park Service
U.S. Department of the Interior
Washington, DC 20240
(This agency administers national parks; monuments; seashores; lakeshores; recreational areas; and other scenic, scientific, and historical sites.)

Forest.S. Forest Service Service
U.S. Department of Agriculture
Washington, DC 20013
(This agency administers national forests.)

Check a library for your state-government directory, which contains addresses of park departments, game commissions, tourism bureaus, natural resources departments, conservation departments, and recreation commissions.

Also contact your county and municipal parks systems, as well as the youth and adult camps in your area. For a complete list of accredited camps, write to:

American Camping Association, Inc.
5000 State Road 67 North
Martinsville, IN 46151-7902.

Sharing Strategies

There are many aspects to being an effective leader. One important skill a leader must nurture is the ability to see the members of the group as individuals. A leader must be able to stand back and observe, not mistaking his/her personality for the personality of the group or of any group member. A leader must realize that there are many differences among people.

You'll find the following differences in almost every group:

Disabilities. Almost everyone has some disabling condition that makes his/her learning and participating different from that of the other group members. Some people wear glasses; some have allergies; some have braces on their teeth. Others may suffer from epilepsy, diabetes, asthma, a heart condition, poor hearing, a speech impediment, loss of sight, or another disability. And even those who have no permanent disability, may have a temporary one: a cold, hay fever, a sprained ankle, or an uncomfortable case of poison ivy. At least one of every ten people has some disability that causes a handicap. Always expect to find conditions such as these in every group.

Varying abilities. Just as disabilities vary among people, so do abilities. The leader's job is to help each member of the group identify his/her abilities and use them to his/her advantage. A leader should never allow any group member to degrade another.

Sizes and shapes. Contrary to what modern advertising wants us to believe, not everyone is thin, tall, and good-looking. The heights of sixth-graders vary by as much as eighteen inches, and weights vary by as much as a hundred pounds. Adults, too, exhibit many differences in size and shape. Some people cannot reach the stepping stones that others use to cross a creek; many cannot wear other people's backpacks without the packs bumping the backs of their thighs. The program leader must remember to plan for the smallest and weakest participants as well as for those who are large and strong.

Energy and strength. Older participants commonly have more endurance than younger participants do. Young participants may have short bursts of energy and speed; older ones may have endurance but no speed. People who are in good shape and those who feel no apprehension tend to move faster than those who are undernourished, obese, out of shape, frightened, or just plain uncomfortable.

Intelligence. Leaders must realize that participants' intelligence will vary and must consider both high and low IQs in their planning. Leaders should meet this challenge with understanding, patience, and absence of predetermined opinions about group members' intellectual abilities.

Experience. Program participants will have a wide range of experience. Some may even be more experienced than the leader in particular aspects of outdoor-living skills. The leader must teach each person carefully, making sure that no one is made to feel stupid or naive to satisfy the leader's ego.

Learning styles. In order to be a good teacher, you must be able to teach the same facts in five different ways. Some people learn best by (1) *hearing;* others, by (2) *reading.* Some learn best by (3) *doing;* others, by (4) *seeing.* And some people need a (5) *combination* of teaching methods. It's always best to use a variety of teaching methods in order to enhance participants' learning experience.

There's no substitute for hands-on experience when it comes to learning. Experience is, in fact, one of the strengths of an outdoor-living skills program. Teaching is not just telling. People learn best when they're interested in the lesson, when they understand the value of the lesson, and when they actually participate in activities and become involved in teaching other people.

Group members, however, may not be as enthusiastic about the program as you are. They may know virtually nothing about the outdoors, and may do or say things that you think are ridiculous. For example, when you tell novice participants to soap a pan before cooking in it, they may soap the inside of the pan. (If you are unsure about how to soap a pan, don't feel silly. You'll find information about this in chapter 6, "Putting It On Your Plate.") Or a participant may pick a beautiful but very rare flower and come running to ask you, "What is this beautiful flower? There was only one in the whole area!"

Learners *will* make mistakes; they'll be amazed by things that you may have taken for granted for years. Just remember that you were a beginner once. Also remember that you're probably still learning a few things yourself. Don't be afraid to ask a more-experienced person questions, or to admit that you don't know the answer when someone asks you a question.

GENERAL TIPS FOR TEACHING/LEADING A GROUP

Leadership is a learned behavior that you acquire through formal and informal experiences. Just as you become an experienced teacher by teaching, you become an experienced leader by leading. The OLS program provides a unique opportunity for developing teacher/leader skills.

Teaching and leading are so intertwined that they're difficult to separate. As you lead, you're also teaching by example. An expert teacher who also happens to be an excellent leader can make the study of any topic a life-changing experience.

Nearly all outdoor-living skills instruction occurs in a group setting. The following sections provide tips on teaching in that group setting.

Preparation

There is no better way to start than to be prepared for all situations. Decide what you'd do in case of rain, snow, wind, blinding sunshine, too many or too few participants, equipment failure, and so on.

Create an outline for yourself, listing the topics you want to cover in the order you want to cover them. Practice presenting the material so that you know both the content and the length of the lesson. Be prepared to make some changes to accommodate your group.

Have all equipment and teaching materials ready and in working condition.

Practice your teaching skills with other leaders.

It would also be valuable to look at your organization's risk-management plan. Ask your program or camp director.

Leading Strategy

Start every new group of campers off with get-acquainted activities to help them learn one another's names and feel more at home.

Know where to stand or sit and where not to stand or sit.

Keep your voice well modulated. Be enthusiastic, even when you don't feel your best, and use humor when appropriate.

Get, and hold the group's attention. Don't start talking until you have everyone's attention.

Listen to participants' comments and try to understand them. Remember that what people say isn't always what they mean.

Participate in learning with the group when appropriate. Don't over-shadow them with your expertise; don't dominate the discussion or activity.

Try to make everything, even mistakes into a learning experience.

Getting Participants Involved

Seat participants so that they can see one another. Try seating people in a circle, square, or horseshoe; such an arrangement makes eye contact easier and gives everyone a sense of belonging to the group. Never stand in the middle of the circle, square, or horseshoe yourself. Join the group. When you use a table for a demonstration, have the group gather around you.

Don't put a barrier between yourself and the group by standing behind the table.

Let participants answer other participant's questions. It's your responsibility, however, to add or to ask for information if a participant's response is not complete or accurate.

When you ask questions, avoid asking those that have "yes" or "no" answers; ask for explanations, suggestions, and alternatives. Don't get impatient — wait for someone to answer. It may take some time at first.

Acknowledge group member's responses, and invite discussion of those responses, whenever possible. Instead of saying that a response is right or wrong, good or bad, ask for other ideas. Get the group to share several answers and discuss why some are more appropriate than others.

Establishing trust

One of the most important components of successful teaching and leading is establishing trust between yourself and the group. Trust can't be bought or transferred; rather it must be earned. One way to establish trust is to admit your own errors. Learners need to know that it's possible to make mistakes without being ashamed and that they can learn from those mistakes. The goal, however, is not to err, but to learn and succeed from positive experiences.

As trust develops, participants find it easier to communicate their thoughts and feelings, and to work together as a group.

METHODS FOR WORKING WITH GROUPS

Leading methods include the following:

- Group leadership
- Group planning
- Group discussion
- Generating and sharing ideas
- Observation
- Demonstration and practice

Some methods are more suitable to particular situations than other methods. For example, holding a group discussion among six-year-olds who are learning to tie knots won't be very useful. Six-year-olds have a relatively short attention span and are more likely to show interest if they are doing something rather than just discussing it. (Besides, discussion probably isn't the best method of teaching knot-tying techniques to any age group.) Group discussion may, however, be appropriate for older campers who are trying to decide whether to build a fire.

Group Leadership

The role you take as the leader is critical to the group's success. For a small group (ten or fewer people), learning depends on the attitude of the group, as well as on your attitude and actions, in terms of guidance, organization, coordination, delegation of authority, respect, and dependability. Group members have greater trust in a leader whom they perceive to be fair, considerate, and consistent.

If you have all these qualities, the group's morale and efficiency will be high, and group members will be inclined to imitate your favorable personality characteristics, such as camaraderie and friendliness.

Your group should see you as both a leader and a friend, not just as a friend. Too often, leaders aspire to be group member's best friend and lose sight of their roles as leaders; when they do, they face making decisions that compromise their responsibility and authority. An effective leader has a delicate balance of traits and skills. Common leadership characteristics are as follows:

- **Decision-making ability.** A good leader doesn't procrastinate in making decisions that he/she can make without seeking additional information. About eighty percent of all situations, (this includes camp and non-camp situations) require decisions that can be made on the spot. An additional ten to fifteen percent require seeking additional information in order to make a quality decision, and the remaining five to ten percent require no decision at all as the situation changes.

- **Confidence.** A good leader is confident of his/her decisions but is open to additional information that could change the decision. Open-mindedness on your part begets collaborative thinking and teamwork in your group.

- **Enthusiasm.** Enthusiasm is contagious. When you're excited and interested, the group becomes excited and interested. It's been said that the difference between a pool of water and a geyser is enthusiasm.

- **Positive attitude.** A leader's attitude is also contagious. If you exhibit a poor attitude toward an activity or task, the group will reflect that attitude. Saying something like "Well, we have to do this, so the sooner we start, the sooner it'll be over" is devastating to a group's enthusiasm and morale. Conversely, saying something like "We have a responsibility to complete this task, and we want to do the best job we can, because our group always does a good job, so let's get started" increases the group's morale and its enthusiasm for other activities as well.

- **Respect for other people.** A good leader respects all members of the group, whatever their abilities, disabilities, and differences. Each member of the group is an individual first, and as such, he/she deserves all the respect you can give. Remember that respect begets respect.

- **Problem-solving ability.** A good leader sees problems as opportunities for growth, rather than obstacles. Too often, groups and leaders spend more time thinking about why they can't do something than they do about how they *can* do it. A task that seems to be impossible and is discussed as being impossible *is* impossible. If you see a glass as being half full rather than half empty, you're likely to view a problem as being a challenge rather than an obstacle.

- **Punctuality.** A good leader respects time and uses it to his/her advantage. You should notify the group when an activity will start, start that activity on time, tell the group how long the activity will last, and end on time. If you find that the activity is taking longer than you expected, don't extend the time without first getting the group's agreement.

- **Planning skills.** A good leader always works from a plan, which is a road map to success. You should remain focused but flexible, to allow for unexpected diversions and complications.

- **Recognition of strengths and weaknesses** — his/her own as well as those of group members. You can accomplish this through self-assessment, evaluation of group members, and continual communication with the group.

- **Listening skills.** Listening is not passive; it requires work. Listening skills are the key to clear communication. A lack of communication between you and your group may result in poor learning, misunderstandings, and reduced enjoyment of the outdoors.

  Communication is a two-way process. While one person is sending a message, the other is receiving. You can communicate in several different ways; in words, in voice tone or inflection, in body language, in facial expressions, and in eye contact. What you say isn't always the only message.

Common obstacles to listening

1. Talking. (You can't talk and listen at the same time.)
2. Getting ready to talk when you should be listening.
3. Mentally arguing with the person who is talking.
4. Mentally criticizing the speaker's grammar, appearance, etc.
5. Failing to receive the entire message (gestures, expressions, intonation, and other nonverbal signals.)
6. Putting your mind in neutral when someone is talking.
7. Being preoccupied with another task.
8. Trying to listen in a poor environment (visual distractions or noise, uncomfortable room temperature or seating, etc.)
9. Being mentally or physically fatigued.

Group Planning

In any group activity, whether it's an OLS group practicing knot-tying skills, or a discussion group, participants should have a purpose or specific task to complete, and they should understand the purpose or task. A stumbling block for many groups is poor definition of, or lack of commitment to the purpose. A gathering of people is a group only when they have a common purpose.

In a group setting, people with different talents and strengths develop into a group as they learn about and from one another and accept a common goal. Quality leadership and planning facilitate this group cohesiveness and intelligent use of differing abilities.

The following items are the minimum steps you should take for productive group planning.

1. Clearly identify the purpose. The discussion topic, problem, or activity may be determined either by you or by the group.

2. Identify the conditions necessary to accomplish the goals. You or the group should consider conditions such as time, space, materials, cost, people, and skills.

3. Revise the goals. After you identify the conditions necessary to accomplish the group's goals, you may find that those goals can't be achieved and must be revised.

4. Develop a plan. Diagram the conditions you identified, including specific elements involved completing the task. For example, if the goal is to prepare meals for an overnight trip, your diagram might look like the following:

What — Plan menus for one dinner, one breakfast, and one lunch. Purchase all food stuffs for menus and pack them for trip.

How — Divide group into three smaller groups, assigning each group one meal. Once meals are planned, all grocery lists will be combined so that groceries can be purchased by a select group of people. After shopping has been completed, food stuffs will be divided and packed with other food stuffs for the same meal.

Who — Entire group will help plan menus in three smaller groups. Entire group will select a small group to go with leader to grocery store.

How much — Food stuffs will be determined by number of people in group. Type of food may be determined by dollar amount allotted to spend.

When — Menu plan must be complete one week in advance of trip. Grocery shopping must be completed at least one day in advance of trip. Packing will take place the morning of departure.

5. Put the plan into action. Follow the objectives that you have created.

6. Evaluate. Evaluation is an ongoing process. As progress or lack of progress is made, information is collected, and decisions are made. (For example, once the menu has been planned, the group determines that there is a group member who is allergic to carrots. The decision is made to add more celery to the stew and leave the carrots out. And, as the group is grocery shopping, they discover that the price of english muffins has gone up and they will not be able to afford them. They decide to replace them on the menu with bagels.) Objectives should be evaluated and reevaluated. Will we meet the time frames? Will we meet the budget? Why? Why not? How can we make it work? Use checklists, reports, observations, comparisons, or other formal and informal methods to evaluate the success of the plan.

Group Discussion

Productive group discussions don't just happen; they depend on participation by all members of the group. Participation in a group discussion, in turn, depends on each member's mental and emotional involvement, motivation to contribute, and acceptance of responsibility for his/her actions. Successful group discussions and participation are directly related to certain conditions, some are personality-related, some environmental. These conditions include the following:

- The group members must agree on, or at least understand, the task, question, activity, or reason for being assembled.
- The group members must be able to communicate.
- The group members must have some interest in the task.

- The group members should have sufficient time to complete the task or discussion.
- The group members should not feel that they're being forced to participate.

Generally, as group members' participation increases, so does the quality of the outcome. As the leader, you must be able to keep the group focused; lack of focus results in wasted time, unproductive discussion, and failure to achieve the purpose of the meeting.

You should facilitate discussion by encouraging group members to participate and by giving them opportunities to do so. Specifically, you should encourage discussion among group members. Asking questions is one of the best techniques for encouraging interaction.

You can do the following to increase participation:

State the purpose of the discussion.

State any rules of conduct.

Encourage and praise participation.

Mediate differences of opinion.

Refocus the group's attention, when necessary.

Clarify definitions.

Provide relevant facts.

Offer new ideas when group members have exhausted theirs.

Check participants' willingness to accept new ideas.

Summarize the discussion.

Seven ways to make a group decision
1. Group consensus.
2. Majority vote.
3. Small group representing a larger group.
4. Averaging opinions of the group.
5. Relying on an expert in the group.

6. Relying on an appointed authority in the group to decide after other members have made their recommendations.

7. Relying on some authority outside the group who has no personal involvement in it.

Generating and Sharing Ideas

Trust must be developed from the beginning if members of a group are to share ideas. In the early stages of group development, members will be somewhat tentative, shy, and perhaps even fearful of participating in the group, and spontaneous discussion won't occur naturally. For example, one person may suggest, "Let's do such and such." Silence follows; the group passively accepts the suggestion, and a course is set without a vote.

The following are some ways to generate ideas and involve group members in creative discussions:

Brainstorming

Brainstorming is a method of generating as many suggestions as possible in a short period of time. Proceed by following these steps:

1. Identify the problem or issue.

2. Set a reasonable time limit for offering suggestions.

3. Tell group members that there are no "wrong" ideas and that there will be no discussion of ideas at this stage.

4. Appoint someone to write down the ideas on a blackboard or other object that everyone can see.

5. Share ideas.

6. Stop when the time limit is reached or ideas are exhausted.

7. Review the ideas.

8. Eliminate obviously inappropriate ideas.

9. Discuss and prioritize the remaining ideas.

Using buzz groups

This technique involves breaking large groups into smaller ones for problem-solving purposes. To use the buzz-group method, follow these steps:

1. Define the problem or issue.

2. Break the group into smaller groups.

3. Assign each group a specific task or part of a task.

4. Set a time limit for completion of the task.

5. Share ideas in small groups.

6. Stop when the time limit is reached or ideas are exhausted.

7. Return to the large group.

8. Ask the small groups to report to the large group.

9. Share any ideas or suggestions.

10. Review.

Using role playing

This technique is useful for visualizing an issue in order to better understand it. To use the role-playing method, follow these steps:

1. Define the problem or issue.

2. Explain what you want the group to achieve — for example, to find more options or to clarify the problem.

3. Establish the situation and the role players.

4. Assign roles to group members.

5. Set a time limit.

6. Allow characters to play out the situation.

7. Discuss and review the role playing.

Observation

Helping people sharpen their observation skills creates excitement and makes learning fun. You can make observation be effective and fun in dozens of ways, including the following:

- Taking a quiet night walk without flashlights so that campers can hear the sounds of night and discover how their eyes cope with darkness. (Make sure that *you* know the trail.)

- Looking at an insect under a microscope.

- Lying on your belly on the ground, looking for tiny creatures.

- Watching the morning sky for clouds.
- Sitting quietly in the woods from dusk until dark, while day animals scurry to their homes and night animals begin to venture out.
- Carefully breaking apart owl pellets to see what the owl has been eating.
- Smelling the difference between pinecones and maple leaves.
- Feeling the difference between granite and limestone.
- Listening for woodpeckers.

Observation games such as "I Spy," "Riddly, Riddly, Ree, I See Something You Don't See," and "Trust Walk" help increase group members' interest, curiosity, and enthusiasm, and lead to other activities or discussion.

Upon completion of a game or activity, ask the group members what they did that increased their observation skills. Help members discuss both what they observed, and how they observed it.

The following tips can improve group members' powers of observation:

- Define what group members will observe. Be as specific or vague as you like.
- Make sure that participants know the rules. Are they to be quiet? Do you want feedback during the observation, or only after the group has finished the observation?
- Build on and encourage comments at discussion time, be that during or after the observation.
- Encourage participants to use all their senses. Set up observations that require techniques other than viewing.
- Demonstrate observation techniques by pointing out various things in nature. Do this even while you are involved in other activities.
- Explain that observation is not identification — that you don't expect group members to know all the names of things.

- Ask participants to observe from different points of view, such as through a magnifying glass or binoculars, and from an ant's viewpoint or a bird's viewpoint.
- Make up stories that make observation fun. For example, tell the group that three-inch-tall aliens have landed at camp, using dragonflies as their airplanes.

Demonstration and Practice

Demonstration and practice help participants learn and retain information. You need to use both techniques, because demonstration alone may bore the group.

Before demonstrating a skill, practice with another leader. It's often hard to demonstrate something you know well; you're so familiar with all the steps that it may be difficult to break the skill into steps that a beginner can understand.

Tips for a successful demonstration

- Understand the skill fully.
- Break the skill into easy steps.
- Consider both right-handed and left-handed participants.
- Demonstrate slowly, matching your actions to your words. For example, if you're saying, "right hand does this," don't stand facing the group; the technique will look exactly opposite to them. In this case, it may be better to have learners look over your shoulder as you demonstrate.
- Enlarge or personalize the demonstration so that everyone can see what you're doing.
- Allow time for participants to practice each step, praising and reinforcing success.
- Repeat and review, and check the group's understanding of each step.
- Help everyone participate by making the demonstration and the practice session fun and nonthreatening.
- Ask some participants to demonstrate a skill. (Demonstrating and explaining a skill always reinforces a person's understanding of that skill.) Make sure you allow different participants to demonstrate different skills at different times; don't leave anyone out. And don't push anyone in

front of the group if he/she doesn't want to give a demonstration.

This chapter presented some methods that will help you share
outdoor-living skills. Test these methods on other leaders. Try
different methods of teaching the same skill. Use them all at
different times.

3

On Your Way

Getting ready for an outdoor activity is like planning any other trip; you're getting ready to go somewhere quite different from where you live. This chapter is about getting ready to go into the outdoors — what to take, how to select it, some things to do when you get there, and what to do so you'll get home safely.

MINIMUM-IMPACT CAMPING

Getting ready includes thinking about how you'll act in the outdoors, considering how being outdoors is different from being at home. You'll need to consider how you'll be affected by the outdoors and how your actions will affect the environment in which you travel.

Twenty years ago, the phrase "minimum-impact camping" was not used; today it's synonymous with good outdoor-living practices. You may wonder why older books don't refer to these practices and why they're so important today. Years ago, relatively few people used the outdoors for recreational activities. So much recreational land was available that few campers thought about the damage they might be doing to one spot or the fact that people coming after them might find those sites ugly and unacceptable. They assumed that there was enough land for everyone and that any land or water left in poor condition would revive itself in a few years.

Today, however, hundreds of thousands of people enjoy camping, and many of them go to areas that have been popular for years, thus wearing them bare from overuse. Much less land is available for outdoor recreation today, and we now know more about what happens to land and water when they're used carelessly. For example, we no longer make beds of soft branches, because we know it takes the trees from which those soft branches come years (sometimes hundreds of years) to mature. Cutting them for one night's use could result in the depletion of that species of tree.

We also know that aluminum cans, which weren't widely used until about 1955, don't break down in the ground or in water. Imagine what a lake would be like if everyone dumped used aluminum cans into the water — after a few years, we could probably walk across the lake on the nonbiodegradable, nonrecycled cans. Even cans buried in the ground don't decompose. And as the rains wash away topsoil and animals dig up the cans for the morsels of food or sugar in them, the land soon becomes littered with trash.

Proper treatment of the environment includes considerations as simple as how you walk on a trail and when, where, and how you build a fire. If we all walked *beside* a muddy trail just to keep our hiking shoes clean, the trails would become unnaturally wide and would have little chance of returning to their original beauty. Imagine searching for a campsite and finding wads of toilet paper, garbage, or charred sticks. Imagine looking into a clear stream and finding strands of spaghetti, left by campers who washed their supper dishes in the stream. Would you like to go swimming in a lake full of soap scum? Or to find the forest floor covered with dust because previous hikers used all the dry wood for their campfires? Or to find nothing but a progression of circles of charcoal, indicating ever-widening fire-pit areas?

Minimum-impact camping means using outdoor-living skills that affect the soil, water, plants, and animals in an area as little as possible. This practice is also called "no-trace camping" or "low-impact camping". The term "minimum-impact", however, is more realistic. You can camp without leaving a visible trace of your presence and still pollute the water. You can bury the cans, papers, garbage, and old socks and appear to leave no trace, but the negative effects may remain even years later. Further, even "low-impact" camping may still have unacceptable effects on the land, water, plants, and animals. The effect of your presence may not be low enough to retain the quality of the environment; it may also not be the lowest you can afford to make. Thus, the term "minimum-impact camping" is the preferred term.

Minimum-impact camping is based on the simple idea of going outdoors to become part of it, rather than to use it for your benefit alone. A scientific term called *carrying capacity* can help you understand your relationship with the environment. Land, water, animals, and plants can stand only so much impact before their quality becomes irreversibly diminished. The point at which a particular environment can take no more is just beyond its carrying capacity. We must, therefore, try to answer the question "How much and what kinds of activity can this place stand before we ruin it?".

We must consider three types of carrying capacity: physical, biological, and psychological.

Physical carrying capacity refers to how much use the land (soils, rocks, etc.) can stand before its quality is permanently diminished.

Biological carrying capacity refers to the amount of use that plants and animals can stand before they are permanently diminished.

Psychological carrying capacity is a new idea that refers to the effect of humans on other humans. When is an area too crowded for privacy? When is it too noisy for others who are camping in the same area? When is our experience diminished by the actions or presence of others?

Choices, Decisions and Values

There are no hard and fast rules for minimum-impact camping; the best way to camp differs from region to region. Camping practices that are best for the land in the Rocky Mountains may not be best for the land in the Sonoran Desert. Appropriate practices for the White Mountains of New Hampshire differ from those for the dunes of Michigan, the Smoky Mountains of Tennessee and North Carolina, the plains of North Dakota, and the Badlands of South Dakota. Each area is unique, and using it in a way that preserves its quality depends on both your knowledge and your desire to do the right thing. The more you practice minimum-impact camping, the more you'll perfect your skills; the more you know about the plants, animals, soil, and water of an area, the better camper you'll become.

Minimum-impact camping is a way of life, a philosophy of caring. Certainly, concerned citizens understand the need to accept responsibility for their actions. If you don't know the best minimum-impact practices for a given area, you can ask an expert what to do. The important thing is that you care and try to learn more and more as you progress.

You should develop a "land ethic". In simple terms, a land ethic is caring for the land in just the way that you try to care for other people, treating others as we'd want to be treated. Treat the natural environment with care, for from it comes all our water, food, and building materials. To destroy the environment is to destroy the human race. So even if you aren't going to spend the rest of your life camping, you too have the responsibility of caring for the land.

What should your actions be? Minimum-impact camping is easy if you always start with that question. Consider the following ideas, which will make your effect on natural resources as minimal as possible.

Litter

In dealing with litter, follow two simple rules:

1. Leave at home as much as you can of what you do need, and all of what you don't need.

2. If you must take something with you, remember that you must carry it home again.

For a day hike, peel the oranges before you leave home, wrap them in plastic, and take the plastic back home with you at the end of the trip. For an overnight trip, leave much of the packaging of foodstuffs (cardboard, boxes, cellophane) at home.

When you're outdoors, package whatever trash you still have so that you can take it back home. Trash cans and dumpsters are appropriate places to dispose of trash; forests, streams, prairies, and deserts are not. Deer and wild rodents may eat a few discarded apple cores, but banana, orange, and melon peels don't decompose easily; they rot, smell, gather flies, and generally attract all kinds of problems.

If you carry something in, carry it out again.

Campsites

In the past, many people commonly camped together at one site. But now we know that large groups of people camping in one place ruin the quality of the environment — and they don't necessarily have any more fun than small groups do. Large groups are noisier and scare away much of the wildlife. Today, eight to ten people are enough for most sites. Maybe eight campers and two leaders should be considered the maximum for one campsite.

You can minimize a large group's effect on the environment in either of two ways. One is to spread the campers into smaller groups approximately 100 yards apart so that they'll have minimum impact on each portion of the site; the other is to concentrate the group so that the group affects a smaller area. Your decision as to which practice is best depends on the environment and on the activities you've planned for the group. You may want to check with the agency that manages the area where you are camping to find out how many people it recommends you have in one group.

Set up camp at least 200 feet away from a stream, pond, or lake. At a popular site, it's best to camp where other campers have camped rather than to camp on the edge of that area; camping on a new site creates a larger, wider area of trampling and causes general environmental change. If you're camping in an area that very few people have used before you, you may want to spread the campers out so that they'll have minimal effect on this rarely used site.

Before you leave a campsite, go over the area carefully to remove all traces of your visit. Leave the campsite in the same condition in which you found it — if not better. (Of course, because you were practicing minimum-impact camping, you don't have many cleanup corrections to make.)

Tent sites

Before the days of plastic and floored tents, campers commonly dug trenches to keep rain from running under the tent walls and the sleeping bags. If it didn't rain, the trenches served only to ruin the land around the tents; if it did ran, the trenches became muddy gullies that contributed to erosion.

Modern campers can use tents with waterproof floors or put tarps underneath conventional tents, so digging a trench serves no purpose today. Digging is not only a lot of work, but also causes irreversible damage to the soil and to plants.

Toilets

What about making a toilet in the outdoors? Chapter 4, "Being Safe " addresses this subject in detail; you may, however, consider a few things right now.

The first rule in relieving yourself outdoors is this: If an existing toilet is available, use it.

Another thing to keep in mind is that toilet paper may not decompose before the next traveler reaches that spot or before it gets washed away by rain or melting snow. If you're going to be camping in an area where no toilets are available, consider disposing of used toilet paper in plastic bags; you can dispose of the bags and their contents when you get home.

It was once recommended that camps burn used toilet paper before covering a cathole. However, soil that is soft enough for digging often contains air and dried roots, and burning paper in a cathole may start small underground fires that could spread to become full-fledged forest fires. If you must burn the toilet paper, be sure to use small quantities.

You may want to consider using natural toilet paper, including both living and nonliving substances. Be careful what you choose; know your environment and its poisonous and bristly plants. Never disturb an entire plant by stripping all its leaves. Recently fallen soft leaves, fallen bark, and pinecones work well; snow is shocking, but it also works well. Be sure not to disturb the area by removing bunches of leaves and lots of rocks; choose your natural toilet paper carefully.

Washing

The goal in washing is to accomplish the task with as little effect on the environment as possible. When you're washing dishes or bathing, you don't need an entire lake, stream, or river, only clean water and a place to pour the dirty water.

Stay away from natural drainage areas so that your soapy water doesn't run back into the lake, stream, or river. Take some water with you for rinsing away from the stream, and do your washing at least 200 feet from the water's edge. Be sure to take enough clean water to wash the soap from your dishes and silverware, because soap in food causes diarrhea.

Always use biodegradable soap, which is available at back-packing stores and many grocery stores. This kind of soap is not harmful to the environment if it's used in moderation.

Trails

Your footsteps alone cause compacting and erosion, so you need to be sure to cause minimal damage to a trail. Proper footwear is important here; it helps you minimize effects on both the earth and your feet. Heavy lug-soled boots are necessary only for hiking on rocks and snow; on forest trails, in deserts, and in grasslands, lug-soled boots do much more damage to trails than do lighter boots without heavy deep treads. Match your boots to the terrain.

Along trails, you may find switchbacks. These sharp curves in a trail are designed to keep water from rushing down and causing erosion; they also provide hikers an easier way to climb up hill. Long gradual climbs are less demanding than short, steep ones, so hikers usually don't mind a switchback going up, but on the way down, nearly everyone is tempted to take a shortcut across the switchback, eliminating several yards of travel at each curve. Short-cutting across switchbacks, however leaves trails that become watercourses causing serious erosion problems. Avoid the temptation to save yourself a few steps!

Maybe even more difficult than restraining yourself from cutting across switchbacks is restraining yourself from hiking on the shoulder of a muddy trail in order to keep your footwear clean and dry. If you are wearing new white shoes, you could have a big problem. Expect to get your shoes dirty. Their purpose is to protect the feet, not to remain pretty. Your role is to walk on the trail and to prevent any further erosion.

Plants

Good outdoors people don't pick plants, not the flowers or any other part of a plant, not even to make the campsite look pretty. If you want to examine a soft leaf or petal, pat it gently instead of picking it; the sensation will be the same, and the plant will stand a good chance of surviving the ordeal.

A rule for young scientists who pick flowers for study is this:

> *Pick, if you must, one flower face*
> *If nine more you leave in place.*
> *A two-foot square must hold that many.*
> *Otherwise, look, and don't pick any.*

This rule should make it possible for those who just can't resist to pick one flower from a mass of buttercups, as long as nine more are left in two-square-foot area.

But why bother? Flowers don't last long once they're picked, and many wildflowers have short lives even if they're left alone. Flowers are an essential part of the environment and look much prettier in their natural location. Their purpose may be to live a short while and then put nutrients back into the earth for the other plants.

In chapter 5, you'll learn that everything in nature is connected. When planning your trip, plan to be part of nature, not to be part of destroying it.

Fires

Minimum-impact camping means that we no longer build campfires to sit around in the evening, for they tend to insulate us from the outdoors that we came to be in. Campfires should not shut out the night. Allow yourself to become part of the night so that you can appreciate what's there, instead of hiding behind a wall of smoke and flame.

The main purpose of building campfires today is for cooking — when it is practical, and when the use of firewood and the fire itself cause no damage to the environment. As you'll learn in chapter 6, "Putting It On Your Plate", you don't need a big fire for cooking.

At times, however, you may need a fires for an emergency signal or to warm a victim of hypothermia.

As you plan your outdoor experience, keep in mind the need for minimum impact. Ask yourself whether a fire is really necessary and, if so, for what purpose.

The human factor

Besides caring for the environment, minimum-impact camping means making minimal impact on other campers. Things that often annoy others include large crowds, people camping too close to them, noisy campers, dogs that bark or bound into other campsites, and loud music. Even certain colors of tents or tarps such as bright orange and pink, may annoy those who went camping to get away from it all. Such colors can ruin someone's photograph of pristine beauty.

In summary, minimum-impact camping means planning to make minimal impact on the environment. Before you step out the door, consider the physical, biological, and psychological carrying capacity of the area and plan accordingly.

RISK MANAGEMENT: PLANNING FOR SURVIVAL

Risk management means controlling (managing) the chance of injury or damage (risk). Plan for the worst case you think you could encounter by creating the best possibility of avoiding that situation. Then imagine the best situation you can and plan how you would maintain it.

When some people think of survival, they have visions of overcoming storms in the Arctic, escaping from crocodiles, or leaping from burning airplanes. They think they don't need to be concerned about survival, for they'll *never* be caught in such situations. Other people think that survival means living off the land during a hike or canoe trip into uncharted wild areas. But most people don't plan to take such adventuresome vacations at any time. If you're one of the thousands who plan to use their outdoor-living skills close to home, near the car, or even in the city park, you may think that you need not read about survival.

Why Plan for Survival?

Two very different types of survival situations may confront anyone. The first type is caused by environmental factors — usually weather, but sometimes fires, earthquakes, volcanoes, or landslides. The second type is caused by people. If you plan wisely, the second situation will be less likely to exist, and you'll be much more likely to survive the first situation.

Environmental factors

Think for a moment about where you live. What kinds of severe weather or natural disasters occur in your area? Tornadoes? Thunderstorms? High winds? Floods? Blizzards? Extreme heat or cold? Fires? Earthquakes?

Anything that would cause electricity to stop functioning is cause to consider how to survive. Assume that the electricity is off and you'll be stranded at home for a day or more. You know you'll need shelter from the elements. If the roof doesn't leak, you need not worry about the rain or snow, but what about the temperature? An electric furnace won't heat or cool you without electricity and neither will a gas or oil furnace. What do you have at home to keep you warm? A fireplace may be available. Is there adequate firewood? Do you know how to start a fire, keep it going, and use it to keep you warm, not just to make a cheerful blaze?

Without electricity, electric pumps won't work and the water will soon stop running. During some natural disasters, pipes could break, and no water will be available from the beginning of the crisis. How will you open a can of juice or food if the electric can opener doesn't work? How will you heat your food if the microwave oven and stove don't work? How will you see without electric lights? And if you live in a tall building, how will you make it up the dark staircase?

Even storms involve survival situations. Do you have shelter, protection from extreme temperatures, extra water, and extra food (plus the ability to prepare it)? What would you do if you were stranded in an automobile on the desert? Or on a four-lane highway during an ice storm, with traffic stopped by a jackknifed semi and your gas tank running on empty?

Never say, "It won't happen to me." Thousands of people suffer every year because they didn't plan what to do in case of emergency. It would be tragic to go without food during a blizzard if you have food in the house but no means of preparing it. It would be tragic to go without water because you can't get a drop out of the faucet. It would be tragic to freeze to death in an automobile because the car ran out of gas and the heater won't work. This is not a recommendation to build a bomb shelter, but a recommendation to plan.

The human factor

Survival also involves the human factor. Will the attitudes of the group members disintegrate, leading to bickering? Will the leader maintain control? Will the group try to complete an activity just to do it, when everyone is already fatigued from other activities, therefore putting everyone at risk? These are the kinds of things that can create negative situations from neutral situations, put people at risk, or even put them in a survival situation.

What Does it Take to be a Survivor?

Many people refer to themselves as "survivors". They're the ones who seem to know what to do and to be able to do it. They're probably the planners.

Essential to survival is *the will to live.* People who want to live don't give up trying; they keep on planning and working to survive. Related to will to live is preparation — having planned what to do if something happens and what supplies would be needed. A good imagination helps here. Think about what could happen, and plan for all *reasonable* emergencies. (Stocking up on snowmobile suits if you might be stranded in the desert in the summer is not reasonable.)

To survive a natural disaster at home, use the list of ten essentials explained later in this chapter. Also consider the following necessities.

Protection from extreme temperatures

The internal (core) temperature of most people is about 98.6 degrees Fahrenheit. If that core temperature rises above 105 degrees or falls below 75 degrees, serious physiological problems, even death, can occur. For that reason, maintaining body heat or keeping the body from overheating is the first thing to consider when you plan for survival. You need adequate clothing and shelter. At home, know where you can find additional warm clothing, as well as blankets.

The second necessity is drinking water. Even when they're resting, people must replace the water they lose water through perspiration, breathing, and urination. When they're exercising, people need even more water; a hiker needs three to four quarts per day just to prevent dehydration.

A person at rest may die of dehydration after three days of going without water. Make sure some liquid is available in the house at all times. A gallon of bottled water is inexpensive and may save a life. Replenish it every six months. (You can drink it, so it won't be wasted.) Soft drinks are also available in most North American homes; juices, however, are better for you and for the very young children.

When you'll be traveling away from home, consider your liquid needs and water availability. Will you be hiking in the August sun? Will there be enough potable (suitable for drinking) water along the trail? Can you carry enough water to make it to a place where there is potable water? Remember the adage "A pint's a pound the world around." How many pints can you carry?

Although food seems to be more important than water, particularly to young people, that's probably because of social habits and enjoyment. Nearly everyone can go without food for up to three weeks — as long as they have ample water. Anyone who has gone without food for that long won't have much energy to move around or think logically, but he/she can survive.

Food is also a good morale-lifter, so be sure to have enough on hand. Make or buy high-energy food that doesn't require cooking, such as dried fruit, nuts, chocolate, and cheese. Cold cereal, particularly homemade or purchased granola, is good to snack on, even without milk. Canned goods, such as fruits, are also excellent, but you'll probably need to use a hand-operated can opener. Read the section on knives in chapter 8 and then practice using the can opener on your camping knife.

In chapter 6, "Putting It On Your Plate," you'll find simple recipes for high-energy foods. Learning how to prepare food for your camping trips will help you prepare food for home emergencies, too.

In addition to the will to live, protection from extreme weather, adequate drinking water, and high-energy foods are required for basic survival. There really isn't any good reason for anyone not to be prepared for emergencies at home, on the road, or outdoors; it just takes common sense and wise planning.

Survival With Some Comfort

You can plan for conveniences as well as necessities to make waiting out an emergency situation more pleasant. One convenience is light. The flashlight you use during camping trips may come in handy. Keep some candles in your home, too, as well as matches to light them with.

Do you have any kind of emergency stove and cooking fuel at home such as a charcoal burner with charcoal or a camp stove with fuel? (You'll also need a well-ventilated place in which to use either of them.) Do you have a fireplace or a chafing dish that uses solid alcohol? Can you cook hot cereal and eat it with brown sugar and raisins instead of milk?

Also plan for possible car emergencies. Convince yourself and others to keep a half tankful of gas in the car at all times, especially in the winter; then if you're stranded, you won't run out of gas so quickly and the heater will work longer.

But what if you do run out of gas? What if you are stranded in a snowdrift in an isolated area where no cars may come for days? Keep an old sleeping bag and/or some blankets in every car in the winter. You should also store an old snowmobile suit, if you have one, or an extra-heavy jacket in each car. Put wool mittens, a wool stocking cap, some heavy socks, and boots in a box in the trunk or the back of the station wagon. Many people who survive in a car in the winter owe their lives to extra planning and extra clothes tucked away for emergency use.

A number-ten can with a candle stuck in the bottom makes an excellent heater, warming your hands and taking the chill out of the air. (Be sure you have matches on hand to light the candle with.) Another number-ten can makes a good emergency toilet. A packet of high-energy food should be available, too. As for water, it may be possible to melt snow to drink. It's difficult to keep water in the car in the winter, because water freezes when the car sits idle.

People who live in rural areas of the northern United States may already take these precautions; their parents may have been following this advice for years. Urban dwellers, however, may not have thought about it, believing that help is always just a phone call away. But there may be no phone service where they're stranded. Also, during a severe traffic tie-up, the next car probably won't be any better prepared, and everyone else will probably be wondering how to survive with only their coats to keep them warm.

What if you are on a trip (camping or otherwise) when some natural disaster strikes? How should you act? Follow this formula: S T O P (**S**top, **T**hink, **O**bserve, **P**lan). This formula is designed to keep people from panicking.

To stay calm, remember: Stop (don't panic), Think (about what you're going to do, what you need, and what you have), Observe (the situation, what you need to do in a hurry, and how to stay where you are, using what is available nearby), and Plan (what you'll do, how you'll do it, when you'll do it and why you'll do it).

By the time you have spent several minutes on the STOP formula, you'll probably be over the panic stage and will be rational enough to act calmly and wisely — particularly if you really *have* planned ahead.

Staying Found

Besides making it through bad weather, the survival situation that worries most parents (and even some campers) is getting lost. Many young campers and their leaders get into trouble because they didn't plan how *not* to get lost. People who get lost on a camping trip are lost not only to themselves, but also to those who will soon start looking for them. This need not be the case if you take the following steps:

1. Plan where you'll be going, and find out as much as possible about the area. Will there be snow on the trail? Is

the water unusually high or low? Has the trail been rerouted or washed away?

2. Make a list of the equipment you'll need and check off each item as you pack it. That way, you won't get halfway to your destination and wonder where you left your rain gear, or something equally important.

3. Tell someone where you're going, where that place is, and when you plan to return. And then stick to your plan! If you don't, you'll waste the time of a great many people who will look for you where you said you would be. If you aren't there, no one will have any idea where to look for you.

   Make sure that everyone in the group also knows where the group is going; don't be the only one with the plan. If something should happen to you, someone else will need to take over. Be sure to let the person you told, know when you return. Otherwise, a group may go out looking for you when you aren't evening missing.

4. Leaders must plan for emergency exits. Plan which trails and other escape routes to take if there is a forest fire, an extremely bad storm, or a medical emergency that requires you to leave the area in a hurry.

5. Take along enough emergency equipment so that if you're lost or injured, you can stay warm, and dry, and comfortable for at least twenty-four hours.

6. Travel in a group. A youth group should plan on a ratio of one leader for every eight campers, plus one extra. This means two leaders for eight campers, three leaders for sixteen campers, and four leaders for twenty-four campers. If you have more than eight campers in a group, plan your travel and campsites for minimal impact on the environment, which may mean splitting into two groups that travel several hundred yards apart. The extra leader can become the tenth member of one of the groups.

7. Never wander away from the group alone. During every rest break, a leader must count in an obvious manner to see that all campers are present before the group starts off again. You may want to make a game of the count.

When someone leaves the group for toilet purposes, that person should be sure how to return. No one should go out of earshot of the group. A buddy system works well, but only if the buddies understand its importance and pay attention to where they are going instead of laughing and giggling until they realize that they're lost.

All campers must be able to take some responsibility for themselves. Being aware of where the group is at all times is the first step. If some members of the group have learning, vision, or hearing disabilities those people should be accompanied by buddies or leaders who can see, hear, and observe where they are going. If the group is made up of people with disabilities, the leader/participant ratio may change, depending on the specific abilities of the participants.

Surviving Being Lost

Now that you've planned how *not* to get lost, you should plan how to survive if you are lost. What happens if you become confused and stray away from the group, or if the group makes a faulty decision and loses the trail? How can you get "found"?

The technique recommended today is called "hug a tree", and it means just that: *stay put*. Remain in one place, keep warm and dry, and make yourself visible. If you stay in one place next to a friendly tree, you'll eventually be found; if you move from place to place, you may move away from seekers and into areas where they've already finished looking for you. Don't play hide-and-seek with your rescuers.

If you hear people, use your whistle or call to them.

At night, you might light a small fire for comfort; the searchers will probably be waiting until daylight to resume their search. There's nothing to fear out there, so get some sleep. Any animals in the area are probably going to stay away from you, because they fear humans as much as you fear them. Remember that animals may be attracted to food, so keep all foodstuffs away from yourself and from the group, possibly even hanging in a tree. If you're with your buddy or in a group, play games such as Twenty Questions, tell jokes, or sing songs.

Summary

Everyone needs to be aware of two different types of emergency situations: those caused by environmental factors, and those caused by human factors. You can prepare for the environmental factors; leaders and campers alike have the responsibility to prevent situations caused by human error.

No leader should ever neglect to take precautions because an emergency didn't occur last time and doesn't seem likely to occur this time. Failure to plan for emergencies is unacceptable behavior for a leader. You must be firm enough to ensure that the campers follow proper precautions and take along the necessary survival equipment.

You can prepare for urban, rural, and wilderness emergencies by planning for adequate shelter, protection from the weather, adequate liquids, and adequate high-energy foods. Other survival items include light and some way to heat food. Following the *STOP* formula, staying in one place if you're lost, and being sure that someone knows where to look for you if you don't get back on time are sure ways to help you survive in the outdoors.

PLANNING YOUR EQUIPMENT

The equipment you'll need for outdoor living depends on how far you'll be going from home base or another place that offers shelter, water, heat, and emergency help. The equipment you'll need for activities in the city park, the backyard, or even the campcraft area of a youth camp is different from the equipment you'll need for a long trip. When you choose equipment, always consider the situation and all possible variations. The weather, the temperature, the season, the campers' stress and activity levels, the sizes and ages of the participants, the distance and method of travel, possible hazards, and group interactions all play a part in planning appropriate equipment.

Look at base-camp equipment first. You'll need comfortable, sturdy clothes that are dark in color so they won't show evidence of soil, charcoal, or just plain dirt. Jeans, cotton shirts, sweatshirts, court or athletic shoes, socks and a windbreaker may be all that you'll need at base camp, so long as you can reach shelter within a few minutes. Find out where the group can go to get in out of the elements or to get additional clothing, rain-coats, or jackets if the weather changes and becomes cold or rainy.

On a trip away from base camp, you must carry everything that you'll need; it won't be possible to return to base camp or go to a store for additional equipment. And if you're injured, you may have to stay out for several hours, even all night, until help comes.

Imagine taking a hiking trip only one hour away from your home base. Just when it's time to turn back, you turn your ankle, and the group decides that you'll need help to get back home. Someone has to travel away from you for one hour, find help, and spend another hour coming back to you. The farther away from base camp you are, the longer it will take for help to arrive. Also, those who are coming to help you will need some time to get their own equipment together. You want to be warm, dry, and fairly comfortable until they arrive.

It is in this situation that the novice may get into difficulty, while the expert is comfortable. It is in this situation that many people get hypothermia or hyperthermia. Certainly, this is the time when many people decide either to continue their interest in outdoor living or to give up on it in misery. What do the experts do? What do the experts take with them?

The Ten Essentials

Be an expert; carry enough of the right equipment to keep yourself warm and dry (or cool and dry) for twenty-four hours. It may take that long for help to arrive! The following ten essentials should be carried by every hiker, climber, cross-country skier, canoeist, and anyone else who ventures away from immediate emergency help.

Clothing and shelter

The first item of essential equipment is proper *extra clothing* — items that can serve as a protection from cold, dampness, or heat, as well as shelter. Plan to withstand the worst weather conditions expected for the part of the country in which you'll be traveling. You may need a jacket, raingear, and a hat with a brim. A poncho, tarp, tent, or rainsuit will offer you protection against sudden storms.

Water

The second thing you must take on any trip away from base camp is *extra water*. Plan to take along an extra quart (unless you'll be in a desert area, in which case you should carry two quarts). Use this water for drinking between water sources, where you'll replenish your water supply. When you drink the extra water, you'll have none for emergency use, so keep refilling that canteen whenever you can.

It's especially important to have extra water in the winter. Streams may be frozen, and eating snow lowers the body temperature to the point that hypothermia may occur. (Hypothermia will be explained in chapter 4, "Being Safe").

You'll also need water bottles for carrying the water. Beware of using bottles that contained anything that you wouldn't want to drink.

If you use plastic bottles from home, be sure that they are sturdy, clean, and hold about one quart of water. Fill the water bottle before you leave home. Commercially purchased plastic water bottles will fit into pack pockets, are sturdy, and have wide mouths for easy filling. They're usually dishwasher safe. When you decide to do more camping, you'll probably want to buy a plastic bottle. Metal canteens are still in use, but are they're much heavier than plastic ones.

Most water must be treated in some way before you can drink it safely. Replenishing and purifying your water supply while on a trip is covered in chapter 4, "Being Safe".

Food

Extra food is the third essential item. The body needs refueling, and in case you must stay in one place waiting for help, you'll need food to keep up your energy and brighten your spirits. Appropriate extra foods are those that do not necessarily need cooking. However, if you have a stove and matches, you may want to cook; at times, you can get along without a hot meal. Consider the area, the weather, the ease of heating food and the possible necessity of spending time and energy purifying water; you may decide to take emergency food that can be eaten cold.

A list of appropriate high-energy extra foods is provided in chapter 6, "Putting It On Your Plate".

Pocketknife

You'll also need a *pocketknife* in good working condition. Selection, care, and use of knives is covered in chapter 8, "Toolcraft."

Flashlight

A *flashlight* with extra batteries and bulb is the fifth essential item. Batteries give out slowly, with warning; bulbs do not. When you put the flashlight in your pack, reverse one of the batteries; that way, the flashlight won't accidentally get turned on inside the pack, wearing the batteries down. Many campers wish that they had remembered this little trick. Reverse only one battery, though; that will prevent a complete current. Reversing both batteries will drain them, even though the light won't shine.

Matches and fire starter

Carry some *matches* in a waterproof container, as well as a *fire starter*. A fire starter is tinder, a candle, or some other purchased material that ignites easily, burns hot, and starts the kindling and fuel of your fire. You'll find directions for preparing your own fire starters in chapter 6, "Putting It On Your Plate."

If you'll be traveling on snow or rock, you won't find any firewood, so add a small stove if you'll want to cook. The main purpose of the matches is to light a fire to heat some food, to provide emergency warmth, or to send a signal. Don't forget to pack cooking utensils, too (see chapter 6, "Putting It On Your Plate.")

Map and compass

A *map and compass* are important pieces of equipment but they're of no use to you unless you know how to use them. Outdoor travelers must know which direction they came from and in which direction they are traveling so they must be able to read both a map and a compass. Read chapter 9, "Finding Your Way", before you add these items to your pack.

Sun protection

Protection from the sun is important no matter where you go. The sun's reflection off snow and rocks can be as bad as, or worse than, sun in the desert. Take along a hat with a brim and some sunscreen. You may decide to wear long pants, to prevent sunburn and scratches, rather than shorts. Also carry a pair of sunglasses and use them whenever the sun is bright.

The sun's rays at higher elevations and on water or sand are much more harmful to the skin and eyes than they are at lower levels or in the forest. No matter where you travel, plan to protect your eyes. A day that starts out cloudy may end up being exceptionally bright, and you could develop a headache from glare, or even snow or sun blindness, which are usually temporary but painful conditions.

First-aid kit

A *first-aid kit* is important for all outdoor travelers. Each camper may want to carry his/her own insect repellant, sunscreen, lip protection, and molefoam or moleskin; all other first-aid equipment must be carried and administered by the leader. (See chapter 4, "Being Safe", for information on first-aid procedures and kits.)

Adults can carry their own prescriptions, but the leader must be aware of all medication taken by any member of the group. Any youth camper should give his/her personal medication to the leader, who can then dispense it properly.

As a leader, you must know about all injuries and treat them with the supplies in the group's first-aid kit, because you're responsible for the health of all the campers. Experienced adults who travel in hiking or canoeing groups may carry some items for treating minor injuries, but it is still the responsibility of the leader to have a well-stocked group first-aid kit available for more serious ailments.

Optional items

Many people also carry folded *toilet paper* in one plastic bag and a *whistle* in another plastic bag. Use a whistle as an emergency signal only; never use it unless you're lost or need help.

The ten essentials everyone should take on every trip are:

1. Extra clothing and shelter.

2. Extra water.

3. Extra food.

4. A pocketknife.

5. A flashlight with extra batteries and bulb.

6. Matches and fire starter.

7. Map and compass.

8. Sun protection.

9. First-aid kit.

10. Optional items (toilet paper and whistle).

Gear for Outdoor Activities

Planning outdoor activities involves planning tools and equipment. Because camping is housekeeping out of doors, you must consider all the things you'll need in order to keep house and the way in which you'll carry these things. Camping equipment must be lightweight, sturdy, and compact — and that all of it must be necessary. One sign of a novice is lots of extra gear tied on to his/her pack, banging, clanging, and jolting as he/she walks down the trail.

Clothing and shelter equipment

When it comes to clothing and shelter, campers, hikers, canoeists, and most other outdoors enthusiasts seem to have their own vocabulary. Like musicians, athletes, and dancers, outdoors experts talk about things that those who aren't part of the group may not understand — "polypro," Goretex, Hollofill, Cordura, parkas, anoraks, Montagna, gaiters, ragg, and other strange-sounding items. The novice may find these names quite foreign, and the dictionary may not list them. This book will discuss only those things that outdoors people commonly use. Materials are changing so rapidly that the many man-made fabrics will be called "synthetics" here.

Cotton. Cotton is the choice of most campers in the summertime. Because it's sturdy, cooler than wool or synthetics, and comfortable. Because of its capability to hold moisture, cotton helps keep you cool in the summer; the breeze that blows over your damp T-shirt evaporates the moisture, taking your body heat with it. But for the same reasons, cotton will not keep you warm in the winter or during wet weather. You may find that cotton socks cause your feet to become very cold in wet or cold climates, as the cotton absorbs the perspiration from your feet.

Cotton underwear, bandannas, shirts, and blouses are particularly good for summer wear. Chamois and flannel are heavy cotton; they're comfortable when the weather is a bit chilly and these materials are kept dry.

Wool. Wool keeps you warm in cold weather and is the choice for hats, socks, mittens, and sweaters. A wool sweater will insulate you from cold wind if you cover it with a windproof jacket. Wool socks can "wick" moisture away from your feet when they perspire, and when they're clean and dry, they also provide your feet with a thick cushion. Unlike cotton, wool retains some of its insulating ability when it's wet, but not when it's matted with perspiration and body oils. You'll need to carry clean socks and wash out your dirty ones every day or so.

Secondhand stores are good sources of extra-large heavy wool sweaters. Forget about a fancy style; find something that will keep you warm. One outdoors authority insists that his campers bring along sweaters that are long enough to sit on.

Synthetics. Synthetics are materials made from something other than plants or animals. One popular synthetic is Polypropylene (commonly called "polypro"), a fabric that may keep you warm when it's wet. Polypro wicks moisture away from your body and is recommended for sock liners (the pair next to your feet) and for long underwear worn during strenuous exercise, such as cross-country skiing.

If you want winter underwear to keep you warm when you're *not* exercising, polypropolene may not do the trick; in that case, you may find that a blend of cotton and wool is better.

Polypro is a good alternative for those who are allergic to wool. Prolypro sweaters and jackets, however, are not windproof but they're warm under wind jackets or parkas.

Other synthetics include nylon, which makes wonderful wind-proof clothes. Nylon is not waterproof unless it is coated with a waterproof substance. Rip-stop nylon is used to keep feathers from sifting out of sleeping bags and to keep shirts from ripping on branches.

Sleeping bags may be insulated with synthetics such as Polarguard, Hollofill, or Qualofill. These materials are easy to launder, retain much of their insulating qualities when they're wet, and dry fairly rapidly. Synthetics are bulkier than down, but they are better when the sleeping bag gets damp. They don't compress as easily as down does however, and they take up more room in a pack.

Pound for pound, down (the fluffy feathers from geese or ducks) is the warmest insulation available . Down is useless, however, if it gets wet. You probably won't need a down bag unless you plan to camp where the temperature goes below freezing and you can afford the higher cost of down.

Goretex is a patented material that is both breathable and waterproof. (Rain can't penetrate the material but perspiration can.) This material is considered to be superior to coated nylon for raingear because coated material retains the user's perspiration and makes the inside of the garments wet and clammy. The micropore material allows the body to "breathe" so the moisture does not accumulate inside the coat.

Footwear

In nearly all outdoor activities, the most important part of your body is your feet, which must carry you to and from your destination. (If you're canoeing, your feet must carry you away from the river if the canoe is damaged.) Your feet must carry your weight plus the weight of your pack or load. You may encounter rough spots, stones, sand, brambles, and many other things that you won't want to step on without comfort-able soles beneath you feet.

You should start out with clean feet and trimmed toenails; long toenails will rub against the ends of your shoes. When this happens, the shoes don't move, but the toenails do. With each step and thrust against the shoe, long nails go backward into the toe until the toenails become bruised and blackened; eventually, they may even fall off.

On one trip, a fifteen year-old lost a toenail on the third day of a seven-day backpacking outing. Whose fault was it that the camper was uncomfortable? The leader can take the blame for not being sure that everyone started the trip with short toenails. He/she should have given all the hikers this tip before they started so that they could all trim their toenails. Remember, "Clean feet and nails neat."

Also consider conditioning your feet. Make certain that your feet are familiar with your shoes and with walking. Walk, wearing the shoes or boots in which you'll be hiking. If you're going to have blisters or any discomfort, it's important to have that experience and to solve the problem before you hit the trail.

Breaking in your shoes or boots can begin with wearing them around the house for a week or so while you do household chores and yardwork. The heat from your feet helps form the boots to your feet, alleviating any hot spots or the beginnings of a blister.

Stop any pain before it gets worse, either at home or on the trail. Take off your boots or shoes, prop up your feet, and relax. Pad the sore spot with a bandage or moleskin so that your skin doesn't continue to be rubbed. Leaders should be sure that participants follow this advice. If they don't, everyone will be sorry later, and the one whose feet are sorest will have the least fun.

Next, consider how well your shoes or boots support your feet and ankles. Shoes will assume part of the responsibility for bearing your weight, so they must be sturdy enough to do the job.

Footwear also must be appropriate for the terrain in order to cause minimal damage to the land. Many boots are designed with smooth soles that don't compact the earth as you walk.

Athletic shoes, particularly ones with thick, rigid soles, may be fine for short trips on fairly soft and even ground. High-top athletic shoes may be even better for the same situations. Shoes marketed as walking shoes are usually good for short trips and light loads, whereas shoes marketed for aerobics have almost the opposite features. Aerobic shoes usually have very flexible soles, designed for easy movement, rather than stiff soles that will bear your load for an entire day. They may be suitable for very short trips, but your feet will be very uncomfortable on longer trips over rough terrain.

For an overnight trip, you'll probably want to take an old pair of lightweight athletic shoes to use for wading or just walking around the campsite. These shoes will give your feet a rest after a day in heavy hiking shoes, and they're less damaging to the soil as you walk around the tent and cooking area.

For traveling long distances or over rocky, hilly, or snowy terrain, you may need a pair of hiking boots. Heavy boots are necessary for hikers above 5,000 feet in the Rockies, Cascades, Sierras, and other mountain ranges, where there are many rough rocks and snow may be on the trail. Lug-soled boots are hard on the trail; they compact the earth and/or carry it off. Hundreds of styles of boots are available. Prices range from $20 to $100 for lightweight boots and from $50 to more than $300 for heavy climbing boots.

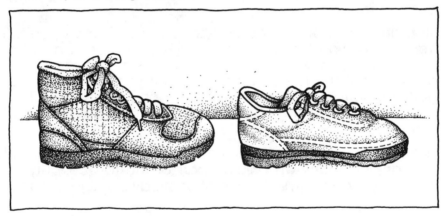

Figure 3.1 Match footwear to terrain.

In summary, consider the activities and terrain before you select your own footwear or recommend any to other people. Find out what is recommended for your area and intended use by asking skilled hikers, knowledgeable leaders, and sporting-goods-store personnel. Beware of any salesperson who just wants to sell you something. Don't buy the most expensive boots until you're sure that you'll use them enough to warrant the expense before you outgrow them.

When you try on a pair of boots, wear two pairs of the kind of socks that you plan to wear on the trail. A thin inner pair should wick the perspiration away to the outside socks, and the outside pair serves as an insulator and cushion. The outside socks also catch most of the dust, mud, and debris of the trail, keeping it away from the inner socks and the feet.

Clothing

The type of clothing you'll need depends on the area and the season. Regardless of the time of year, dark sturdy materials are usually preferable to thin material in pastel colors because they don't show dirt or wrinkles and are harder to tear. In the summer, you might want to stick to cotton unless you're traveling in those parts of the United States that are noted for cold nights and occasional summer snow, such as high elevations and northern areas. If you camp in the northern half of the country or over 3,000 feet, you're bound to encounter the cold, fog, rain, and brisk wind.

Denim jeans are not suitable for canoeing or high-country hiking; they get heavy when they're wet, and as the moisture evaporates, you can become very cold and contract hypothermia. For canoeing or hiking at high elevations, consider wool or Polypropylene. If the only pants you have are denim and you don't want to buy new ones for your first trip, be sure to have rain pants that you can put on before the jeans get wet, and try not to wear jeans in a canoe.

For cold-weather travel, wear several layers of clothing: long underwear, a shirt, a sweater, a wool or synthetic jacket, and a wind jacket. You can add or remove one garment at a time when the temperature changes. The dead air space between the garments insulates better than one heavy coat can.

Some hikers and wear tights or shorts during the warm part of the day and slip long pants over them as the weather gets cold. Be sure that your long pants are large enough to fit over your shorts or tights.

Another important article of clothing is a hat. A hat with a brim can keep off hot sun and may prevent sunstroke; it may also shed rain or snow. A stocking cap can keep your head and ears warm. When you exercise, most of your loss of body heat happens through your head. To stay warm, put on a hat. To keep cool, take off the cap or change to a hat with a brim.

Rainwear

Plan for rain by taking along waterproof clothing. Inexpensive plastic raincoats are widely available but they may tear in the wind and on little branches. Try an inexpensive urethane-coated nylon rain jacket for your first trip. You may perspire in it but it *is* waterproof, and you can wear it for walking in the rain when you get home; you can always buy a more expensive breathable rain jacket later.

A poncho, while not terribly stylish, is an excellent choice for a rainproof hiking garment. It can cover you and your pack, and also serve as a ground cloth or tarp under your tent or over your eating area, or as a tent extension. You won't outgrow a poncho. It fits all sizes and is relatively inexpensive. A poncho is not good for canoeing; if you fall out of the canoe, the poncho will weigh you down and is hard to remove in the water. Nor is a poncho good for activities in which you use both arms and legs, as in climbing. But a poncho is wonderful for hiking. If the wind blows it around, you can tie it around your waist with a belt or rope, and it will still keep you dry.

You should also consider the color of your clothing. If you'll be traveling during hunting season in an area where hunting is permitted, you'll want to be clearly and easily identifiable as a human, so bright red and orange are very appropriate colors. In other situations, you may want to think twice about wearing bright colors; they're offensive to travelers who want things to look as natural as possible. Review the material on psychological carrying capacity earlier in this chapter before you make up your mind. What is available on the market may dictate the colors you wear, but the topic of color on the trail always makes for a good discussion.

Tents and other shelters

Tents and tarps are available in many sizes, shapes, fabrics, and weights. When considering tents, your group can discuss where you will be traveling, for how long, and in what season. It's possible to make a very useful tent for three or four people from a   9-foot by 12-foot   nylon or polyethylene tarp, and a

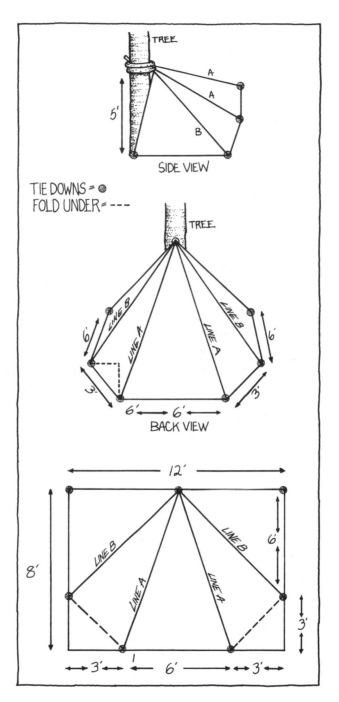

Figure 3.2 Making a tarptent.

poncho makes a small shelter for one person in a pinch. These shelters won't be mosquito-proof, but will suffice in a rainstorm, on an unexpected cold night, or when someone is injured and needs shelter while waiting for help. All you need is a tree, some rope, and the tarp.

Making a tarptent

You can make an excellent tarptent from a 9-foot by 12-foot piece of four- to six-mil polyethylene. This inexpensive material usually comes in black or white and is available at most hardware stores. Don't buy anything lighter.

Stretch the material out on the ground and mark the tie-down spots with a waterproof marker or plastic tape in a contrasting color. When you get to your campsite, attach tie-downs to the seven appropriately marked spots. To make tie-downs, use small round pinecones, stones, or wads of some soft material. (Moss, bunches of leaves, or grass will do only in an emergency; try not to destroy the area.)

To make the tarp tent, you'll need a small tree and seven nylon cords, each about three feet long. Put a pinecone under a tie-down spot and wrap part of one nylon cord around the tie-down spot so that it looks like you're holding the pinecone inside. Secure it with a clove hitch or a double half-hitch. (see chapter 7, "Tying It Up.") Tie the loose end of the cord to a tent stake, and tighten the tarp with a taut-line hitch.

To pitch the tent follow these steps:

1. Tie the center of the front to a tree at a point about five feet from the ground (about chin level for an adult).

2. Stretch the back out to meet the ground, and secure it at the tie-down spots (three feet in from each corner).

3. Adjust the front corners as desired, and tie them down.

4. Adjust the sides to tighten the tent, and tie them down.

5. Tuck the back corners under. The corners make a good ground cloth for your gear and serve to tighten the back of the tent.

This tent doesn't cost much and is very lightweight. Up to four youngsters can sleep in it easily, and in a pinch, even four large adults can squeeze into it.

Synthetic tents

Canvas tents are common in youth camps, where they're used for semi-permanent shelters, but most hikers today carry tents made of lightweight synthetic materials. Canvas tents are heavy and leak when they're subjected to long rains; they're also hard to keep clean and are likely to mildew and rot.

Tents are usually manufactured from lightweight nylon. Regardless of the style, a good tent has a waterproof floor and waterproof "rain fly" that covers breathable lightweight nylon tops and sides. If the top is made of uncoated material, it will leak; if the top is made of coated material, it will sweat and drip condensation on the occupants. The rain flies serve as water barriers and insulators, permitting moisture to escape through the top of the tent and dissipate into the air. Flies should be long enough to cover all the uncoated areas of the tent so that no moisture can seep in.

Tents for two or three people can weigh as little as five pounds. All tents should be waterproof, sturdy enough to withstand wind and hard rain, and easy to pitch and pack. Tents also should be in dark unobtrusive colors (see the material on psychological carrying capacity earlier in this chapter). Match your tent by the kind of environment in which you plan to travel: the season, the presence of mosquitoes, and the possibility of rain, wind, or snow.

Plan to have one person carry the tent and his/her buddy carry something of equal weight, such as cooking gear, or food. If the tent fly is separate from the tent, one person can carry the rain fly, poles, and stakes, and his/her partner can carry the tent.

Sleeping bags

Like tents, sleeping bags come in hundreds of kinds, shapes, designs, weights, and materials. You'll probably select a rectangular bag, a mummy bag, or a modified mummy bag. Before you select a sleeping bag or recommend one to others, review the material on synthetics and down earlier in this chapter.

Rectangular bags are roomier, heavier, and bulkier than the other shapes, and are usually used in situations where the camper has access to motor transportation. These bags are less efficient in cold weather because the large pocket of air around the feet is hard for the body to heat.

Mummy bags are smaller, easier to pack, and lighter in weight than rectangular bags. These bags are narrow at the foot, where the body is narrow, and wide at the shoulders, where the body is wide. Your body heats only the small area around it when you're in a mummy bag.

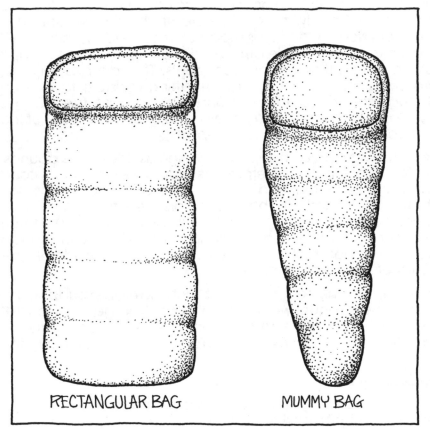

RECTANGULAR BAG   MUMMY BAG

Figure 3.3 Sleeping bags.

Sleeping bags are rated by temperature and are recommended for use at or above the temperature rating when there is no wind. For summer use, sleeping bags rated for warmth to 65 degrees are fine for most parts of the country; those rated to 40 degrees are better for the northern sections and higher elevations. A rating, however, is subjective and only a rough average. You may need a warmer sleeping bag than your tent partner, who can get along with a really light one.

Most people wear modified sleeping garments in sleeping bags. Clean T-shirts used just for sleeping are fine in warm weather; long underwear is a good choice in colder regions. Sleepwear must be different from the clothes you wear during the day. Those garments are likely to be damp from perspiration and won't keep you warm. (Besides, they'll need a good airing out for the next day.)

Sleeping pads

In the past, campers slept on the hard ground, made little indentations in the sand or soil for their hips and shoulders, or made beds out of boughs. But today, the ground is too hard for most people, indentations ruin the land, and cutting boughs to make a soft bed is one of the fastest ways to destroy the environment.

If you don't want to sleep on the ground, you can take a sleeping pad with you. Backpackers and boaters want to keep their hips and shoulders off the ground because those parts hurt after a long night without padding. Sleeping pads, therefore, are usually only forty-eight inches long — just long enough to keep the shoulders and hips comfortable. Three-quarter-length pads are economical and can be used from year to year. Pads made of closed-cell foam are preferable to open-cell foam, which soaks up moisture. Sleeping pads range in cost from $5 to $50 or more.

Cooking gear

For an overnight trip, you'll need many of the same things you have in your kitchen at home. A complete list of these items appears in chapter 6, "Putting It On Your Plate".

Packs

Although there are many types of packs in many sizes and shapes, you'll probably need only a basic day pack and a backpack.

Day packs

The day pack is often called a knapsack although technically, a knapsack is something that hangs over one shoulder. A day pack is carried on the back and held in place by two shoulder straps through which the wearer thrusts his/her arms. Useful day packs are waterproof and have one to three outside pockets for extra clothing, water, food, rain gear, and other essentials. You can use a large day pack for a one-night trip, but you'll rarely have room for a sleeping bag, tent, stove, sleeping pad, and extra food.

Some people who make long backpack trips add a lightweight day pack to their load for short hikes away from their overnight sites. Many mountain climbers add heavier, larger day packs to their backpacks to carry their climbing gear and emergency supplies in case they are stranded on the mountain.

For most day hikers, a pack that weighs about one pound is heavy enough. It may be hard to find a one-pound day pack in a highly durable material, though, so you may find it desirable to sacrifice material in favor of weight. Small hikers shouldn't be burdened with so large a pack that carrying a light load becomes drudgery. Padded shoulder straps and hip belts make day packs much easier to carry, so they should be considered basic equipment, not frills.

Day packs come in sizes ranging from approximately 12" x 10" x 8" to 22" x 14" x 13". Their capacity may be from around 1,000 cubic inches to more than 3,000 cubic inches. The smaller ones are adequate for most day hikers.

Features to look for in day packs include pockets into which your water bottle will fit, adequate space for clothing, and a place to carry your lunch so that it won't be squashed into a pulp.

Backpacks

For overnight trips, you'll need a backpack to carry your shelter, food, cooking equipment, clothing, and all the other supplies you'll need for living outdoors on the trail or along the river for one or more days and nights. Many backpacks are large enough to hold supplies for a month.

Before you buy a backpack consider where you're going, what you need to carry, and how much weight you can easily manage. Many hikers forget about leaving it all behind and end up taking it all with them.

Simple backpacks have one main compartment and two or more pockets on the outside. These pockets should be useful. If they accomodate things that you'll need easy access to, such as your water bottle, first-aid kit, map, compass, and maybe lunch, perhaps that pack is not the one you want. More elaborate packs have two or more compartments with sections arranged from top to bottom or side by side. Some people carry a sleeping bag inside a backpack, while others strap it on the bottom.

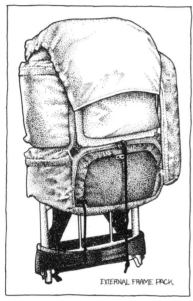

Figure 3.4

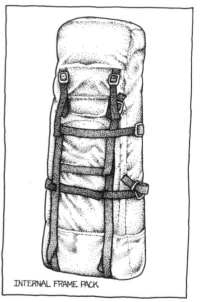

Figure 3.5

A hip belt is a necessity for holding the bag snug against your hips so that the load won't sway, throwing you off balance. You'll get far less tired carrying a load that is secured close to your body by a hip belt than you would carrying a load that wobbles back and forth with every step.

Pack frames

When you select your packs, you'll need to decide between internal and external frames. External frames, which are outside the pack bags, are usually aluminum and are padded with webbing to keep the frame from hitting your back, hips, and shoulders. The pack bag is attached to the external frame by a suspension system that keeps it steady. Internal frames are modifications of the external frame, placed in sleeves inside the pack.

Most backpackers find an external-frame pack very suitable. The frame keeps the pack stiff so that items can be packed neatly; it also keeps the pack away from the back so that there will be some ventilation when the hiker perspires. One of the best reasons for using a frame pack is that the frame helps distribute the load over your hips, thus eliminating strain on your back.

Internal-frame packs have aluminum stays placed in sleeves inside the pack. Internal-frame packs fit closer to the body, and because they're narrower than external-frame packs, they permit more freedom of body movement. These packs may be the better choice for cross-country skiers and climbers, and for anyone else who travels off the trail in rough country where free movement and tight control of the load is necessary.

If you plan to backpack in the summer and want some air separating your back from your pack, you'll find the external-frame pack to be superior. If you plan to climb with a heavy load or do some cross-country skiing, consider an internal-frame pack.

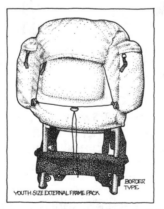

Figure 3.6 Youth sized external frame pack.

The size of the pack is very important. A pack should not extend above the head or below the buttocks, and the shoulder straps should wrap around, not gap at the shoulders. A pack that is too short or too long is very uncomfortable. Pity the poor hiker who strides down the trail with the bottom of the load going bump, bump, bump against the backs of his/her thighs with every step!

No one should be permitted to travel with a pack that is too big or too small. After a few miles of discomfort, he/she might well decide never to go backpacking again!

Packing the pack

Heavy things should generally be at the bottom of the pack and as close to your body as possible. Items that you won't use during the day should also be at the bottom, as close together as possible. Always put your lunch where you can easily get to it, and be sure that a sweater or jacket, as well as your rain gear, hat, and sunglasses are at the top of the pack.

Sleeping bags that are strapped onto the bottom of a pack need waterproof covers. If you don't have a waterproof cover, you can make a good cover from a plastic garbage bag; just put the sleeping bag inside and tie the bag shut. Take care of the plastic cover so that it doesn't rip. Put it away carefully at night, or use it to cover your pack against rain.

Pack dirty clothes in a cloth or plastic sack away from your food and clean clothes. Put your eating and cooking tools together in a separate bag.

Plan your packing before you go, and stick to your plan. Where will your ten essentials be? Are the map and compass easy to reach? Where are the trowel and the toilet paper? Will you reserve a separate pocket for garbage and trash? (Be sure to keep other things out of that pocket!)

Packing food is important and is covered in chapter 6, "Putting It On Your Plate".

Have a discussion with others in your group about sharing equipment and how to pack things. No single way is best, but there are lots of unsatisfactory ways. For example, too many heavy things at the top of a pack may unbalance the load, and box of crackers shoved into a corner may yield cracker crumbs and disappointed companions.

Pack weight

How much weight is too much? The answer to that question depends on the age, size, and physical condition of each person. A good rule is to carry no more than 25 percent of your body weight. That means that a 100-pound camper should carry a maximum of twenty-five pounds of gear in a backpack if he/she is in reasonably good physical condition. A 150-pound adult may be able to carry forty to fifty pounds for some short trips; the pack gets lighter as the trip progresses and the food is eaten.

It may be questionable though, why any adult would carry more than forty or forty-five pounds on a trip of two or three days. Are all the things you want to take along really necessary? Think about it, and plan carefully so that the effort of carrying a pack doesn't ruin your trip.

Summary

Planning your outdoor-living skills experiences requires planning for minimal effect on the environment and safety for the participants. Before gathering equipment and going anywhere with it, you need to ask, "Is this the best plan?"

Minimum-impact camping means using the land and water so that they remain in good condition. Safety means knowing how to survive in emergency situations, and choosing and using appropriate supplies and equipment.

Leaders also need to know as much as possible about the area in which the group will travel, so that they'll be able to make good recommendations about clothing and equipment to the participants.

4

Being Safe

In this chapter, you'll learn about four seemingly unrelated topics: weather, drinking water, toilets, and first-aid. This information will contribute to your health and safety in the outdoors, just as careful planning and preparation will help you get ready to venture there.

Related to all four topics are basic safety rules that every group should discuss and every camper should respect.

Safety Rules

1. Always travel with a buddy. Two people can assist, watch out for, and warn each other of trouble.

2. Never leave the area where the group is without an adult's permission.

3. Know the areas in your camp where you can't to go without an adult (for example, the waterfront or any natural-hazard area.)

4. Know how to recognize any poisonous plants in the area.

5. Avoid strangers.

6. Carry a whistle so you can signal for help when you're in trouble. Never use the whistle when you're not in trouble.

7. Tell an adult about suspicious sounds, activities, or people in the area.

8. Move toward familiar people and/or lights if you are in trouble.

9. Know where to go if you become injured or ill, whether that's to the camp infirmary, to the school nurse, or to the phone to dial 911. [1]

Have your campers discuss the importance of traveling with a buddy, being aware of strangers, and staying away from certain places unless an adult is present. Make up a skit about how the buddy system works, or have your campers write a buddy agreement. Such an agreement might say:

"I, _____, agree to watch out for _____. I will help if he/she is in trouble, and he/she will help if I am in trouble."

WEATHER

People who are planning any outdoor activity learn to read the weather so that they won't be surprised by rain, snow, excessive heat or cold, or high wind. Weather changes can cause discomfort, even danger. Fortunately, most people can get the weather information they need from the local newspaper or from television. If, however, you're on a trip of two or more days, you'll have to rely on your own ability to understand potential weather changes. You'll need to know the prospective high and low temperatures, the wind direction and intensity, the amount of cloud cover, the humidity, and the possibility of precipitation. *Weather* means daily changes in temperature, humidity, wind, cloud cover, and precipitation. In the United States, most weather comes from the west and moves east. In mountainous areas, however, you may encounter storms caused by changes in air temperature as the elevation increases. These weather changes may be quite different from those in the valley from which you came.

Although some weather signs are easy to read, they don't always mean the same thing throughout the country. For example, cloud formations that foretell rain in the north may mean nothing in the arid southwest. Thunderhead clouds,

---

1. Adapted from *Outdoor Education in Girl Scouting*. New York, NY: Girl Scouts of the U.S.A., 1984.

however, usually precede storms no matter where they may appear.

In order to understand the weather — and in particular, rain — you need to understand the water cycle and the way in which clouds form. A good way to begin is to perform a simple experiment with cloud formations.

Bring a tea kettle of water to a boil. If you look carefully, you'll see an area of clear air just above the spout and just below the plume of steam. The air that is warmed by the boiling water rises; this air holds moisture from the evaporating water in the tea kettle. As the warm, moist air rises, it cools. Cool air can't hold as much moisture as warm air; consequently, the moisture condenses and forms steam, creating a miniature cloud.

Clouds are like steam, except they are much cooler. When warm air rises from the ground, laden with moisture from rivers, streams, oceans, and plants, it cools, creating clouds. As these clouds rise higher and higher, the air becomes colder and colder. When clouds are so cold that they can no longer hold moisture, that moisture falls back to earth in the form of rain or snow. The probability of rain, then depends on how moist and how cold the air is.

CONVECTION CURRENTS
IN HEATED WATER

Figure 4.1 Convection currents.

Try a different experiment. Fill a metal or tempered glass pan halfway or more with water and place it on a stove burner. After the water comes to a boil, drop small bits of paper into the water. You'll see the paper swirl, drop to the bottom, and rise to the top again. This is because the water, heated by the burner, warms and moves to the top, while the cooler water on the top moves down to take the place of the warmer water.

You're seeing a *convection current* — a miniature weather pattern.

Try to imagine a similar current in the air. The warm air, which is full of moisture, rises, condenses and forms clouds.

Most weather systems in the United States come from the Pacific Ocean and move east in convection currents. When air moves east and meets the Cascades, the Sierras, and the Rocky Mountains, it has to rise in order to get over the mountains. As it rises, the air cools, and clouds form. If the clouds are heavy with moisture and the air cools to the point of condensation, rain or snow falls. After the air crosses a mountain range, it keeps going east, and because the air has already dropped much of its moisture, the eastern side of the mountain range is relatively dry compared with the western side. Of course, as the air passes over the prairie states, it picks up new moisture rising from fields, lakes, rivers, and forests; rain falls again when the air is sufficiently cool and saturated.

On the East Coast, the morning sun warms the air along the beaches and continues to warm it as it passes inland. In the eastern mountain ranges, a band of clouds often rises from about 8 to 10 in the morning, accompanied by gusts of wind. The wind is created as the warm air rises over the eastern sides of the mountains. Late in the afternoon, when the sun goes on over the western side of the mountains, the air on the eastern side cools and sinks. As the cooling air falls, warmer air rushes down the mountainside after it, causing afternoon breezes from the west. This *diurnal* (daily) sequence of breezes is the natural weather pattern for this area; stronger winds from the west bring storms and higher wind.

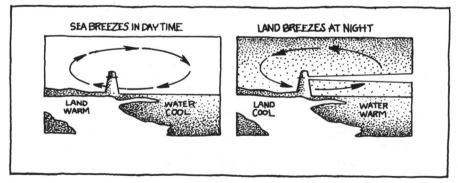

Figure 4.2 Breezes.

The following sections describe air currents and the water cycle. Try to imagine what happens in your camping area, and you'll start to understand weather.

Humidity

The amount of water vapor in the air is called *humidity. Relative humidity* means the amount of moisture in the air compared with the maximum amount that the air can hold. "Relative humidity of 65 percent" means that the air contains 65 percent of the moisture that it can hold at the current temperature. While humidity isn't necessarily a weather sign, it indicates how comfortable or uncomfortable the temperature is, given the amount of moisture in the air.

Air is like a sponge. Sometimes, a sponge has no moisture; at other times, it's damp, very wet, or so saturated that it can't hold any more moisture. If a sponge is 80 percent full of moisture, it contains more moisture than a sponge that's 60 percent full and less than one that's 100 percent full. When humidity reaches 100 percent, the clouds can hold no more moisture, and the excess moisture falls as rain or snow.

You may be surprised to learn that even while rain is falling, relative humidity may be only 70 percent or 80 percent. Remember, though, that the cloud above you may contain 100 percent of the moisture it can hold, and the rain may be falling through air that is *not* saturated.

Most scientists agree that relative humidity between 40 percent and 60 percent is comfortable for most people. (We are always more uncomfortable in extremely high and low temperatures, though, regardless of the humidity.) If the temperature is 75 degrees Fahrenheit, you'll be more comfortable when the humidity is between 40 percent and 60 percent than you'd be if relative humidity were 20 percent or 80 percent.

One reason for this is that perspiration evaporates faster when humidity is low than it does when humidity is high. Evaporation helps you stay cool. However, if your body moisture evaporates faster than you can replace it, you may suffer heat exhaustion or heat stroke. If the relative humidity is high, your body perspiration evaporates slowly, making you feel sticky.

Understanding relative humidity, therefore, can help you decide what to wear and the amount of exercise to do, as well as how much drinking water to take along.

Clouds

Clouds formed by rising air currents are classified as *cumulus clouds,* because they're piled-up, or "accumulated" formations. Sometimes clouds form without any vertical movement, as fog does; these sheet-like formations are called *stratus clouds.* Other kinds of clouds include *nimbus* (rain), *fracto* (broken or fractured), *alto* (middle range), and *cirrus* (ice crystals). Can you think of ways to remember what "nimbus" and "cirrus" mean?

We can classify clouds as being high, middle, or low. *High clouds,* which form in the cold upper part of the atmosphere, are made up of tiny ice crystals. High clouds come in various forms. *Cirrus clouds* are thin, wispy, feathery clouds forming above 25,000 feet; they're often called "mares' tails" because they resemble the tails of horses streaming out in the wind. *Cirrocumulus clouds,* which form between 20,000 and 25,000 feet, are rippled and thin. Many years ago, fishermen called these clouds "mackerel scales" because they looked like the scales of the mackerel these men caught off the coasts of New England and Canada. *Cirrostratus clouds,* which are sheets of high ice clouds, are responsible for the halo you sometimes see around the sun or moon. Light shines only so far through the thin layer of clouds, producing the halo effect.

High clouds are usually followed in a day or two by middle clouds. *Middle clouds* form about 10,000 feet above the earth. They're classified as being either *altostratus* (veils or sheets, with some stripes) or *altocumulus* (patches or layers of puffy clouds). To some people, middle clouds look like cottage cheese.

Middle clouds are usually followed in a day or two by low clouds. *Low clouds,* which form anywhere from just above the earth to about 10,000 feet, are usually sheetlike formations. *Stratus clouds,* which are low clouds that can produce drizzle, are dull gray and resemble fog. *Nimbostratus clouds* are just what the name says they are: rain sheets. They even look wet. If nimbostratus clouds are broken by wind, they'll look broken and are called, logically, *fractostratus. Stratocumulus clouds* are irregular masses of clouds in rolling or puffy layers. These clouds don't produce rain, but they can change into nimbostratus clouds, which may.

Other clouds range from very low to very high. The common thunderheads, or *cumulonimbus clouds,* are good examples. Their bases may be almost on the ground, and their heads may rise to 75,000 feet. The top of a growing thunderhead often looks like a head of cauliflower. Many times the wind at high elevations flattens the top of a cumulonimbus cloud, making it look like an anvil.

CUMULUS

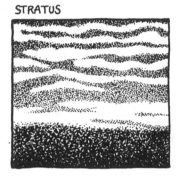
STRATUS

Figure 4.3 Clouds.

Figure 4.4 Clouds. [2]

Cumulus clouds are puffy clouds with changing shapes. For centuries, people have seen imaginary figures, such as animals, in them. Cumulus clouds are often called "fair-weather clouds," because they form during the day, rise, and disappear at night. You needn't worry about storms when you see cumulus clouds unless they keep growing, becoming cumulonimbus clouds.

2. Adapted from Reifsnyder, Wm. F. *Weathering the Wilderness.* San Francisco, CA: Sierra Club Books, 1980.

Knowing the different kinds of clouds and what they mean can help you enjoy weather patterns and, more importantly, predict the weather. Cloud watchers know when to leave an area, when to expect showers, when a storm may hit, and what to wear on any given day.

Wind

Have you ever wondered how fast the wind is blowing? Many times, you may think the wind is blowing much faster than it really is. One way to check wind speed is to use an *anemometer,* an instrument that measures the velocity of the wind.

If your group is building a weather station, they may want to add this easy-to-build wind direction finder. To build a wind direction finder, you'll need a metal coat hanger, a tin-can lid from a number 10 tin-can, an eyedropper without a bulb, rubber cement or masking tape, a nail, and a wooden dowel.

Start by cutting an arrowhead and a counter weight out of the tin-can lid. Then bend the coat hanger so it's straight and cut off the badly bent ends. Next, bend an oval loop in each end of the straightened coat hanger. Use the rubber cement or the masking tape to stick the arrowhead against one loop, and the counterweight against the loop on the other end. Then find the balance point on the straightened coat hanger by resting it on one finger to see at what point it will balance (it won't fall off in either direction). Next, bend a loop, the diameter of your eyedropper, at the balance point, and insert the eyedropper into the loop. Now drive a nail into the top of a dowel and clip the head off the nail. Set the eyedropper down over the nail. You now have a wind direction finder.

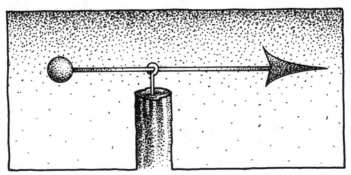

Figure 4.5 Wind direction finder.

Stick the dowel of your wind direction finder in the ground. Then locate north with a compass, and place a peg in the ground on the north side of the wind direction finder. You can also place a peg for east, south, and west. When the wind blows, the arrow should always point to the direction the wind is blowing. But remember, wind direction is always stated by where the wind is coming from.

Thunderstorms

Thunderstorms generally follow a buildup of thunderhead clouds. In the mountains, thunderstorms can be especially severe, because hot air from the valleys rushes up the sides of the mountains and cools dramatically.

Whenever you see thunderhead clouds building up, even if the sky is otherwise clear and blue, be prepared to take cover. If you're on a lake, go to shore at once. If you're on a rocky area on a mountain, retreat to a lower elevation immediately. If you're in a meadow, lie down or go to the edge of the forest. If you're in a forest, take cover under shrubs or low trees. Never stand near the highest tree or the only tree in a field; lightning tends to strike the tallest object in the area.

Water is an excellent conductor of electricity, so you want to avoid it during thunderstorms. Hiding in a crevice in the rocks of a mountain may be safe, but not if water is running through the cracks in the rocks of your hiding place. That water may conduct the electricity to where you are standing.

You'll be safe in an automobile, an airplane, or a steel-frame building. But if you don't have access to any of those places, look for the next safest place: a clump of low trees.

The best practice during a thunderstorm is to get away from high places and water and to seek shelter under small trees until you're sure that the storm has passed. There may be lingering lightning strikes, so don't rush right out into the rain; wait at least twenty minutes. If you don't hear a thunderclap for twenty minutes, you can venture out and go on your way.

Tornadoes

Tornadoes often follow thunderstorms in the Midwest. West of the prairie states (North Dakota to Texas), tornadoes rarely occur. Most tornadoes strike in the lower Great Plains States, although they occasionally occur in the other Midwestern states and in the East.

A tornado moves relatively slowly across the ground, but the winds whirling around in the funnel itself may travel at 300 or more miles per hour, and the speed of the updraft may be 100 to 200 miles per hour. The tornado won't be very wide however — probably about 1,000 feet in diameter.

Signs of an approaching tornado include changes in the sky — it may turn a blackish green — and rising wind. When you observe those signs, seek cover. The safest place is the basement of a building, against an outside wall; when you're on a trip, though, no basement may be available. In that case, look for the lowest place you can find — a gully, a ditch, or a dry riverbed. Get away from large trees. Small branches are less likely to seriously injure you if they fall on you, and small trunks are easy to hang on to with both arms.

Your chances of being caught in a tornado are very slight because the storm has a small diameter. Nevertheless, you must be prepared for a tornado and know what to do if one springs up.

Weather sayings

Before the days of sophisticated weather instruments, pioneers, explorers, sailors, and trappers predicted weather by what the sky and clouds looked like, and they followed the advice given in well-known sayings. Some of these sayings follow.

Red sky in the morning, sailors take warning.
Red sky at night, sailors' delight.

If the sky is red in the morning, a thin layer of cirrus (icy) clouds is blocking the sun. Cirrus clouds are followed by alto clouds, and alto clouds carry rain. Therefore, rain will probably come by nightfall, and possibly a storm during the night. If the sky is red at night, the thin layer of icy clouds is far to the west, where the sun is setting. Weather probably won't be troublesome until the next day or the day after that.

Mackerel scales and mare's tails
make lofty ships carry low sails.

This saying refers to those high, wispy cirrus clouds that are the forerunners of storms. When sailors saw these clouds, the storms were closer than when they saw just the red sky peeping through a thin layer of high cirrus clouds mentioned above. The sailors then lowered their sails so they wouldn't be blown about by the storm.

When swallows fly low over a lake, it's going to rain soon.

When air pressure starts to fall, insects fly closer to the water, and the birds that eat them have to do likewise. Falling air pressure is usually followed by rain. Usually, some cloud action verifies this prediction, but sometimes the clouds are too thin to see.

Find some other weather sayings or local ideas and see whether they are accurate or nearly accurate.

Now that you know what makes up the weather, you can try to predict it. You should be able to predict changes in the temperature and cloud cover from day to day. It's equally important, for safety reasons to be able to predict thunderstorms, tornadoes, heavy rains, and other weather that can cause serious problems for campers.

You can predict the weather fairly accurately for a short time by following cloud cover, from high to low clouds. Try to predict tomorrow's weather, and then check the local newspaper, radio, or television to see how accurate you were.

DRINKING WATER

At home, it's easy to find good drinking water; all you have to do is turn on the faucet. Outdoors, it's not quite as simple. If you're at a youth camp or a state, national, or city park that has faucets, by all means, use them. You can expect good drinking water to come from pipes that can be easily turned on and off. Health regulations in the United States mandate that water pumped through pipes from which the general public will drink must contain no disease-bearing organisms.

At one time, streams, lakes, rivers, and springs also offered safe drinking water. Until about the 1970s, most canoeists, backpackers, mountain climbers, and rafters simply drank from rivers and streams, giving little thought to any impurities in the water. Today, it's foolhardy not to take precautions against disease-causing organisms in even the most remote streams. Because there are thousands more outdoor enthusiasts today than twenty years ago, disease is much more likely to be spread by water. People and their pets travel farther and to many different places today, transmiting organisms to areas where they never existed before.

A good example of this is a water-borne organism named *Giardia lamblia* that causes a disease called giardiasis. This disease, which has been around for many years, is now found even in the most remote high mountain areas; the organism seems to thrive in the cold waters of mountain streams.

No one knows how Giardia came to the United States or where it evolved. The organism is spread to water sources by human and animal fecal material, and anyone who drinks Giardia-contaminated water suffers a very painful complication of the intestinal tract; Giardia acts as a powerful laxative. The illness may take up to two weeks to show up and victims may be ill for many days. They often wish they had never gone into the beautiful country where they contracted the disease.

What's the solution to the dilemma of choosing between beautiful country and the possibility of this or other diseases? The answer is water purification. Purifying water takes a little time and a little planning, but you're in the outdoors to enjoy yourself, not to rush through everything as fast as you can.

You'll need to purify all water that you'll be using for drinking, cooking, and washing dishes unless you use melted, newly fallen, clean snow. Most people, however, participate in outdoor activities long after the months in which snow falls, and old snow can be as contaminated as a stream or pond.

Boiling Water

Boiling dishwater is a simple task. It takes a little while for the water to cool, but you can be doing other chores or appreciating the sunset while you wait. Purifying drinking water is also easy; simply boil stream water for 10 minutes. If you don't have time to wait for your drinking water to cool to a refreshing temperature, you can use other simple water purification methods.

Assuming that pollutants are living organisms, not chemicals, boiling will provide you with safe drinking water as long as you boil it *at least 10 minutes at sea level* and *up to 20 minutes at 5000 feet* (even longer if you are above that elevation). Be sure to sanitize your water bottle by rinsing it out with some of the boiling water. It's a waste to pour purified water into a bottle that may have had even a small amount of pollutant in it.

Remember that one of the ten essentials is extra drinking water. Common sense should tell you to save some water to drink while you are preparing the next batch. It would be silly to drink all the water, get thirsty, and then try to find a source of new water that you'll have to purify; by that time, you'd be really thirsty. A good rule is to drink before you're thirsty; another good rule is to replenish your water supply before you're thirsty.

Water Purifiers

If you use commercial water purifiers — halogens, iodine, a bromine or chlorine compound, or even common bleach — you'll be able to kill Giardia cysts if you use the purifiers properly. The directions on the bottles usually assume that you're using these materials in room-temperature water. If you're taking your water from a mountain stream, its temperature may be only 30 degrees, so you must allow the purifier to work for longer than the directions suggest — at least 30 minutes.

Water Filtration

The third method of water purification is filtration, a process that is becoming very popular. Your youth camp, outdoor program or group may need to purchase commercial backpacking water filters. Unfortunately, the best is probably the most expensive. Other very good models are available, however, and the secret is not the price as much as it is the size of the filter; it must be small enough to catch the Giardia organisms. Filters are described by size, and the .06 micron size should filter Giardia.

Filters must be replaced or cleaned at intervals in order to keep them efficient. Be sure to follow the directions that come with your group's water filter. Keep these directions in a readily available file at home or at your camp so that you can refer to them each time you prepare for trip.

No matter what method of water purification you use, practice it at your base camp before venturing forth on your trip to learn how the method works and how long it takes. Then when you get to a water source, on the trip you'll be able to act with confidence and assurance that you know what to do.

Don't take water from streams that may contain agricultural or chemical wastes. Free-flowing streams may not purify themselves of chemicals; no matter what you may have read. Don't use streams carrying runoff from farms, forestry operations, and factories, because you have no way of knowing what kinds of chemicals the water may contain.

When you're hiking in a snowy area, particularly in the early spring, you may see red or pink snow patches. Although the color may simply be pollen from nearby conifers, it could also be red algae, which contains a chemical like Giardia — a very powerful laxative. Anyone who drinks melted snow that contains even small portions of this algae will suffer severe diarrhea. Beware of red snow! Find clean white snow, if you can, and melt that instead. (You may have to dig to reach a spot where the snow has not been covered by branches or dust.) When you melt snow for drinking water, it's best to pack it tightly before you put it in a pan over the heat source. By doing so, you'll use less fuel and end up with more drinking water.

Water flowing from a glacier probably won't be contaminated by pathogens, or disease-producing materials, but you can be sure that it contains fine particles of worn rock. This material resembles liquid sandpaper as it moves through your system. Although the water may look and taste great, the rock particles will make you ill. You may decide that drinking water from a melting glacier is not such a good idea after all.

Water sources vary in different geographical areas. Talk with forest rangers, expert campers, and experienced outdoor leaders in the area where you'll be traveling; they can give you the best advice.

Gadgets are probably unnecessary. Some outdoor experts believe that a solar-still works well in the desert, where the sun is intense. However, building a still takes more energy and perspiration than the resulting small amount of water it can replenish. It's better to conserve your energy and natural body moisture. Even in a survival situation, a solar-still may not give enough water. If you plan appropriately before you leave base camp, you'll never need one.

TOILETS

As cultured people, we have been taught that the discussion of human waste and its disposal is neither pleasant nor even acceptable in polite groups. Yet we must recognize that one of the biggest challenges of using the outdoors for recreation is disposing of human waste. Certainly, if any toilet facilities are available, you must use them, no matter how unpleasant they may appear to be. Not using existing toilets or latrines is extremely insensitive to other people and to the environment.

Your base camp may offer some sort of latrine or outhouse. But you must make other arrangements in remote areas. Can you construct your own toilet? How can you be sure that your toilet won't contaminate the soil or water, spread disease, or leave unpleasant residue for other people to find after you've gone?

Human waste carries many forms of bacteria that are harmful to the environment and to humans, and it's just plain disagreeable to people who encounter it by accident. Urine, however, doesn't cause bacterial problems; it's a sterile waste product that usually carries no parasites. It does, however, contain uric acid — which, when crystallized, has a taste that bears, skunks, and particularly porcupines enjoy. Many old-fashioned outhouses have been ravaged by porcupines who gnawed the wood to taste the uric salts. Urine also has a disagreeable odor, particularly when it gets on clothing or accumulates in one place.

When you urinate, do so at least 200 feet from water and preferably on rocks or dry areas. This practice will help the urine evaporate, keep animals away, and disperse any damage to plants.

As for fecal material, no single way to dispose of it can be recommended for every situation. You'll need to consider the size of the group, the type of soil, the location of the trip, and the time of year. You have the challenge of deciding which method will contaminate the water supply the least, will not be discovered by later campers, and will still result in rapid and maximum decomposition. Regardless of the disposal method you use, remember that the *pathogenic,* or disease-producing, material may survive in the ground for more than a year after you leave the area.

Because you'll be traveling in a group, you must figure out how to disperse the waste, not concentrate it. [3] The best way may be to have each person locate an area 200 feet or more from the water supply and, with a trowel, dig a cathole several inches deep to receive the fecal material.

When you finish using a cathole, mix the feces and the soil with a stick, and cover the area with an inch or two of topsoil, the way a cat does. Then camouflage the cathole so that it's not obvious, but identify it somehow so that the next camper won't make the mistake of digging another cathole in the same place. Many campers mark a cathole with two crossed sticks. This looks fairly natural and signals other campers that this area has been used.

You might consider making a group latrine if you're in an area where digging is fairly easy. Dig a long trench twelve inches deep, and ask users to start at one end and cover their waste as they use the facility. When the trench is full to within four inches of the surface, cover it and start another one.

A latrine may be the best option when the campers are inexperienced and having difficulty finding suitable individual catholes. It may also be the best option when you have a large group and don't want to surround the camping area with catholes.

A person traveling alone or with one or two others in a dry, rocky area might best leave feces scattered on the rocks to dry if there is little possibility that someone else will be coming along soon; fecal material deteriorates rapidly, and the bacteria die quickly in this type of environment. But this type of situation is extremely rare.

Keep in mind the idea of carrying things out of the woods with you. When you camp in a snowy area, or when the air temperature is below freezing, you should use plastic bags to carry fecal material back to the area from which you came; you can dispose of the waste in the toilet facilities provided there.

3.   Hampton, Bruce and Cole, David. *Soft Paths.* Harrisburg, PA: Stackpole Books, 1988.

As a matter of fact, when large groups camp under these conditions, one common practice is to designate a common area for the latrine; deposit all frozen feces, toilet paper, and other material in a double plastic bag and transport the material to the trailhead for disposal in a landfill. The material remains frozen and odorless as long as the temperature stays below thirty-two degrees.

Cold acts like a preservative, much like a refrigerator, and keeps many things from decomposing. Human waste is one such thing. Disease-producing material may not survive, but the physical waste will remain, creating a terrible mess when the snow melts. In all cases, regardless of temperature and climate, carry tampons and sanitary pads out in plastic bags; they won't decompose in the woods or the desert.

In desert areas, it's very important to keep a cathole or latrine shallow. Few organisms will help decompose the fecal material, but the heat of the sun on sandy, light soil creates a sterilization oven of about 105 degrees if the hole is not too deep.

Minimum-impact camping on river trips begins with the planning stage. Each river has a different management plan. Check with the U.S. Forest Service, the National Park Service, or the Bureau of Land Management (if the river you plan to travel is managed by one of these federal agencies) to find out how you should dispose of human waste. Where there are no established rules and regulations, take the following steps:

1. Urinate and defecate above the high water mark and at least 100 feet away from the river. Keep away from natural drainage systems.

2. Dig a cathole.

3. Carry out all toilet paper in plastic bags.

You can make a rocket-box porta-potty large enough for twelve people to use for five days by using a surplus ammunition can or box, available from Army-Navy stores. You'll also need a toilet seat, large heavy-duty plastic bags, a chemical deodorant (such as the kind used in motor homes) or chlorine bleach to prevent methane gas production, toilet paper, and a handwashing bucket.

To build and use a rocket-box porta-potty follow these steps:

1. Line the box with two plastic bags, folding the excess plastic over the edges of the box.

2. Pour in the deodorant.

3. Use the toilet for fecal material, not for urine. Urine will increase the amount of liquids that you must transport from your campsite.

4. Place used toilet paper, tampons, and sanitary napkins in the toilet.

5. Keep the handwashing bucket nearby (covered with plastic, if flies are a problem).

6. To dismantle the toilet for the next day's trip, remove the plastic bags from the box, squeeze out excess air, and tie the tops of the bags shut.

7. Place the used bags inside other bags, and store them in the ammo box for transportation in one of the canoes or rafts. As other bags are used, add them to the carrying bags.

8. At the next stop, remove the bag containing the used bags from the ammo box and line the box with two new plastic bags.

9. When the trip is over, dispose of the plastic bags in a landfill.

As you would for any outdoor activity, always ask the question "Am I disturbing the environment unnecessarily?" Practicing minimum-impact camping may also make a difference in your own health and safety.

FIRST-AID

First-aid is *immediate* and *temporary care* given to the victim of an accident or sudden illness. It is not the purpose of this book to give the reader a complete first-aid course. There are many excellent books on first-aid and on wilderness first-aid. They will not be duplicated here. You should get training from the American Red Cross or some other recognized first-aid organization. Every leader must consider it his/her personal responsibility to complete an advanced first-aid course *before* taking any group outdoors.

The following section provides basic information on treating some common problems. This information is by no means complete; get further training in these areas.

Minor Injuries and Illnesses

Bleeding

Place the cut or bleeding area above the heart, if possible, unless the victim has other injuries that require him/her not to be moved. No matter how minor or how severe the bleeding is, put pressure on the wound to stop the bleeding, using a clean cloth if one is available. If the bleeding is severe enough to saturate available clean bandages, use a bandanna, a shirt, or anything to stop the bleeding. It may take anywhere from fifteen minutes to five hours, but keep putting pressure on the area until the bleeding stops.

Blisters

Eliminate any friction that caused the blister and clean the blistered area. Cover the area with a bandage and tape, or molefoam and moleskin to prevent further trauma to the area. Do not remove the skin from the blister; it will help prevent infection. If the blister is large, it may need to be drained. The best treatment for blisters is avoidance — make sure that campers' boots or shoes fit and are broken in, and that they are wearing the appropriate socks. Gloves should be worn when there is any possibility of blistering to the hands.

Minor burns

Immediately remove all surrounding clothing. If the burn is superficial and localized, and involves less than 20 percent of the body surface, the following steps should be taken. Apply cold immediately. Wash the area thoroughly with non-medicated soap and water. Apply Betadine ointment. Cover loosely with a sterile dressing to avoid further trauma. Aspirin may be given to relieve pain. Leave dressing secure while on the trail to reduce the risk of infection. When the bandage is removed, check for blistering. If none is visible, cover the area only to protect it from trauma. Keep the area clean.

More serious burn victims should be given fluids to help reduce the chances of shock, then evacuated immediately. There are other considerations in evacuation; please read a more in depth resource or get further training on burn treatment.

Chapped hands and lips
Protect the chapped parts of the body from further exposure to the elements. Apply lotion, Vasaline, or a commercial chapped-lip treatment.

Dehydration
Replace body fluids with any nonalcoholic, noncaffeinated drink. Fruit juices, Gatorade, and noncaffeinated soft drinks are especially good because they also help replace lost electrolytes. (Potassium, salt, and bicarbonate together, make up electrolytes; your diet should include a balance of these things.) Do not treat dehydration with salt tablets, especially if the victim has a kidney disorder. Treating dehydration with salt tablets can create a lethal imbalance in the kidneys.

Common headaches
Make certain that the camper has not been injured. If no injury is present, a non-aspirin pain reliever may be given in the proper dose, and the person should be kept still and quiet for 30 to 60 minutes. Headaches are common after a rapid ascent to high altitudes.

Minor insect bites and stings
Remove any stinger or remaining poisonous insect parts. Cold compresses may decrease absorption of the venom. Desensitize the injured area with some mild antihistamine. Keep the area covered with a bandage if victim is likely to scratch it.

Insect bites and stings can cause severe allergic reactions in some people. The treatment for these cases is much different and you should be properly trained by medical personnel for them. Some campers are already aware of their allergy to bee or wasp stings and will have their own medication. If so, they will know how to medicate themselves, possibly by injection. It may be prudent to get permission to teach that camper's buddy how to give the medication, in case the victim is unable to do it himself/herself.

Muscle cramps

Stretch the muscle where the spasm is occurring. Do not knead or pound the area; that may cause other soreness. To help prevent cramps, make sure that campers get enough water and salt in their diets.

Nose bleeds

Keep the victim upright — either sitting or standing, but not lying down — and do not let that person tilt his/her head backward. That won't stop the bleeding, and the blood could run backward into his/her throat. Have the victim tilt his/her head forward instead, to let the blood drain. Cold application may help stop the bleeding. Have the person pinch his/her nostrils firmly with his/her thumb and forefinger so that there is pressure on the place where the bleeding is. Usually the bleeding will stop in one to two minutes.

Poison ivy, poison oak, poison sumac

Wash thoroughly. Relieve the itching by applying an over-the-counter topical antihistamine.

Sprains

Apply a cold compress to the area immediately to prevent further swelling. The camper should rest the joint for 24 to 48 hours. Support the ankle, wrist, or other joint by wrapping it with a well-padded compression bandage or tape. If the injury is a sprained ankle, you may need to wrap the boot as well as the ankle, so that the ankle won't have to support the weight of the boot.

Hypothermia

Hypothermia (low heat) and hyperthermia (high heat) must be a primary concern of leaders and participants. In almost all situations, you can prevent these problems by making sure that everyone has proper clothing and equipment.

Hypothermia is the lowering of the temperature of the inner core of the body faster than the body can replace the heat. The average internal temperature of the human body is 96.8 degrees Fahrenheit. When the exterior of the body becomes cold, the heat from the interior moves up to warm the surface. If you put one finger in an icy stream for a few seconds and examine it after you pull it out, you'll see it has become red.

This redness is the result of the body's inner heat rushing to warm the finger in the cold water.

When the external body temperature goes below about 75 degrees, the internal temperature drops significantly. This results in a decrease in vital bodily functions such as digestion, circulation, breathing, and even thinking.

As the core temperature continues to decrease, the symptoms of hypothermia change. Although not all cases are the same, the following indicates the usual symptoms of hypothermia at specific body temperatures.

96 to 99 degrees
Shivering becomes intense and uncontrollable. Ability to perform tasks is impaired. The victim can't walk heel to toe down a thirty-foot line scratched in the ground.

91 to 95 degrees
Continued shivering. Difficulty in thinking and speaking. Loss of memory is evident.

86 to 90 degrees
Shivering stops, and muscles become rigid. Motions are jerky and erratic. Skin may be blue and puffy. Thinking is less clear, but the victim may *appear* to still be in contact with reality.

85 to 81 degrees
Muscles continue to be rigid. Pulse slows. Victim loses contact with the environment and may drift into a stupor.

78 to 80 degrees
Victim loses consciousness. Heartbeat becomes erratic.

Below 78 degrees
Cardiac and respiratory control centers fail, resulting in heart and lung problems and possible death.

Hypothermia that occurs over a period of time is called *systemic hypothermia*. If the body is immersed in cold water, hypothermia is almost immediate; that type is called *immersion hypothermia*. The two types are similar, except immersion hypothermia may set in after only five to ten minutes.

The best protection against hypothermia is following good outdoor practices, especially by providing adequate protection from wind, rain, and snow. In addition, make sure that campers get adequate nutrition and liquids. You'll recognize these as the first three items in the list of ten essentials and survival tips provided in the previous chapter.

Other safeguards include physical conditioning, wise use of wool and insulating materials, adequate rest, and enough exercise to keep up the body's production of heat.

There are two treatments for hypothermia:

1. **Reduce the heat loss.** Shelter the victim from the wind, weather, and cold ground. Replace his/her wet clothing with plenty of dry clothing so that he/she won't lose any more body heat. Increase the victim's exercise level slightly to maintain heat (for mild hypothermia). Get the victim into a tent or other shelter immediately.

2. **Add heat.** Give the victim warm or hot drinks and high-energy foods, such as sugars and breads. Apply heat from a warm rock or canteen full of hot water. (If the heat source is too hot for you, it will burn the victim, so be careful.) Exercise the victim by having him/her walk with you toward a lower elevation, warmer area, or the trailhead.

If the victim is in a state of confusion and can't respond or get warm, put the victim naked or nearly naked into a sleeping bag with another person who is also naked or nearly naked. The warmth from his/her body will warm the victim. The experience will be very chilling for the person who is helping, but there's no better way to transfer body heat back to the victim. If you can zip two sleeping bags together, add a third person so that the victim is sandwiched between two warm bodies.

It's extremely important that you not warm the body of a severely hypothermic person too quickly. Warming the extremities too quickly will dilate the blood vessels, sending previously stagnated cold, low-oxygen blood back to the body core, where it will shock the organs. This can be fatal.

Assuming that you caught the hypothermia in time, as the victim becomes warm, he/she will need to urinate frequently. Be sure to have some pan or bottle available in the tent for this purpose; the victim can't go outdoors yet. The treatment for even mild hypothermia may take several hours.

A victim who seems to be fully recovered should be evacuated to the trailhead and given medical care slowly but steadily. If the victim does not respond to early treatment, you must immediately send for emergency medical care.

Hyperthermia

Hyperthermia, which is just as serious as hypothermia, may set in more rapidly. Your body contains a built-in cooling system, but if the body core reaches 106 degrees Fahrenheit or more, death may occur.

Your body gains heat in two ways: through *absorption* (external heat from warm air, radiated and/or reflected sunlight, and direct contact with warm objects) and *internally* (heat produced by working muscles and normal body metabolism).

Hyperthermia may result in either *heat stroke* or *heat exhaustion*. Heat stroke is characterized by high body temperature; hot, red, dry skin; rapid, strong pulse; and possible unconsciousness. To treat it, cool the victim with cool or cold water. Avoid overchilling him or her.

Heat exhaustion is characterized by approximately normal body temperature; pale, clammy skin; profuse perspiration; weakness; headache; and possible nausea and vomiting. To treat it, give the victim sips of mildly salted water (unless he/she is vomiting) and apply cool wet cloths. This victim should not be exposed to warm temperatures during the rest of the trip. It's probably best to return all victims of any type of hyperthermia to the home base immediately.

Preventing heat-related problems involves drinking water whenever you are thirsty. In hot weather, two to three quarts per day is the minimum amount you need to maintain normal body functions. Have plenty of salt in your normal diet; salt tablets are not a good substitute. Stay out of direct sunlight. Cover your body; wear a hat; protect your neck. Imagine the covering worn by Arabs who must be protected from hot, dry desert conditions, and follow their example. Eat lightly but well, and slow your activities.

If all goes well, your trips will be uneventful as far as injuries are concerned. As a leader, though, you must be prepared to treat minor problems so that they do not become major ones.

First-Aid Kit

A well-stocked first-aid kit is a good starting point for handling common first-aid problems. Your first-aid kit should include the following items:

A first-aid manual
Permission forms from parents or campers, for providing
    medical treatment
Matches
Flashlight
Paper and pencil
Change for making phone calls
Adhesive bandages of assorted sizes
Adhesive tape
Antacid tablets
Aspirin and/or non-aspirin pain reliever (to relieve pain and
    reduce fever)
Butterfly bandages (to protect small, deep cuts)
Antibiotic ointment (small tube)
Liquid antibacterial soap (for cleaning wounds)
Elastic bandage, four inch wide (to support sprains or strains)
Sterile gauze compresses, two inches and four inches wide
    (to protect open wounds)
Rolled gauze bandages, one inch and two inches wide
    (to protect open wounds)
Telfa pads (nonadhesive)
Molefoam and moleskin (to protect blisters)
Needles (to open blisters)
Oral thermometer
Safety pins
Scissors
Sunblock lotion
Sunburn lotion
Triangular bandages
Tweezers (for removing splinters, bee stingers, etc.)
Poison-ivy or poison-oak remedy

Snakebite kits are recommended only if an adult who has been trained in their use is present. Snakebite kits can be as dangerous as the snakebite itself if they're used incorrectly.

Before you go on a trip, discuss the possible accidents that could occur. Practice the first aid you would administer. Try role-playing simple first-aid situations with campers.

In all cases, remember to get first-aid training before you provide any first-aid. It is recommended that leaders be certified in American Red Cross Standard First-Aid.

Summary

In addition to making and following sound plans for a trip into the outdoors, you can help ensure safety by learning about weather, water, toilets, and first aid. Understanding the weather will help you keep campers from getting too cold and wet, too hot and dry, or ill under cold, damp, windy conditions. Understanding how to get safe drinking water and dispose of human waste can keep your group from contracting painful and sometimes fatal diseases. And knowing how to care for victims of accidents or illness will prevent the problems from becoming major ones. *Be safe. Take care of yourself and your environment.* By doing both, you and the environment will remain safe and healthy, and you can take another trip with confidence.

5

Exploring Your World

The first part of this book focused on safety and minimum-impact camping skills. There is more to outdoor living, however, than just keeping campers and the environment healthy. The main reason why people go outdoors — to a city park, a youth camp, remote mountains, winding rivers, deep forests, or vast deserts — is enjoyment.

Some people find that the outdoors is a marvelous place for socialization, games, exercise, and other forms of recreation because it seems to give them a feeling of freedom and cleanliness. But not everyone feels the same enthusiasm for the outdoors. When it gets cold, rainy, windy, humid, or hot; when insects bite, bees buzz, dust flies; and even when darkness falls, lots of people want to go indoors.

Before people can enjoy being outdoors, they need to feel comfortable and secure. Many youngsters at youth camps — and many camp-staff members — don't feel at home outdoors. And even those who are comfortable outdoors may need to have that comfort nurtured so it doesn't disappear.

All children have natural curiosity about the outdoors — about plants, animals, odors, textures, colors, and many other things. If this curiosity is squelched by the time the child reaches the age of ten, however, it may stay dormant for years and years, possibly reviving when that person is in his or her twenties or thirties, or maybe never. What a shame that these people will never know how fascinating nature really is.

This means that as a leader, you have a triple responsibility:

1. You must be sure not to destroy anyone's natural curiosity.

2. You must be able, in some situations, to revive lost or stifled curiosity.

3. You must nourish the curiosity of those who already feel comfortable outdoors.

Nourish any existing curiosity, revive dormant curiosity, and don't destroy natural curiosity — that's the challenge. This task is especially challenging if only a few members of the group know anything about the outdoors.

Fortunately, there are relatively few things you need to know in order to understand and appreciate the world around you, and many activities can help campers enjoy learning them.

Physical comfort

The first criterion for comfort in the outdoors is physical comfort. If the members of your group are not warm enough, or are too warm for example, no one will have much fun. This situation is not conducive to learning, because campers will be wondering how soon they can go back indoors where it is comfortable. Therefore, you must ensure that they have appropriate clothing to keep them warm or cool enough and dry.

Even if the temperature is comfortable, wind may affect people's learning. Voices don't carry well; papers get blown away; leaves, branches, or insects may not stay in place for observation. The sun also plays a role. When you face the group, you should also be facing the sun, so that group members don't have to squint, shut their eyes, or look away.

A thoughtful leader always attempts to get his/her group out of the wind before trying to explain any type of activity and never makes the group face the sun.

Psychological comfort

When people are in a new place, they want to know where things are, what they are, and what they do. They also want to know whether anything out there can hurt them. Their fear is mostly fear of the unknown. When people don't understand something or aren't sure what's going to happen, they often become afraid, or act disinterested, or silly — anything to mask the fact that they are uncomfortable.

We are secure in cities and towns, in our own houses and backyards. We are less secure in unfamiliar surroundings, where we may encounter strange animals and plants, or unusual sounds. To many of us, the outdoors is a confusing green or brown world filled with unknown things that bite or sting. Make your group members comfortable. Tell them what's there. Explain the grounds of the camp, campsite, or park. Tell them where the bathroom is, where the food will be stored, and what insects and other creatures are there.

The fact is that there are very few, if any, things in the outdoors that demand such extreme caution. One of those things is grizzly bears, which live in remote regions of some of the Western states. There are usually adequate warnings about grizzlies in those areas; leaders who are unfamiliar with grizzlies, however, should be sure to get advice from experts on proper human behavior when traveling in grizzly country. (This is just one more aspect of planning: knowing your environment and checking the situation out thoroughly.)

Another legitimate fear is poisonous snakes. Statistics indicate that there are very few cases of snakebite in the United States each year and that nearly all the victims recover; in fact, you may be hundreds of times safer in rattlesnake country than you would be in big-city traffic. Qualified leaders, however, should have first-aid training to prepare them for cases of snakebite. (Snakebite kits, if left to untrained hands, can be more dangerous than a snakebite. Know what you are doing.)

Finally, leaders should maintain a healthy respect for alligators (in the swamplands of the south), and for scorpions and large centipedes (in the desert). If you are planning an excursion to such an area, talk to the local experts about how to avoid

Figure 5.1

problem animals — and about what to do if avoiding them isn't possible.

In the rest of the country and its millions of square miles of recreational lands, there are very few problem animals that will harm people. Convincing some people of that fact, however, may be a major task, one that requires patience, understanding, and positive personal experiences outdoors. To a novice backpacker sleeping outdoors for the first time, the rustling of a meadow mouse in the weeds may sound like the tramping of a hundred ferocious buffalo. Understanding companions (and a flashlight) will show him/her that there really is nothing to fear. (This is not to say that there aren't specific things in nature that can cause some people harm. For example, one bee sting can be fatal to a person who is allergic to bee stings. Make sure you know your campers medical history.)

Most people find frogs fascinating — but only when they're not used in practical jokes. If a leader uses small harmless animals to frighten timid campers, those campers will have a difficult time adjusting to the idea that larger animals, such as rabbits, squirrels, porcupines and raccoons won't hurt them if they don't hurt the animals. It's helpful to explain that most animals are afraid of people. Animals' homes are outdoors, where people are merely visitors. When we go outdoors, we may frighten an animal as much as a dinosaur would frighten us. If you treat animals with respect and the members of the group with equal respect, the fears should go away.

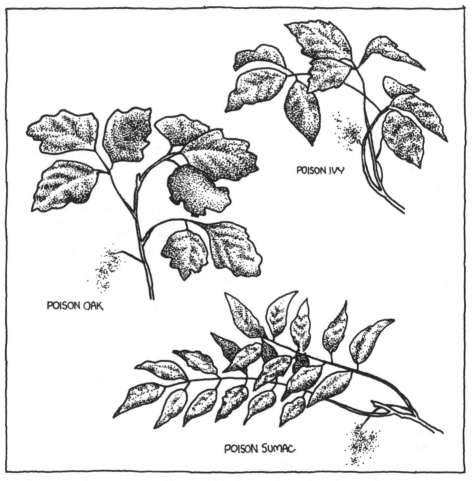

Figure 5.2 Poisonous plants

There are a few common plants that grow in many parts of the country that can cause humans problems. They include poison ivy, poison oak, nettles and some cacti. You should know the troublesome plants in your area and point them out to participants so that they can be avoided. Participants will be more comfortable knowing what to and what not to touch.

IDENTIFYING UNFAMILIAR THINGS

Many people are reluctant to learn about the outdoors because they think they'll have to identify and memorize long lists of plants and animals — seemingly a rather boring and useless activity. There are so many different birds, flowers, trees, ferns, insects, and shells to study that many people panic. "There's too much to learn," they complain.

They are right. There are more than one million different kinds of insects alone and no one can learn them all. Nor can anyone learn everything there is to know about trees, flowers, birds, or even just one kind of plant; some people spend their lives studying only roses or dandelions.

How can a camper be expected to learn all the different kinds of trees or birds? You may not know all the species yourself. It would be like trying to memorize the names and addresses of all the people in your school, and then the names and addresses of all the people in your town, county, and state.

Whose names do you remember? Those of your friends, relatives, and other people who are important to you. The same is true of plants and animals. If you want to remember some of the names, you will. Even if you can't find out what their names are, invent nicknames for them; later you can try to find out what their real names are.

Many plants carry names that were given to them by the people who first saw them. In the early days of exploration in the American West, for example, a pine tree that was straight and small enough for one or two men to lift into place for the side of a cabin was called lodge-pole pine. But the scientists who first saw that species of pine on the Pacific Coast, where the trees were gnarled and twisted by the wind, called it *Pinus contorta* (twisted pine). How can the twisted pine of the west coast be the same as the straight lodge-pole pine of the interior? One name may be wrong, but no one seems to care. Non-scientists usually give trees and other plants names that mean something to them. Eventually, the plants get official scientific names, such as *Pinus Contorta*, but in different parts of the country, they carry different common names, such as lodge-pole pine. The same is true with birds and fish.

Figure 5.3 Lodge-pole pine.

Can you think of any plants or animals that have more than one name? What about vegetables or fruits? Did you know that some people call green peppers, *mangos*?

Even people who know a great deal about plants give some of them strange names. For example, four adults who like to remember the names of wildflowers were visiting Great Smoky Mountains National Park when they saw patch after patch of a flower they had never seen — so much of it that they felt they should call it something, so they referred to it as "that white stuff." Everyone in the group knew what "that white stuff" was; it made no difference that they didn't know its real name. They thought of the flower as being pretty and plentiful, and they had a great time seeing it and laughing about its nickname. They'll always remember that plant with pleasure. It doesn't matter that it has scientific name that they never learned.

You probably do the same thing with people whose names you don't know, calling someone "the man who wears the hat" or "the woman who drives the Volkswagen."

It is not necessary for campers to learn the names of everything they see outdoors. For starters, they need to know only a few common trees, flowers, and birds.

You can reach most people through your enthusiastic presentation of fascinating facts. Explain to your group that nicknames are how many things got their names. Have fun making up nicknames. If you know the proper name for something, talk about the name and decide if it has some connection to how that plant or animal was originally seen or used by people. Having fun nicknaming things in nature can help nourish interest in nature. The following material can also help you begin to nourish that interest.

Learning to "See" the Outdoors

As we said earlier, many people see the outdoors as a confusing green and brown world. Perhaps that's because they've been conditioned not to touch unfamiliar objects or get dirty. Why not help them become explorers?

Ask the members of the group what they'd do if they found themselves on a strange planet. They'd probably do the same things they'd do if they were examining a new house. They'd smell the fresh paint, stand on tiptoes to look in the cupboards, get down on their hands and knees to look up the chimney, feel the carpet, and perhaps listen for noises from next door. They'd investigate the closets, the basement, the attic, and the garage. In short, they'd use their senses of sight, smell, hearing, and touch, varying their positions, looking in cracks, under and inside things, really getting acquainted with their new environment.

Your group members should examine nature the same way. Have them touch things, smell things, and listen to things. Have them look under, into, and on top of things, getting down on their hands and knees, or on their stomachs, or even looking at things upside down. Even getting wet or dirty is all part of getting acquainted with nature.

Then help them to focus. First, have them practice looking at large areas. Then ask them to pretend they are camera lenses looking at smaller areas. By making frames with their fingers, they can focus on what they see in that space. Next, make the spaces even smaller. Ask, "what's the largest plant you can focus on? What's the smallest plant?" Have them pretend they're looking from an ant's view.

Seeing Familiar Things in Unfamiliar Ones

Part of teaching campers about the outdoors is teaching them to be at home there. You can help them see that many of the things they see outdoors are very much like the things with which they're already familiar. You can lead the following exercises indoors, in fields, in forests, or at your campsite. The point is simply to find familiar things and learn to be at home.

Lines

Start with something simple, such as lines. The following figure shows types of lines that campers can find in both man-made and natural settings. They can experiment further by finding half-circles, and wavy lines.

LINE		MAN-MADE	NATURAL
HORIZONTAL	—	CLAPBOARDS ON A HOUSE; ROWS OF BRICKS; SLATS OF BLINDS	THE HORIZON; BRANCHES OF SOME TREES; BRANCHES LYING ON THE GROUND
VERTICAL	|||	FENCES; SIDES OF BUILDINGS	TREE TRUNKS; GRASSES; VEINS IN IRIS LEAVES
DIAGONAL	///	RAMPS; ROOF LINES	SOME BRANCHES; HILLS
INTERSECTING	X + ✳	CROSS ROADS; CHURCH CRUCIFIX; TELEPHONE POLES	BRANCHES, FLOWER PETALS, APPLE CORE

Figure 5.4

Shapes

Your group members should already recognize squares, circles, triangles, rectangles, spheres, and cones. What can they find in nature that is square, or round, or triangular? Or any other shape?

Next, have the group try to find three-dimensional forms, such as cubes, spheres, cones, and pyramids. Pretty soon, they'll be seeing shapes all over the place, and suddenly, leaves and branches and trees will become much more interesting.

Colors

That confusing mass of green really isn't what it seems to be. If you've ever used a paint-by-number art kit, you'll remember that the artist put orange and green in the sky, pink and yellow in the ocean, and blue and purple in the trees. Nature's like that. You can find a wide variety of colors in every landscape.

Colors are subtle, with many variations in *hue* (red, orange, yellow, green, etc.), *intensity* (brightness or dullness), and *value* (lightness or darkness). Thus, orange can be light bright orange or light dull orange, dark bright orange or dark dull orange. Participants can find virtual rainbows in nature by examining leaves, flowers, stones, clouds, tree bark, grass, and insects.

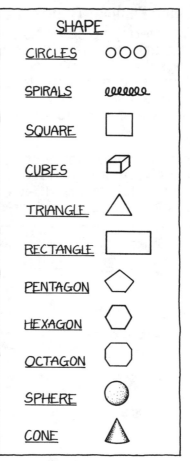

Figure 5.5

Remind campers to look very closely; some things in nature are *camouflaged.* Their colors match the colors of other things around them, so that they won't be spotted as easily.

Textures

Your campers may not be ready to touch every object they find in nature, but they can tell by looking at most objects whether they are soft, hard, fuzzy, prickly, or tickly. Later, they can feel them to make sure their perceptions were correct. Ask how many rough things, or smooth things they can find?

Remind campers not to pick flowers, pull bark off trees, or turn rocks over. Touching is enough.

Symmetry

In some tree species (maples, ashes, dogwoods, and horse chestnuts), every branch or bud is opposite another branch or bud. This arrangement is called symmetry, or balance. But not all tree species are symmetrical. Some are asymmetrical. In these tree species, no branch or leaf bud is opposite to another one; the buds of these trees alternate up the twig (see figure 5.6). These asymmetrical species have balance too.

Other examples of symmetry are the petals of a daisy or a dandelion. The fins of a fish are also symmetrical — there's one on each side. Are the veins of the right half of a leaf symmetrical with the veins of the left half? Ask your campers to decide.

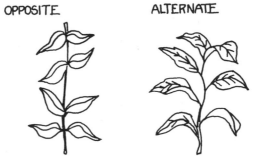

OPPOSITE   ALTERNATE

Figure 5.6

Contrast

Ask your group members to compare what they see in light areas with what they see in dark areas. The difference is called *contrast*. Have them look at shadows and bright patches, and notice how things look as day turns to twilight, and twilight turns to night. Contrast is marked by changes in colors as well as changes in light.

Patterns

Once people learn to recognize lines, forms, colors, textures, symmetry and contrasts in nature, they start to notice designs and patterns created by repetition. For example, the zigzag line of certain evergreen trees against the sky and the rounded tops of a single species of deciduous tree make patterns. One rainstorm after another after another seems to be a pattern of storms. Waves make patterns of lines on the shore. Just look for repeating designs, events, or forms, and you'll see patterns.

As you ride in a car or bus, you and your group can find patterns and share them with one another. As you walk along a trail, you can find other patterns.

The preceding sections list seven things your group members can look for outdoors: lines, shapes, colors, textures, balance, contrast, and patterns. Finding each will help them get better acquainted with nature.

Trying to make all these observations in one morning or even one day won't be much fun, so spread them out over a period of time. You can be doing other things to help acquaint campers with the outdoors while you're introducing these exercises.

Finding Analogies in Nature

Another way to help people feel at home in a natural setting is to relate nature to familiar things through the use of *analogies*, or comparisons.

You may already know many analogies in nature. The jellyfish is neither jelly nor a fish, yet we call it that because it looks like swimming jelly. You could describe a porcupine by saying that it looks like a pincushion. Sea urchins, found in coastal tide pools, look like pincushions, too. Elm trees are shaped like vases or feather dusters; certain clouds look like sheep or heads of cauliflower. There is a flower that some people call a Shooting Star and others call a Bird's Bill. Dutchman's Breeches is a flower that looks like a pair of trousers hung up by the ankles.

Some analogies are rather scientific. One of them is "palmately veined leaves," which means leaves that have veins arranged like fingers — five veins, like five fingers, joined at the base or palm.

Your campers may find many other analogies, such as a rock that looks like a monkey's face, or a cloud that resembles a dog, a horse, or even someone you know. Looking for unfamiliar things that resemble familiar ones, will help your group feel more at home outdoors.

Using all Five Senses

Once the members of your group feel comfortable finding familiar forms and shapes and imaginative analogies, they're probably ready to get involved with the outdoors firsthand by using their senses.

Because of our convenient way of life, we are not encouraged to use our senses. We look, but we don't really see. We don't listen carefully, and we rarely touch unfamiliar things. In short, we've been conditioned not to use our senses in everyday living. You can help your campers train their senses, in such a way that they can get better acquainted with nature.

Sight

Most people look at things while they're standing up; they seem to think that the best vantage point is eye-level. Have your group look at things from different vantage points. Some plants are nicknamed belly plants because if you really want to see them, you have to lie on your belly. Some things are best seen by looking *under* something else; others are best seen by holding them close or by using a hand lens. If you use a hand lens, it's best to hold the lens very close to your eye and to move the object toward the lens.

Ask you campers to look under, over, and behind things — and to notice lines, shapes, colors, textures, symmetry, contrast, and patterns at the same time.

Hearing

The next sense may seem easy; to hear, you just listen. But hearing isn't quite as simple as it seems. Our sense of hearing may be dulled by our habit of wearing headphones to listen to loud music. When we remove the headphones, we aren't as aware of natural sounds. Our ears tend to want to hear the sounds that we heard last, such as a drumbeat.

It works the same way outdoors. If you spend a few minutes listening to the drone or hum of a hive of bees, and then leave that area and try to hear crickets or grasshoppers, you probably won't hear them. That's because you're still hearing the humming of the bees. If, however, you "listen higher" — that is, let your auditory imagination go up the scale to a higher pitch — you'll hear the crickets or grasshoppers. You just have to concentrate on different pitches.

Some people have trained themselves to hear the little voices of birds over a human conversation. If the pitch of the human voice is low, a practiced listener can also hear the higher pitch of the birds. This takes practice, but it can be developed.

Smell

Seeing and hearing are relatively simple, safe activities. For the most part, so is smelling. At times, however, you may not want a good whiff of something. A strong inhalation of ammonia, for example, will probably gag you, but a faint sniff may help revive a person who has fainted.

The way to teach people to smell objects is to have them sniff gently at first. If they sense no odor at all, they can sniff harder and harder until they pick up the odor.

Most people enjoy the aroma of honeysuckle, roses, and lilacs. But it may surprise them to learn that the flowering blossoms of poison ivy and poison oak are also very fragrant. If these plants grow in thick clumps and the sun reaches the blossoms, they send forth an odor that can be appreciated as far away as ten feet. Smelling the air near the blossoms will cause you no harm; just don't stick your nose into the plant!

In many parts of the country there are small, shiny black insects called *millipedes* or "thousand legs." These slow moving insects curl up into a circle when they're picked up, and at that point, they emit an odor of folic acid. This is a protective act that prevents birds from eating them. If you sniff a millepede when you pick it up, you can understand how it protects itself from predators. After all, the millipede is too slow to run away from danger; it can't fly; and it has no way to bite or sting its opponent. The odor seems to repel any bird or animal that might otherwise eat it.

Our sense of smell is stronger in moist air than in dry air. Foxes and coyotes lick their noses to enhance their ability to smell. Ask your campers whether they think it would be helpful to wipe their noses with a damp cloth before smelling things. Then have them try it.

Touch

Thousands of people have missed wonderful opportunities for learning about the world around them because they've been conditioned not to touch. Put it down, don't touch it, keep your hands to yourself, it's dirty, sticky, slimy, and on and on. It may be time for them to learn to touch. Touching doesn't mean grabbing something; actually, the cheek is more sensitive than the fingers. Use the fingers to touch gently. Pat things. Have participants touch things lightly to their cheeks.

If you want to understand a plant, you needn't pick it. The saying, "patting prevents picking" means "get acquainted with the *feel.*"

Of course, touching can have serious consequences. Burns, cuts, or rashes can result if you touch some things improperly. First, touch gently with the fingertips; then touch large areas with the palm or back of the hand.

It's easier to determine the shape of some things by touching them than by seeing them. For example, identify for yourself some sedge plants, rushes, and grasses. Then, have your campers look at them. Have them touch these plants. Even though they all look a lot alike, they'll find that sedge plants have triangular stems, while both rushes and grasses have round stems. They'll also find that if they run their fingers along the round stem of a grass, they'll feel the nodes, or joints, whereas rushes have no nodes.

Or ask campers to try to roll the needles of spruce trees between their finger and thumb. The needles look flat, but they feel diamond-shaped, and they are.

Taste

Using the sense of taste to examine objects in nature requires great care. You *must* do some research before campers begin tasting. If you aren't absolutely positive about a certain kind of plant, don't let them taste it! Certainly, you wouldn't want them to put poison ivy, or thorns, in their mouths, either.

Tasting is not eating, swallowing, or chewing. Except for a few things, which are tasted only by the back of the tongue, tasting occurs on the tip of the tongue.

Tasting involves the following steps:

1. Touch the tip of your tongue against an object with which you are familiar, such as lemon, onion, sugar, or bread. Then try raw vegetables, such as lettuce, spinach, celery, carrots, turnip, and cucumbers. You probably can't taste them with the tip of your tongue.

2. When no taste is evident, bite the object gently with your incisors (front teeth), and then touch the tip of your tongue to it.

3. If you still can't taste it, chew some of it and spit it out.

If you're very familiar with the plant life in the area, you can have participants try the tip-of-the-tongue taste test on such things as clover blossoms, mint plants, blackberries, blueberries, and grasses. A word of caution: No one should try taste testing unless he/she is very familiar with poisonous plants in the area. White and red berries tend to be poisonous so never try them. Also, never, never swallow a plant. That's not tasting — that's eating, and people *can* become ill from eating.

Remember too, that not all names are reliable indicators of the plant's edibility. Skunk cabbage, for example, is neither a cabbage nor edible. Never put it in your mouth or bite it; it will burn you all day!

UNDERSTANDING THE ECOSYSTEM

Now that individual objects don't seem so strange to them, what should campers learn about nature that will help them understand it wherever they go? You certainly can't teach them *everything.* You can, however, present a few facts that will help them understand any ecosystem in the world.

What Is Ecology?

Hundreds of books and articles have been written on ecology, and the subject seems to become more and more complex as we learn more and more about it. But isn't there a simple way to understand what the word "ecology" means? Certainly. *Ecology is the study of the interrelations of all plants and animals and their environment.* That's all there is to it.

To put it simply, ecology is the study of how things in the world depend on one another. Ecology studies can get very complex, involving chemistry, physics, reproduction, and nutrition. Here, however, we're interested only in the basics of how plants and animals depend on one another, and on the soil, water, and climate for survival.

What Are the LAWS of Nature?

The LAWS of nature are **L**ight, **A**ir, **W**ater, and **S**oil. No matter where you go, you can explain different types of plants and animals by explaining the LAWS in their environment. In the deserts, jungles, forests, prairies, swamps, lakes and seas, plants and animals depend on four things. **L**ight refers to the amount and intensity of sunlight. **A**ir refers to the quality and temperature of the air. **W**ater stands for the amount and quality of water. And **S**oil refers to the quantity and types of soil or rocks in the area.

Why are there no plants or animals on the tops of many mountains? A lot of sunlight may reach the mountain top, and light is good for plants. But on rainy days the cold **A**ir carries **W**ater in the form of snow, and that snow covers the **S**oil, preventing plants from growing. All four LAWS affect plant and animal life, and on a glacier-topped mountain, the LAWS make plant and animal life almost, if not impossible.

By contrast, jungles provide a lot of warm air, warm water, and hot sunshine for plants, so many plants can grow there. But in some areas of the jungle there are no small plants under the large trees. Why not? Sunlight can't shine through the large trees to the ground, so only plants that don't require much sunlight can thrive there. Similar relationships with the elements ar true for deserts. Deserts offer abundant sun and fresh air, but the very small amount of rainfall drains rapidly through the porous soil, leaving little moisture for plants.

Different plants need different environments. Your camping area probably supports plants of all kinds in various areas — areas that are wet, dry, rocky, etc. The LAWS determine which plants grow in which areas.

What Are Forces?

Closely related to the LAWS are forces — natural phenomena that affect the power of the LAWS. These natural forces include such things as wind, gravity, volcanoes, earthquakes, fires, lightning, ice, and temperature.

Sometimes, forces appear to negate the affects of the light, air, water, and soil of an area. If the slope of a hill is too steep, gravity pulls things down, causing landslides or even plant slides, no matter how good the light, air, water, and soil are, plants won't grow there. Or if the wind in an area is so strong that the tops of plants are trimmed off and entire trees are blown down, the LAWS are not very effective. As a result, you may find that natural forces make some areas very different from what you had expected.

Imagine the surprise of the people who discovered Yellowstone National Park's Norris Geyser Basin. They probably stepped out of a lush green forest into a barren landscape, even though the light, air, and soil were just the same in both places. The water in the basin area was different — great streams of hot water filled with natural chemicals that prevent plants from growing. The hot water gushing from the ground is a force that changed the environment. The hot water released from the soil some chemicals that otherwise wouldn't have effected the plant life in the forest.

To see the different effects of hot water and cold water, try putting a teabag in a cup of cold water and another teabag in a cup of boiling water. Which cup brews tea sooner? Try it with water of different temperatures.

Remember that both the LAWS (light, air, water and soil) and natural forces determine the plant and animal life of any area.

What Is the Food Chain?

The *food chain* diagram below shows that all energy comes from the sun and is used by everything on earth. Plants, which are low on the food chain, use energy from the sun to make their own food. Animals and humans, which are higher on the food chain, eat the plants, including grains, vegetables, and fruits. Insects eat plant leaves and stems, cattle eat grass, mice eat seeds — thousands of living creatures depend on plants for their survival.

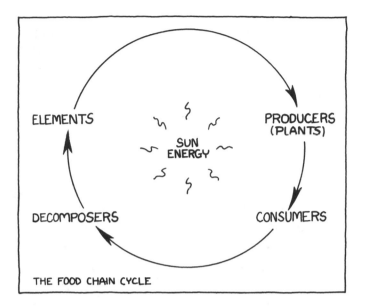

Figure 5.7

In ecology, anything that eats something else is called a *consumer*. Consumers that eat plants are called *herbivores*. Some herbivores are, in turn, consumed by *carnivores*. Many animals, including humans, are both plant eaters (herbivores) and meat eaters (carnivores), so they are called *omnivores*. When you eat a hamburger, you are consuming an herbivore. Likewise, when a hawk devours a mouse, it is consuming an herbivore. Both you and the hawk are omnivores because you eat plants and animals.

All forms of life must eat in order to grow. Eventually, though, they all die, and are in turn, are decomposed by *decomposers*. Decomposers break down the organic material in plants and animals into basic minerals and chemicals, returning these substances to the soil — where they nourish more plants to produce more energy to be eaten by more herbivores, and so forth.

Each link in the food chain is related to the next, and all phases contribute to all others. Understanding the food chain helps us understand the interrelationships between the sun, plants, animals, and decomposers, as well as the cycle of life and death. In nature, all things are connected.

Understanding ecology, the LAWS, the forces, and the food chain gives you a basic understanding of the natural world. This understanding should be an ample foundation for more advanced activities and studies of the ecosystem.

Understanding Ecological Principles

In many youth camps, outdoor-education programs, schools, youth groups, church programs, and community centers, you'll hear people chanting, "E-C-D-C-I-C-A, E-C-D-C-I-C-A, E-C-D-C-I-C-A." What on earth are they saying? What do all those letters mean? They stand for the first letters of seven basic ecological principles that help us understand the world. This little chant is an easy way to remember them.

E-C-D-C-I-C-A [5] stands for Energy, Cycles, Diversity, Community, Interrelationships, Change, and Adaptation. The following sections explain those seven principles.

Energy

All energy comes from the sun, which affects every form of life on earth. For example, plants cannot grow in the dark. If you put a houseplant in a dark closet for several months, it will die, even if you open the door occasionally to give it a drink of water. Without sunlight, plants cannot produce energy.

Now that you understand the food chain, you also understand why sunlight affects (directly and indirectly) the health of animals too. Because plants get their energy from the sun, animals that eat plants get their own energy from the plants, which got energy from the sun. Animals that eat the animals that ate the plants, get energy from those animals, which got their energy from plants, which got *their* energy from the sun.

To illustrate this principle, make up a skit about energy, Show how energy is transferred from the sun to plants to herbivores to carnivores to decomposers and then back to the soil, where the sun gives plants energy from which they produce more energy, and so forth.

Cycles

The sun comes up in the east every morning, goes down in the west at night, and comes up again in the east the next morning. Day and night are cycles. So are the seasons and the years. It is very reassuring to know that spring follows winter and

5.   VanMatre, Steve. *Sunship Earth*. Martinsville, IN: American Camping Association, 1979.

that summer and autumn follow spring. Other cycles include the migration of birds and the blooming of trees.

Perhaps the most important cycle in the natural environment is the air cycle, because we use the air over and over again. Animals inhale oxygen and exhale carbon dioxide; plants take in carbon dioxide and produce oxygen for animals to breathe. The cycle goes on and on. This cycle is one of the reasons why people are so concerned about the cutting down of the rain forest, where one third of the world's oxygen is produced. [6]

When rain falls, the water goes into soil, streams, rivers, lakes, and oceans. From those places, water evaporates and rises into the sky, where it forms clouds. When the clouds become saturated, the evaporated water becomes rain again and falls back to earth. This water cycle maintains moisture, providing water for our wells, our rivers, and our oceans.

Understanding the water cycle is important to any outdoor-living activity, because this cycle affects the weather, as you learned in chapter 4, "Being Safe."

Diversity
Diversity means difference. People differ in size, shape, color, race, religion, background, intelligence, and athletic ability, among other things. Plants and animals also differ. Not only are there many species of trees, but also there are many subspecies. Needle-bearing trees, for example, include pines, spruces, hemlocks, cedars, firs, and junipers. There are about a hundred different kinds of pine trees alone. When we consider the number of different types of plants and animals there are, we realize how diverse nature is.

Diversity has great value in nature. Just as human communities need people with all sorts of abilities, interests, and personalities, plant and animal communities need diverse members. If one species becomes diseased or is devoured by insects, there may also be a loss of other species in the area. Each species provides a home for some other, provides nutrients for something, provides moisture for some plant, provides protection for some animal, or something for someone. The diversity of species makes it possible for plants and animals to live in all different ecosystems created by the varying factors of Light,

6. *The International Book of the Forest.* New York, NY: Simon and Schuster, 1981.

Air, Water, and Soil. Furthermore, diversity makes natural resources much more interesting to us.

Community

Plants and animals live where the LAWS and forces best suit them, and each plant and animal has a *niche* or role in that area. Roles may include holding soil in place, breaking rocks into smaller pieces, storing water, providing shade, pruning leaves and branches, or feeding birds.

We know that certain animals depend on certain plants for their food, and that those animals and plants live only where the environment is suitable for them. How many roles can you think of in a natural community?

Interrelationships

It must seem obvious by now that each ecological principle is connected to every other principle and that all the principles are connected to the LAWS (light, air, water and soil). *Interrelationships* is the principle that recognizes this fact.

Animals depend on several different kinds of plants for their food. Plants also depend on one another. Some plants shade others, protecting them from the scorching sun; some plants, such as vines, use others for physical support. And certainly, people depend on one another. For example, you depend on parents, friends, teachers, police officers, shopkeepers, farmers, manufacturers, and on many others. Everything on earth is connected.

For thousands of years, people have asked questions such as, "What good is it?," "What good is poison ivy?," "What good are mosquitoes?," and "What good are dandelions?" These questions really mean, "What good is it to *me*?" If we understand that all things are interrelated, we might instead ask, "What roles do poison ivy, mosquitoes, and dandelions play in the world?" "What is their niche in the *world*?" Poison ivy makes shade for other plants, holds soil in place, and provides food for some birds. Mosquito larva help purify the water in high mountain lakes, and provide food for birds. Dandelion leaves are used as food by many people, and young rabbits like the new leaves.

Everything is related to something else. All things are inter-dependent. To demonstrate this principle, name something (a person, plant, or animal), and ask another person to name something (another person, plant, or animal) that depends on it. The next person then names something that depends on the previous thing, and so on.

Change

In nature, everything changes. The energy from a plant becomes an animal's energy. Live leaves become dead leaves. Seeds become plants. Little trees become big trees. Even mountains change, growing smaller through the process of erosion. Everything is changing.

People also change — our friends, our families, our homes, our classes, our interests, our knowledge. Can you think of anything in the environment that is *not* changing?

Adaptation

Adaptation, is the capability of a plant or animal to change so that it fits the environment. You can see many examples of what is called *situational adaptation.* A tree that lost its top during a windstorm may have adapted by straightening one of its branches, which reached toward the sun and became a new top, or *leader.* Or a tree that had its trunk bent and broken by a heavy snowstorm may have adapted by growing straighter above the crooked trunk. You'll find many of these trees in the forests of the American West where there are heavy snowfalls. Their trunks are called pistol-butt trunks, because they reminded the early settlers of the grip of an old-fashioned gun. (This is another example of how people use analogies to name things.)

If you hike along a trail, or along a country road that was dug a little below the level of the forest floor, you'll see that the trees on either side look as though they started to grow sideways but then turned and grew straight. Why? When the road was built, gravity caused the trees along the cut to slump toward the lower level. Their roots kept the trees from falling down, and their capability to adapt caused them to straighten.

These three examples demonstrate that trees are *phototropic* or sun-loving and can adapt to various negative situations.

Camouflage is another example of adaptation. Some animals who have little other protection from predators, are colored in such a way that they blend with their surroundings. Their predators then have a difficult time seeing them. Some animals even change colors depending on where they are — a Chameleon is green when it's on a leaf, and brown when it's on a tree branch.

Long-range adaptation is called *evolution*. In this case, evolution refers to the fact that over the centuries, many species of animals changed to adapt to their environments. Bills, for example, adapted so that birds could feed on certain nutrients. A hummingbird's bill would not do for a hawk, and a duck's bill would not do for a seed-eating bird. Another evolutionary adaptation is elephant's ears. African elephants have larger ears than Indian elephants do because large ears are better air-conditioning devices than small ears and it is hotter where the African elephant lives.

Much of the diversity you see among plants and animals is a result of adaptation. Again, you see the interrelationship of two ecological principles — diversity and adaptation — and again, you understand that everything is connected to everything else.

Summary

In this chapter, you learned the basic information you need for understanding nature, and even if you don't read any further, you'll still be way ahead of most people. Now you understand what you are observing.

Learning about nature is like making friends; the better you understand new acquaintances, the closer you become. But in one way, nature may be less challenging than people are: nature is fairly predictable.

No one can learn about the outdoors all at once. If this chapter seems to cover too much material, study it section by section. Maybe you won't be ready to tackle the ecological principles until you understand the rest of the chapter. In summary, there are four simple steps to understanding the environment.

- Seeing things that you already recognize (lines, shapes, colors, textures, balance, contrast, and patterns) in nature.

- Inventing analogies.
- Using your senses (sight, hearing, smell, touch, and taste).
- Understanding ecology (LAWS, forces, the food chain, and ecological principles).

Try some of the activities explained in the following pages, and you'll soon be able to enjoy the world around you.

ACTIVITIES

Tuning in the Senses

Concept: To provide an opportunity for the concentrated use and development of each of the five senses.

     To increase participants' awareness of the value of using all five senses as tools for observation.

Time: 1 hour and 30 minutes

Season: Any — during dry weather

Location: Anywhere outdoors — preferably a level surface

Number: One to five groups with maximum five participants in each group

     One leader per group

Materials: Paper (2-5 sheets per person)
Pencils (one per person)
Tape (scotch/masking)
Blindfolds (one per person)
Five rings of different sizes
Natural objects: rocks, flowers, pine cones
Optional: table, bench, or flat surface (3' x 6')

Procedure: Arrange five stations around tables or in an open area.

     Divide participants into groups — five maximum per station.

     A leader at each station involves the participants in activities oriented toward a particular sense.

After 15-20 minutes, the leader rotates stations and leads the same activity with another group at the next station.

Variation: the leader and group rotate together to a new station with a new activity.

Continue until all groups have participated in each of the five sense activities.

1. Smelling: Ask participants to explore, find and describe five different smells (soil, flowers, fungi, pine cones, etc.) List the descriptions of each smell on a piece of paper. If desired, tape items on a piece of paper.

2. Seeing: Ask participants to find and describe (color, shape, design, etc.) objects of a specific size. Pass out rings of various sizes so participants can find items that fit through each.

3. Touching: Ask participants to find and draw or describe:

   a. the hairiest leaf around
   b. the softest leaf
   c. the smoothest twig
   d. the roughest twig
   e. something cool
   f. something warm
   g. something bumpy
   h. something dry

4. Listening: Use natural objects, such as rocks, leaves, and pine cones, to make sounds for participants. Keep the objects from their sight.

   Have participants close their eyes, or blindfold them, as you make each sound. Then have participants try to describe the sound and the object using analogies and imagination. Write each description on paper.

   After the activity is completed, discuss the descriptions and/or tape the written descriptions next to each object.

5. Tasting: Arrange a variety of tasty, natural objects (miner's lettuce, licorice fern, sour grass, pine needles, ginger, etc.) on a table or level surface. Know your areas plants!

Blindfold the participants.

Pass out pieces of each item to the participants, one at a time, and have them taste the items. Record responses as they taste the items.

Encourage analogies and descriptions of the tastes.

Tape each item next to its written description.

Safety: Define boundaries.

When tasting, allow no swallowing.

When choosing natural objects for each sense activity, do not disturb the environment.

Organize — make sure groups stay together.

Adopt a Tree

Concept: We can see things with more than just our eyes.

Time: 45 minutes

Season: Any

Location: A natural wooded area

Number: 12 maximum

Materials: 1 blindfold per participant
40' rope

Procedure: 1. Blindfold participants to heighten the other senses.

2. Evenly space participants along the rope and lead them into an area with a lot of trees. As you guide the group along by the rope, "drop off" one participant at a time at different trees. Variation: Blindfold participants after a short spin to erase their sense of direction. Then guide each participant to a tree.

3. Have participants remain blindfolded and use all of their senses (except sight) to really get to know their tree friend.

4. Ask them to explore it. Hug it. Rub their cheeks against it. Listen to it or try to hear the life inside it. Smell it. Explore its skin with their fingers, nose, or skin. Check out its base. Feel the patterns on the trunk. Is anything living on it? How big is it? Instruct participants to be silent and stay with their tree until a leader comes back for them.

5. Round up all the participants on the rope, lead them back to the starting point, and ask them to take off their blindfolds. Then ask participants to go and find their friendly tree, using all of their senses. Variation: Ask participants to listen to your voice and turn to face the direction it is coming from. Continue talking and ask them to walk from their trees to you, taking off the blindfolds only when they reach you. When all participants have found their way back by listening to your voice, ask each participant to remove his/her blindfold and go find his/her tree.

6. Once each participant finds his/her tree, ask them to take a moment and really see how beautiful the tree is.

7. Discuss the activity:

What feelings were experienced?

What different methods were used to identify trees?

Have participants describe what they felt, smelled, heard and tasted.

Safety: Keep everyone in sight.

Don't allow anyone to wonder off blindfolded.

Walk slowly and carefully when leading the blindfolded group on the rope.

Before leaving any participant alone, make sure he/she is touching the tree you want him/her to explore.

Once You've Seen One, You've Seen 'Em All. Haven't You?

Concept: To have participants understand the strength of the sense of touch. To have participants understand that no two things are identical.

Time: 15-20 minutes

Season: Any

Location: Any — outdoors preferable

Materials: One small rock per person (leaves or twigs may be used depending on ability of group)

Procedure: Have participants stand or sit in a circle, blindfolded or with their hands behind their backs. Give one rock to each person. Tell everyone to get to know his/her rock through touch only. If participants are not blindfolded, make sure they keep their hands behind their backs. Let participants feel, scratch, pat their rocks. Let them find grooves, edges and any other qualities that their rock may have.

Then collect the rocks and redistribute them in a different order. Instruct participants to feel the new rock behind their back to see if it is theirs. Have participants pass the rock on to the next person if the rock they hold is not their own. Have them continue to pass the rocks until they find their own. Try to get each rock back to its original owner. Let participants keep their rocks or ask them to find a home in the woods for it when the activity is over. To make it easier, let them look at their rock for one minute before collecting and redistributing the rocks.

My Leaf

Concept: To develop participants sense of touch to help fully know natural objects.

Time: 20 minutes

Season: Spring, summer, fall

Location: Woods or meadow

Number: 5-15

Materials: One leaf per person

Procedure: Instruct participants to close their eyes and leave them closed until you say they can open them. Give each participant a leaf and tell them to get to know the leaf by using their hands. Let them feel the leaves for five minutes. Then gather the leaves and put them in a pile. Instruct participants to open their eyes and find their leaf in the pile. Discuss the different details that could be felt with hands, but might be missed with the eyes.

Scavenger Hunt

Concept: To develop participants' awareness of their sense of observation, and knowledge of their natural environment.

               To provide a nature exploration experience.

               To use nature for recreation.

               To operate in a group with good sportsmanship.

Time: 1 ½ to 2 hours

Season: Any — preferably a dry season

Location: Any outdoor site

Number: Maximum of five groups with 3-4 people in each

Materials: A container (bag or sack)
               A list of natural objects
               Pencil (one per group)
               Paper (one per group)

Procedure: Divide participants into groups (informally) and give each group a container.

               Set a time limit (1 ½ hours) and boundaries for exploration.

Hand out a list of items to be found and collected.

Suggested list:

the hairiest leaf
the softest leaf
the smoothest twig
the roughest twig
something cool
something warm
something bumpy
something dry
something with grooves
something triangular
something sweet
something fuzzy
something circular
something bright
something symmetrical

Instruct groups to stay within the boundary and find as many of the items on their list as possible without disturbing the environment.

Call the groups back together at a designated place and share the items found.

Let participants use these items for a craft project.

Have participants discuss the objects that weren't brought back to the group. How would bringing them back have disturbed the natural environment?

Safety: Define boundaries for the scavenger hunt.

Prevent disturbance of the natural environment by instructing participants not to destroy an object's habitat area.

When tasting, allow no swallowing.

Instruct participants to draw or describe an object and its location if the object cannot be brought back without disturbing anything.

Outer Space Visitor

Concept: To increase participants' observation skills, use of descriptive language, and analogies.

Time: 10-15 minutes

Season: Any

Location: Any (good fill-in activity while waiting)

Materials: None

Procedure: 1. Have participants pretend they have just arrived by rocketship another planet.

2. They are standing on a planet that is completely foreign to them. They are looking at things for the first time!

3. Ask each participant to select an object (a tree, rock, flower, cloud) and describe it without using words that would ordinarily apply. Words such as trunk, bark, leaves, twigs, buds, petal, blossom may not be used.

4. Have the group try and guess what object is being described. The participant who first recognizes the object takes the next turn.

What Is It?

Concept: To have participants describe an object with clues. To have participants work as a unit. To have participants really think about the features of an object.

Time: 30 minutes

Season: Any

Location: Outdoors

Materials: None

Procedure: Divide the group into smaller groups of five or six with one leader per group. Instruct each group to gather four or five natural objects (plants or insects, etc.) without destroying the environment. Once the materials are gathered, discuss each object within the smaller groups without letting the other groups see. Once all groups have discussed their objects, start the contest.

Have group A offer two clues about an object they have. Then have groups B and C try to guess the object. If the other groups can't guess, have group A offer one more clue and again groups B and C guess. Continue until group A has offered six clues. If groups B and C are still unable to guess then group A tells them and receives a point.

Now group B offers two clues and groups A and C guess. The above process is repeated if groups A and C are unable to guess the object. The game is continued until each of the objects has been presented.

At the conclusion of the game, have each group draw their objects from memory. Discuss why each object was found where it was and if there is any inter-relationship between the objects.

Back to Back Observation

Concept: To develop participants' ability to describe precisely. To develop participants' use of analogies in describing things.

Time: 30 minutes

Season: Any

Location: Any

Materials: 2 bags of identical natural materials, five items per bag (pine cones, leaves, rocks, twigs, acorns, etc.)

Procedure: Divide into the group in two smaller groups or two to ten people. Have each group stand or sit with their backs to the other group. Give each group a bag of items to spread out in front of them.

Instruct one group to start by selecting an item from their bag, describing it so the second group can pick the same item out of their bag. Then have group one explain exactly how they are placing the item on the ground in front of them, and group two must place their identical item in an identical position in front of them.

Group one then selects another item, describes it to group two, and explains how to place it in relation to the previous item. Continue until both groups have placed all their objects.

Next, compare to see if group two's objects are in the same relative position as group one's objects.

Trade roles and use different objects.

Rules for describing:

Groups may not use words to describe the object's name, color, or material. They may use words to describe the object's size, shape, feel, or odor.

This activity may also be done with different items of varying descriptive difficulty such as five different leaves, all kinds of rocks, or five flowers, of different species.

Leaf Rubbings

Concept: To have participants make leaf rubbings and begin to understand differences in leaf types.

Time: 20 minutes to one hour

Location: Any area with different types of plants

Season: Late spring through early fall

Number: Any

Materials: Thin paper
A flat surface
Leaves (to be collected by participants)
Natural rubbing materials (charcoal, fleshy leaves, bark, soil, etc.)

Procedure: 1. Explain that there are many kinds of plants with leaves of varied shapes and sizes.

2. Instruct participants to collect different leaves and natural drawing materials.

3. Have participants:

Place a leaf vein-side up on a flat surface.

Place a sheet of paper over the leaf and hold it firmly in place.

With the other hand, rub the charcoal or other rubbing material in parallel strokes over the leaf. The outline and venation of the leaf will appear on the paper.

4. Have participants make a booklet of rubbings.

Safety: Avoid poisonous plants. Make sure participants know what the local poisonous plants look like.

Diving Bell

Concept: To allow participants to explore life in the water and watch animals being attracted to light.

Time: 30 minutes in late evening or at night

Season: Late spring through early fall, depending on the climate. In some places this activity could be used anytime.

Location: Pond, lake or any still or slow moving body of water which has a dock or a pier.

Materials: Gallon jar with a tight fitting lid (a mayonnaise jar)
Weight (rock)
Flashlight
Rope

Procedure: 1. Have participants assemble the diving bell by placing a flashlight and a weight in the jar; sealing the jar tightly; and tying the rope around the jar leaving one long end of the rope free.

2. Lower the diving bell into the water.

3. Watch animals being attracted to the light source. Observe and discuss animal life.

Cinquain Poetry

Concept: To introduce participants to an easy, enjoyable writing experience utilizing the outdoors.

Time: 30 minutes

Season: Any

Location: Any

Materials: Pencil and paper

Procedure: Have participants observe features in the outdoors, then compose a cinquain as a group, Next, let individuals try their skills.

A cinquain follows this form:

raccoon	1 word naming subject
playful, funny	2 describing words
creeps slowly onward	3 words of action
silently stalks the grasshopper	4 words of activity, effect
hunter	1 word synonym for the subject, or a summary

Have participants share their poems or display them on a bulletin board.

Haiku Poetry

Concept: To introduce participants to an easy, enjoyable writing experience about the outdoors. To use syllables to write a poem about nature.

Time: 30 minutes or more

Season: Any

Location: Any

Materials: Pencils and paper

Procedure: The haiku is a form of Japanese poetry about nature. It needs not rhyme. It is based on numbers of syllables in each of three lines.

A Haiku poem follows this form:

Winter

The star studded tree	5 syllables
Shivers in the pale moonlight	7 syllables
The wind rushes by	5 syllables

After writing, it is fun to illustrate the poems with sketches or pen and ink drawings.

Art Form Hunt

Concept: To expose participants to art forms in nature. To have participants become aware of patterns, shapes, lines, textures, and colors; relate natural forms to man-made forms; look for similarity and variety.

Time: 30 minutes to 1 hour

Season: Any

Location: Any outdoor location

Materials: Pencils and notebooks
List of art forms to look for
A leader in each group

Procedure: Have groups of four to five participants plus a leader explore patterns, art forms and colors in a natural environment, recording what and where they are found. Find examples of: five shapes, ten shades of color, three horizontal lines, four vertical lines, four diagonal lines, five patterns (repetitions), and five textures. Discuss findings.

Peanut Patch

Concept: To have participants learn that living things adjust and change, or adapt, to cope with their environment, even in one lifetime. Introduce the D.A.M. Law: Die, Adapt or Move.

Time: 20 minutes

Season: Any

Location: Any

Number: 8-12 participants

Materials: Large bag of peanuts in the shell
                Empty bag for storage of empty shells
                Masking tape
                Scissors

Procedure: Divide group into two smaller groups. Have of the
            groups watch carefully while the other group
            does the following:

            Have group one stand or sit in a line. Then throw
            some peanuts to them and ask them to crack and
            eat the peanuts. (Group two should be watching
            group one as they do this.)

            Tape the thumbs of the group two participants to
            their palms, and have them stand or sit in a line.
            Then throw some peanuts to them and ask them
            to crack and eat the peanuts. (Group one should
            be watching as group two tries to eat the pea-
            nuts.)

            If the people in group two were able to eat the
            peanuts, even without their thumbs, they have
            solved a problem. The way they solved their prob-
            lem is an example of adaptation. Discuss the
            importance of an opposable thumb. Could they
            have adapted in any other way? Found some
            other food that didn't need to be cracked open?
            Discuss plants and animals that have adapted.
            (Adaptation is a change of function in one life-
            time while evolution is the process by which ad-
            aptation is passed on to following generations.)

Circle of Life (Building Images)

Concepts: All plants, animals, and substances in nature are
            interrelated with others in some way (for example,
            some things feed on others, some are eaten by
            others, some protect others, some decompose
            others). Humans are ultimately the chief predators
            in the natural environment. "There is no free
            lunch" means that nothing in nature gets some-
            thing without a consequence. "Everything is
            going somewhere" means that the natural envi-

ronment is always changing, nothing remains in the same state over a long period of time.

Time:	20-30 minutes
Season:	Any
Location:	Any — around a table, campfire, or outside in a circle.
Number:	12 maximum
Materials:	None
Procedure:	1. Have your group sit in a circle.

2. Pick up an object from nature, such as a pine cone, a leaf, an insect, etc., and show it to the group.

3. Have one person start the game by taking the object and naming a plant, animal or other object in nature that feeds on, is eaten by, protects, is protected by, or decomposes the object you picked up.

4. Have the participant pass the object to the next person. That person then names something else that would be associated with the object in any of these ways.

5. Failure to give an answer within a given time earns a participant the first letter of the word "DEAD." If a person receives all of the letters from the word "DEAD," they're out of the game. Any answer may be challenged by any person in the game. A challenge can be accepted or denied by the group. If the group accepts the challenge, the person who was challenged receives a letter.

6. Other rules may be added later to increase the difficulty of the game: such as, not being allowed to repeat any previously mentioned object.

Safety: Do not pass objects which are pointed or can be harmful. Do not use fragile or delicate objects such as bird eggs, etc. — help protect nature.

Forest Community

Concepts: A city community and a natural community (forest, meadow, marsh, etc.) have similar items that help the community thrive. There are different functions that allow the community to coexist and function. Each item is related to another — each has a function and is dependent on another for survival. Plants and animals that need one another live together in communities, similar to the way humans make use of and live with each other and natural resources.

Time: 1 hour

Season: Any

Location: Outdoors in a natural area

Number: 8-10

Materials: Pencil and paper

Procedure: 1. Have the group discuss the parts that a town or city has and make a list. Relate this to participants' hometown or neighborhood.

Suggestions for the list:

inhabitants
plumbing
communications system
factories
stores
cafeterias
apartments
garbage collectors
energy sources
traffic
streets
transportation

2. Divide the group into smaller groups.

3. Send each group out to locate items in nature that are similar to those on the list.

4. Bring the group back together to share their findings. Discuss how things in nature depend on one another, work together, and live interdependently. Discuss what things participants found in nature that play roles that are similar to those found in a city.

Safety: Set boundaries for exploration. Set a time limit for returning to the group. Do not collect the items, simply look and make note of things.

What Eats?

Objective: To illustrate to participants the concept of the food chain.

Time: 20-30 minutes

Location: A room with a blackboard

Materials: Blackboard
1 piece of chalk per team

Procedure: For one game, divide the group into teams, with no more than ten participants on a team. On the blackboard, write a column of numbers, one to ten, for each team. Give each team a piece of chalk. Have each team stand away from its column of numbers.

At a signal, the first person on each team should dash to his/her team's column of numbers and writes the name of a plant or an animal by the number one. Then he/she should dash back and give the chalk to the second person on the team. This person should dash to the column and write the name of something that eats what was written in the number one spot. The chalk is then passed to the third person, who rushes up and writes the name of something that eats what was written in the number two spot, and so on until one team has reached number ten.

If a player writes down an incorrect name, it may be erased, but only by the very next player, who loses his/her turn to write a name. This means that a turn is lost each time a team makes an error.

To determine the winning team, allow one point for each correct link in the chain represented in the column. If an item is incorrect, a point is lost, but the scoring continues from that point.

The first time a group plays this game, scores probably will be low. There may also be considerable discussion about right and wrong answers. Using books to answer questions and settle arguments is one way to learn about food chains. Each time the game is played, participants will know more and more about what eats what, the competition will be more exciting and the game more fun.

Once a group has developed some skill at playing, try limiting the habitat to that of the forest, a brook, a marsh, a pond, the ocean, or some particular community. Perhaps you can even limit the season of the year, or the time of day.

6

Putting It On Your Plate

Picnics! Cookouts! Hamburgers, hot dogs, pizza, spaghetti, chicken, ice cream, hot chocolate! Everyone likes to eat, and eating outdoors seems to be especially appealing, even to people who aren't interested in being experts in outdoor-living skills.

Cooking outdoors is much easier today than it was for our pioneer ancestors. Of course, we can't cook everything outdoors as easily as inside. Microwavable entrees are out of the question; so probably is anything involving meringue. And baking in a convection oven isn't possible either. But many of us go through life without making lemon meringue pies or roasts anyway, and the main advantage of microwave cooking is speed. You'll have plenty of time for cooking outdoors. You're there to enjoy yourself, so be patient.

The types of food that you can cook outside depend on the type of fuel and cooking implements available, and on the amount of effort you're willing to expend. It's possible to bake pies and cakes, roast chicken on a rotisserie, bake beans in an earth oven, and even make ice cream in a hay hole in the ground. Most of the time though, outdoor cooking consists of simple meals requiring only simmering, boiling, and heating, or maybe frying or grilling.

COOKING METHODS TO USE OUTDOORS

The following are descriptions of the choices you have for cooking outdoors. These are the same choices you have at home, in your kitchen.

Boiling: A process in which boiling water bubbles around the food that's being cooked. Bring the water to a boil, place the food (such as spaghetti) in it, allow the water to come back to a slow boil, and then adjust the heat down to a simmer.

Very few things need to actually boil in water — food usually needs only to bubble gently.

Simmering: Another process in which food is cooked in bubbling water. The food cooks at the same temperature as when it's being boiled, but it cooks more slowly and gently. This process prevents food from sticking or boiling over, and also conserves fuel.

Simmering is used to warm food, such as soup and canned vegetables. If you simmer food for a relatively long time (one hour or more), you're stewing it.

Frying: Cooking food in hot fat or oil. Fried foods usually get crusty and brown on the outside, but stay moist inside.

You can fry both meats (such as hamburger, steak, and chicken) and vegetables (such as onions, potatoes, zucchini, and mushrooms). *Stir-frying* means frying food rapidly in a little oil, while stirring the ingredients to keep them from sticking to the skillet and to make sure that everything cooks evenly.

Baking: Cooking with dry heat in a boxlike structure. At home, you'd probably bake a cake in a conventional oven. There are, however, ovens that sit on top of the stove, as well as box ovens and reflector ovens for use outdoors. (More about these later.)

Grilling: Cooking food directly on, or very close to, a fire or coals, without using a pan. Commonly, food is placed on a metal grate above the flame or coals.

Grilling (also called *barbecuing*) is the usual method of preparing meats, firm moist vegetables, and fruits outdoors. Most people are familiar with grilled hamburgers, hot dogs, and chicken.

The only real differences in these cooking methods involve the fuel, or cooking surface you use. At home, your stove probably uses either electricity or natural gas, or wood (if you have a wood stove). Outdoors, you will have neither electricity nor gas but, nevertheless, can find fuels that are just as effective.

FUELS FOR OUTDOOR COOKING

Fuels used for cooking outdoors include wood; charcoal; solid alcohol; and liquid or gaseous substances such as kerosene, white gas, butane, and propane. There are pros and cons for using each fuel for different types of cooking and in different situations.

Before deciding what to cook, consider the type of fuel that is available and the situation in which you'll use it. Let's analyze some possible outdoor-cooking situations.

At your base camp, you can set up a well-stocked kitchen and use any cooking method you want to try. You may have access to several kinds of fireplaces, stoves, and fuels, as well as to equipment for making more stoves, ovens, and rotisseries.

Away from base camp, however, you'll have less equipment — you'll want to keep your load light. Stick to simple recipes and cooking processes — one-pot meals are the easiest.

Practice all trip cooking at base camp before trying it out on the trail. You may find that you want to change the menu, or the ingredients, learn to cook some dishes better, or not take some equipment along on the trip.

The following sections describe the uses of various fuels. Before you actually use any of them, be sure to understand the section of this chapter that relates to the specific fuel you have in mind.

Butane and Propane Stoves

Today, many campers use small stoves that burn some type of petroleum product. There are many types and some are safer than others. Generally, the safest and easiest to use are the butane and propane stoves. The fuel comes in a gaseous form, in a pressurized container. These stoves light much like a kitchen stove that uses natural gas; once a canister of butane or propane is loaded onto the stove, you need only light a match, and turn on the gas.

Butane and propane stoves are easy to regulate, and therefore are excellent for cooking many types of foods. Because these stoves are so easy to operate, they are sometimes used for heating lunches. They may even be used on day hikes, where a stove is not normally carried. As well, propane and butane stoves are easy to pack, don't require messy priming like some liquid-gas stoves, and they're not as volatile as liquid-gas stoves.

There are, however, some drawbacks to these stoves: they do not work well at high elevations or at temperatures below 50 degrees, they sometimes suffer malfunctions (for example, the knob that turns the stove on and off can get stuck), and many butane stoves are awkwardly tall and prone to tipping if not placed solidly on even ground. Additionally, the fuel canister must be replaced frequently (always carry used canisters out to be disposed of properly). On the whole, however, these stoves are an excellent way to teach beginners about camping stoves because they are easy to operate.

A few tips and warnings about butane and propane stoves

- Always read the manufacturers directions before using any type of stove.
- There should be little activity around any stove; that activity should be directly related to operating or supervising the operation of the stove.
- Always place these stoves on a level surface to avoid tipping. This will also help to avoid boiling food over the side of a pot.
- Always make sure the fuel canister is *seated* correctly so there is no fuel leakage.
- Never put your face over a stove while lighting or operating it. Never allow any camper to put his/her face over a stove while lighting or operating it.

- Never remove a fuel canister while the stove is on.
- As long as nothing is spilled on the burner plate of this type of stove, they require little cleaning.
- The fuel for propane and butane stoves comes in canisters. Take enough canisters with you. Always carry empty canisters out with you.
- Some types of fuel canisters can be removed and then replaced. Others will allow any remaining fuel to leak if they are removed before they're empty. Know your stove.
- Propane and butane stoves should not be used inside of a tent where they may tip over and ignite the tent fabric.

Liquid-Gas Stoves

In America, the stove most commonly used at parks and established campgrounds is the two-burner white gas stove; although, recently, it has been replaced with the two-burner propane stove. Many types of smaller one-burner stoves are also available, and much more popular with backpackers. These stoves come in all shapes and sizes; some are compact and easy to pack; some are not. Some even come with a small cooking pot that fits over or around the stove.

Almost all liquid-gas stoves work relatively well in cold temperatures and at high elevations, which makes them popular with mountain and winter campers. But these stoves can be very dangerous. White gas, one of the liquid gases, doesn't actually burn; the fuel is in a liquid state in the fuel reservoir of the stove, and it must be pressurized into a gas before burning. As tiny droplets of the liquid are pressurized and become gaseous, they explode as they mix with the air and flame. If handled incorrectly, liquid-gas stoves are prone to flare-ups, and may even explode, setting tents, forests, and people afire. If handled correctly, cleaned properly and regularly, treated with care, these stoves can be as safe as any other.

Some liquid-gas stoves burn white gas; generally the most dangerous of these fuels because it's very volatile. Kerosene stoves are generally safer because the fuel burns at a lower temperature than white gas does. Other stoves use automotive gasoline, which falls between white gas and kerosene in terms of heat and safety. Still other stoves accept multiple kinds of fuel. Always read the stove directions before using any fuel.

Kerosene and automobile fuel, which are more oily than white gas, must be handled carefully. Because of their oiliness, if kerosene or automobile fuel is spilled on fabric, such as clothing or a tent, it won't evaporate as quickly as white gas will. Should a match or a burning coal come into contact with this saturated cloth, the fabric will catch fire very easily.

For risk-management purposes, only group leaders, 18 or older who have been trained in the use of liquid-gas stoves should supervise the use of these stoves; younger people should be permitted to use them only under the **direct supervision** of a leader trained in the use of such stoves. *Direct supervision,* in this case, means the leader should have his/her full attention on the stove and persons operating it. There is no recommended minimum age for the use of liquid-gas stoves. However, there is enough risk involved in the use of such stoves that a group must be able to exhibit mature behavior while using them. If you believe that a group is not or can not exhibit mature behavior, do not allow them to use liquid-gas stoves.

A few tips and warnings about liquid-gas stoves

- Always read the manufacturers directions before using any stove.
- There should be very little activity around any stove; that activity should be directly related to operating or supervising the operation of the stove.
- Always place these stoves on a level surface to avoid tipping. This will also help to avoid boiling food over the side of a pot.
- Always fill a liquid-gas stove away from the actual cooking area, and away from other activity.
- Use an eye-dropper to place liquid fuel around the priming area of the stove. This will allow you to place only as much fuel as needed, without any spillage.
- After filling a liquid-gas stove, allow it to sit for at least five minutes before lighting it, to allow any spilled fuel to evaporate.

- Never fill the fuel reservoir of a liquid-gas stove completely full — leave room for the cap to fit back on and for the gas to pressurize.

- Never put your face over any stove while lighting or using it. Never allow any camper to put his/her face over a stove while lighting or using it.

- Liquid-gas stoves are prone to flare-ups if they are not treated properly and cleaned regularly. These stoves will need to be cleaned less frequently, if you avoid boiling food over onto the stove.

- Never turnoff a liquid-gas stove during a flare-up. Let the excess fuel burn off.

- Never take the cap off the fuel reservoir during a flare-up, while the stove is burning, or while the stove is still hot after it has been shut down.

- Clean white-gas stoves regularly so they will burn evenly.

- Keep fuel for liquid-gas stoves in a container made specifically for it. Never put anything else in that container.

- Liquid-gas stoves should not be used inside a tent where they may tip over and ignite the tent fabric.

Alcohol Stoves

You may have seen someone use a chafing dish to cook fancy meals at the table at home or at a restaurant. Alcohol chafing dishes use a semisolid type of wood or denatured alcohol that is sold in grocery stores, often under the name *Sterno*. Both chafing dishes and liquid-alcohol stoves can be used for outdoor cooking.

These stoves have some advantages: they're relatively inexpensive; they're compact; they're very quiet; and if they're unopened, they are not likely to leak except in extreme heat. The popularity of some kinds of alcohol stoves is growing because they burn so quietly.

However, they also have four drawbacks that limit their popularity and usefulness:

- Alcohol stoves that are nonpressurized, generate a relatively low heat; limiting their use to cooking very simple meals.

- The fuel burns quickly.
- The alcohol is extremely poisonous. (In some states, it is impossible to buy wood alcohol without a permit because of its poisonous properties.)
- When there is leftover fuel in a container, it can be hard to light a second time, thus wasting the remaining fuel.

Charcoal

Charcoal is wood that has been partially burned so that only the hard fuel remains. It is made from wood that was grown and cut specifically for this purpose. Hardwood charcoal, which burns slowly and generates a lot of heat, is the preferred type.

Some charcoal is impregnated with an easily ignited material so that it can be lighted with only a match. This type of charcoal may be the easiest to use; however, you'll get a better bed of coals if you use the ordinary kind, which contains no ignition fluid. Ordinary charcoal is more difficult to light and requires some sort of starter.

Before you build a charcoal fire, decide what you want to cook. Many Asian families can cook an entire meal for four over four or five charcoal briquettes. North Americans tend to use too many briquettes, and the coals keep burning long after the cooking is over, the meal has been eaten, and the area has been cleaned up. Four briquettes are enough to cook hamburgers for two people. Twenty briquettes will cook an entire meal for eight, and you can use the leftover fuel to heat the dishwater.

Starting a charcoal fire

There are several ways to start a charcoal fire. The easiest way is to use treated charcoal. Place the briquettes in a neat pile and light one or more with a match, so that others will ignite from those. After all briquettes are ignited and before you cook, use a pair of tongs to space the briquettes evenly. A well-controlled bed of coals generates heat at the correct temperature for cooking most foods. After spacing the briquettes, place a metal grate over the coals, then set your pot on the grate. Or, you may place the pot directly on the coals if they have burned down enough.

Whenever you place a pot over coals or a flame, be sure to soap the pan. Rubbing liquid soap over the outside of the pot will make it easier for you to clean the black soot off when you're finished cooking.

Nontreated charcoal requires some starter — and appropriate risk-management strategies. Starter fluids are liquid petroleum products that are sprayed onto the charcoal, allowed to sink in for a minute or so, and then ignited with a match. If you use starter fluid, make sure to let it be absorbed before you try to light the briquettes; otherwise you may burn the fluid off the charcoal as you try to light it and will have to add more fluid.

The danger of adding starter fluid to charcoal that you've already tried to light is that a few briquettes may already be burning. As you release pressure on the starter-fluid can, the fluid is drawn back into the can — along with air and possibly flames from the coals. The result can be an explosion that burns the person who was lighting the fire.

As the leader, you should be the only person in the group to add starter fluid to a charcoal fire. Pour the fluid into a paper cup before putting it on the charcoal, so that when you pour the fluid on the coals, only that fluid will burn, not the remainder in the cup. Even this practice is dangerous, because the flame could move up the stream of fluid that you're pouring and ignite the cup.

Here is a simpler, safer method of lighting a charcoal fire that is also a true camping skill: make a tiny campfire out of tinder, paper, and wood chips, and light that with a match. If you put a small pile of charcoal on top, this little fire will light the briquettes.

Tin-can fire starter

You can also make a tin-can fire starter. Open a tin can, (any size from a number 2 to a number 10 is appropriate), use the contents, and wash the can carefully. Then turn it upside down and punch triangular holes in the sides and the closed end with a juice-can opener. Punch similar holes in the sides near the open end. Partially fill the can with charcoal, using four to ten briquettes, and finish filling the can with crumpled paper. Place the can on the ground upside down, so that the closed end is at the top, and light the newspaper through the holes you punched at the bottom. The heat from the burning newspaper will be concentrated enough to light the charcoal. When the briquettes are glowing, use a pot-lifter to remove the can. You can now spread out the charcoal for cooking, or add more briquettes to make a larger, hotter fire.

Other fire starters

Other ways to light charcoal include using *heat tabs,* which are cubes of solid alcohol, or *fire ribbon,* which is a gelatinous alcohol product that can be squeezed out like toothpaste. People on backpacking trips, and those who use liquid-gas stoves but don't want to prime them with liquid fuel, usually take fire ribbon along as emergency fire-starter and stove primer.

In the past, you may have seen charcoal being lighted with paper milk cartons. This was an excellent practice when the cartons were covered with paraffin, which burned like candle wax. Today, however, milk cartons are covered with a poly-plastic and do not burn well.

You can make your own heat tabs by taking a cardboard egg carton (not a plastic or foam one), filling each egg compartment with small pieces of charcoal, then pouring melted paraffin over the charcoal pieces. Be sure to handle the paraffin carefully; if you let it get too hot, it will burst into flames. As soon as the paraffin melts, pour it over the briquettes, and then allow it to dry thoroughly. Later, when you need a heat tab, simply tear off one of the egg compartments, put it under some briquettes and light the cardboard, which serves as a wick for the charcoal "candles."

To melt paraffin, follow these steps:

1. Place the paraffin blocks in a tin can.

2. Place the tin can in a pan of water.

3. Place the pan of water on a stove or fire, and heat the water to a simmer. The hot water will slowly melt the paraffin. Never place a container of paraffin directly over a flame.

You can also make fire-starters from strips of newspaper, rolled tightly into cylinders about one inch thick. Tie the cylinders together with string and dip them into melted paraffin. The end of the string will serve as a little wick for your homemade candle. (Or you may want to carry stubs of purchased candles in your pack for use as emergency fire-starters.)

To extinguish a charcoal fire, either let it burn out, or sprinkle water on it, a little at a time, until the coals are cold. Save the unused portion in a sack for use the next day. If the leftover charcoal doesn't dry out completely, you'll know to use less charcoal next time. It's much easier to add one piece to a dying fire than to lug wet leftover charcoal around until it dries.

Wood

For the veteran outdoors person, wood is the ultimate cooking fuel. It can be regulated. It is relatively safe and can be used for virtually any type of cooking, and it can be collected at the campsite. Collecting wood, however, is a trickier matter than it may seem, and may be the greatest drawback to using wood for fuel. **When you take wood that you find on the forest floor, you may be destroying future forests.**

When there were very few campers and outdoor cooks, plenty of wood was available for cooking. Native Americans used wood most of the time; some prairie Indians also used buffalo chips. (*Buffalo chips* are dried buffalo droppings made up of partly digested grass; these chips generate great heat when they're burned.) Some people living in the African deserts got the same result by using camel dung. These materials, sanitized by drying in the hot sun, are essentially compact pieces of processed grass.

Today, wood fuel is no longer as plentiful. In the central United States, where there are many farms, forests have been re-placed by fields. Even in the North and West, where large forests still stand, fuel is short. Too many people camping in the same spots year after year have depleted the supply of downed wood, particularly small sticks, which are useful for cooking. And because of campers' fascination with blazing campfires, the supply of logs has been depleted also.

If you camp in a state or national park, you may see signs warning that campfires are prohibited. There are two reasons for this: the danger of forest fires set by careless campers, and the depletion of forest nutrients.

Trees derive much of their nourishment from decaying plant materials. If the fallen timber, sticks, and branches are burned, no material will be there to decay, in order to feed new small trees and replenish the soil's nutrients for existing trees. In some parts of the country, it takes up to one hundred years for downed trees and limbs to decay and nourish growing trees. If campers take all the dead materials for use in their campfires, the growing trees will soon die of starvation. Therefore, where there are many campers, there are usually restrictions against using wood from the forest floor for campfires and cooking.

An ethical issue

Whether to gather fallen wood for a campfire is not only a legal question, but also an ethical issue. There are some places where there are no restrictions on fire building. The land is vast and in theory, the number of campers visiting the area wouldn't greatly affect the land, if they spread themselves throughout the natural area. In practice, however, many campers seek the same popular sites. Often, these sites are places that have a naturally stressed existence — they may be mountain lakes at tree line, or beach sites on barrier islands. The areas around these sites are then damaged by a continuous stream of campers, while other areas of the same managed forest go virtually untouched. So, even though fires are permitted, there is still a question of whether or not to be part of the wear and tear on that popular site by building a fire. People have damaged the earth in hundreds of ways — by depleting forests of downed wood, by discharging industrial pollutants, by using chemical fertilizers, and so on. Challenge yourself and your group. Do you want to damage the environment or help protect it?

Before you answer this question, consider the possibility of forest fires and the depletion of forest nutrients. Plan to bring your own wood to a site if you are at a base camp. This wood has been cut from a managed forest where new growth is replacing cut trees. Plan, also, to use a stove for cooking meals when ever possible. Fires should be considered a luxury.

There is more information provided in this chapter for building wood fires than for any other single fuel source, because of the nature of the fuel — there are no manufacturers instructions on this package. Should you be in a situation where the above criteria can be met and decide to build a wood fire, you should know as much as possible about them in order to make the least impact possible on the environment.

It is recommended that wood fires be used only when the following conditions can be met:

1. Any removal of fallen wood for a fire still leaves *more* than adequate downed wood for continued decay into the soil for replenishment of forest nutrients. (If you have to search for wood, this condition is not being met.)

2. The fire can be built in an existing fire pit and/or will leave no visual scaring.

3. The fire can be built and used without any danger to participants or the surrounding natural environment.

Gathering wood

Despite the fact that cooking over wood in a forest has a certain amount of glamour, at times it is neither easy nor pleasant to do so. Gathering wood and cutting it into short pieces takes time and effort. It may also be difficult to find wood that burns easily. On a rainy day, you may not be able to find any dry wood; if there is snow on the ground, the only wood in sight may be the tops of living, non-burnable green trees. A lush, humid forest may offer no dead wood, or that wood may already be rotten and soggy; a hardwood forest may offer no small tinder with which to start a fire. You may be in an area where you have no idea what kind of wood burns easily and well; or where the wood contains some natural chemical that causes your food to taste strange (for example, certain cedars make food taste like mothballs). Or, the available wood may be too hard to cut.

To gather wood, take a buddy and a compass, and travel about 100 yards from your campsite in one direction. Gather wood, **being sure not to take all you find,** then return to your campsite, traveling in the opposite direction. Gather just enough wood for your own use. The days of leaving firewood for the next camper are over. Step lightly while you are gathering wood, so that you disturb the forest as little as possible.

If you are camping in an area where wood fires are permitted and environmentally ethical, your cooking fire should be small. It's almost impossible to prepare dinner over a roaring fire. Small sticks (between the size of your finger and your arm) are large enough for all outdoor cooking; anything larger makes too big a fire, burns too hot, and wastes wood. Consider the fact that you really want to be part of the outdoors. A roaring fire may detract from the sounds and sights of the natural world, which you're visiting for only a short time.

Selecting a fire area

The next step in building a wood fire for cooking is selecting a site for the fire itself. If you are in a park, at your basecamp, or in a campcraft area, you'll probably find an existing place for a fire, such as a charcoal stove, a fire pit, or a fireplace. Many fireplaces have a layer of heavy metal under them to keep the fire from spreading to plant roots. In any case, if a designated fire pit is available, use it.

When you have to build your own fireplace, the recommended places to do so are on rocks, on sand, or in shallow pits. To make a *shallow pit*, remove the *duff* (organic material on top of the soil), and the topsoil down to mineral soil. Be very gentle, so that you don't destroy the topsoil and duff; you'll scrape them back over the shallow pit when you leave the area.

If the only place you can find to build a fire has a thick layer of duff, is under low branches, or is surrounded by heavy vegetation, try making a *mound fire* instead of a pit. The purpose of the mound is to protect the soil and its inhabitants. Find an area with exposed mineral soil (a stream bank, an uprooted tree, gravel near rocks), and use this soil to build a mound at least three inches deep on top of a large rock or several rocks piled together. Again, be very gentle and conservative with the amount of soil you take; exposed soil houses many tiny creatures, so help them maintain their homes.

A mound of twenty-four inches in diameter is sufficient for a cooking fire. You can even make a mound fire on top of a plastic or nylon sheet covered with at least three inches of mineral soil. Be sure to use at least three inches; less than that will allow the fire to melt the sheet, cook the lichens on the rocks underneath, and scorch the rock itself. Building a fire directly on a large rock is not recommended because of the visual scar it leaves.

After building the mound of soil and laying the fire, place a small, lightweight grate on top. When you use a grate, your fire will burn more evenly, leave less ash, and pans will be less likely to tip over and put out the fire.

Consider taking along a large frying pan and building your fire in that (still on top of the protective layer of mineral soil). This "portable fireplace" will keep the fire contained and the area around it clean. Many people on canoe or boat trips carry some sort of fire pan, such as a metal garbage-can lid, oil drain pan, or barbecue pan.

Building a fire

To build a fire, you'll need tinder, kindling, and small fuel. *Tinder* is small, easily lighted material that gets hot enough to light the *kindling* (wood larger than tinder); the kindling, in turn gets hot enough to light the fuel. The *fuel* is what actually produces enough heat to cook on. Allow the fuel wood to burn down to coals before cooking. The heat from the coals is much more even than that from the fire.

A match doesn't burn with enough concentrated heat or long enough to light anything larger than tinder, so find a variety of tinder materials before you think about lighting that match. Tinder may be birch bark; wild grapevines; small sticks; dried spruce; tamarack; pine branches; or other wood that you find lying on the ground or dead on trees. *Never remove bark from living trees, and never use living branches for tinder.* You may bring tinder from home in the form of wood scraps, paper (although it doesn't burn as well as wood does), or purchased or home-made fire starters (described in the section on charcoal). Don't use rotten wood, which crumbles, or green wood, which bends but does not break. And *always* be gentle with the environment when you gather wood and build fires.

Gather some pencil-size sticks for kindling and assorted larger sticks up to baseball-bat-size, for fuel. Fuel wood should never be larger than your arm. If you need a saw or ax to break a stick in half, that stick is too large for your cooking fire and would be a waste of wood — not a good minimum-impact practice.

Your cooking fire need not be fancy. Put down a base of three fuel-size sticks, arranged like the letter *A*, with the crossbar placed on top of the others. Put the tinder in the middle of the *A* and the kindling on top. Then you can add small pieces of fuel wood. Don't worry about covering the tinder and kindling; you won't put out the fire. On the contrary! The fire won't burn at all unless you put something flammable on it.

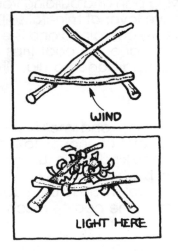 

Figure 6.1 Fire building

Of course, you don't want to smother the tinder or kindling, so leave small spaces through which air can move in and out. Put eight to fifteen pieces of kindling and three to five pieces of fuel on at the beginning so that the heat from the tinder lights the kindling, which in turn lights the fuel. Try making a small tepee of your tinder; the flame will burn upward in a concentrated cone, following the shape of the tepee.

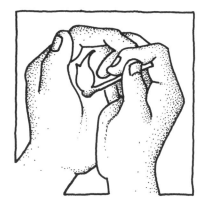

Figure 6.2 Fire building

To light your fire, strike a match (shielding it from the breeze by cupping your hands around it), and insert the flame under the crossbar of the A where there is air space. After the match lights the tinder, throw it in the fire to serve as another piece of tinder. Add fuel and let the fire burn down a bit; you'll get the best results if you cook over coals instead of flames.

When you finish cooking, let the fire burn out. You can burn waste paper, but not garbage. Burning garbage requires much more fuel, produces debris and odors, and is not satisfactory minimum-impact practice. Remember, if you carry something in, carry it out again.

Once the fire is out, sprinkle water on it and stir the ashes with a stick until you're sure that both the ash and soil are cool. Then return the leftover ashes and soil to the environment by scattering it widely.

Sprinkling water on a burning fire is generally safe, but very young participants should never do this without adult supervision. Pouring water on a fire creates steam, which can burn people and scatter the burning wood, possibly creating another fire.

If you're at a base camp, leave the fire pit and leftover materials where they were used. (In a frequently used primitive site, you may want to leave the fire pit and some ashes so the next person will use the same site, rather than digging another hole.) If you're in a pristine area, be sure to practice no-trace camping. Remove all evidence of your presence, return the topsoil, and scatter the duff around on top of the fire pit.

When you're camping beside a river, put the fire out with water, drain the coals, and put the coals into a bucket or sack to dry out so you can use them again at your next stop. Again, leave no trace of your visit.

FOOD

While you consider the type of fire and fuel you'll be using, keep in mind the types of meals you'll be preparing. The food served outdoors should be as nutritious as food served at home. This chapter provides only general dietary information. Make it your responsibility to be aware of the special dietary needs of every member of your group, and keep this information in mind when planning menus.

The food you choose to prepare will depend on where you'll be preparing it. If you'll be in base camp, you need not worry about ingredient weight, because you won't be carrying the foodstuffs. You can cook anything you want. (But remember to consider the cleanup time involved, so that you don't get carried away with glorious ideas.)

On trips, you'll want to prepare food that provides enough energy for you to carry out the day's activities. Commonly, 50 percent of your caloric intake should consist of carbohydrates, 25 percent of protein, and the remaining 25 percent of fats. These percentages are average, however, and will change depending on the situation. In very cold weather, you'll need a higher percentage of fats than you would during hot weather. And don't forget the four food groups; dairy, meats, fruits and vegetables, and grains.

Good sources of *carbohydrates* include: cereals, grains, pasta, starchy vegetables (such as potatoes and corn), fruits, honey, and flavored gelatin. *Proteins* come from meat, cheese, milk, and eggs. *Fats* are found in oil, margarine, butter, nuts, cheese, and meat.

Carbohydrates provide quick energy and are easy to digest. This energy doesn't last long though, so you'll need the benefit of proteins and fats, which require more time and effort to digest but stay with you to provide energy over a longer period of time. Never eat large amounts of protein and/or fat just before participating in strenuous activity. Chocolate, for example, should not be eaten in great quantity as an energy-booster, because it contains a lot of fat. When you need quick *and* long-lasting energy, such as in cold weather, you'll do best to eat some oatmeal, dried fruit, and maybe a granola bar sweetened with honey.

Planning Meals for a Trip

Let's start our discussion of meals with those to take on a trip, because they're usually the simplest to prepare. Fancy cooking at a base camp is an activity all in itself, but food preparation during a trip is just one part of a many-faceted activity.

Good hiking, canoeing, or trip food should be nutritious, simple, easy to prepare quickly, lightweight, compact, inexpensive, nonperishable, and tasty. On a trip, you may find that you want three meals a day plus snacks. But you may want to serve *less* per meal than you would at home. For one thing, we all tend to overeat at home. And, after a big meal, you need to sit still while your body digests some of the excess food; you won't be able to start a hike right away. Eat light, and eat often.

You'll need more carbohydrates when you're active; and during cold weather, you may need more fats. Only experience can tell you exactly what your dietary needs will be. (Suggestions in this chapter are for average appetites; you may want to modify menus and recipes for your group.)

You have many choices of trip food: expensive packaged freeze-dried foods; foods you prepare and package yourself before the trip; or foods bought at the neighborhood grocery store. An adult carrying 1 ½ to 2 pounds of prepackaged food per day may be living quite expensively. A packaged breakfast for four might cost more than twice as much as a breakfast you make yourself, and a packaged dinner may cost 80 percent more than a dinner you packaged yourself.

Planning the menu is one of the best parts of preparing for a trip. In your menu planning, consider the length of the trip, the types of activity, the probable weather conditions, the availability of water, the type of stove and fuel you'll use, the number of people you'll be feeding, the time allotted for cooking, and the cost and variety of the ingredients. For example, you may want to plan an elaborate heavy dinner as a rest day in the middle of a long trip, because such a meal may be just what you need to lift your spirits and lighten your load for the rest of the trip. And if you'll be traveling during cold weather (a natural refrigerator), you may want to take fresh foods in spite of their weight. Some people freeze meats and take them along well-wrapped so that they'll defrost slowly the first day out and can be eaten the first night. Serving defrosted hamburgers on the first night of a five- to seven-day trip is a great way to make novice campers feel more at home.

Although food that requires no cooking may be all right for many days, it's imperative to plan some meals that must be eaten hot, particularly during cold or rainy weather or any time you expect the members of your group to be very tired. Hot food wards off hypothermia, is easy to eat and digest, and refuels a tired body faster than cold food can. Always plan to serve some thick soups, hot casseroles, or one-pot dishes.

Depending on your situation, you can plan meals in a variety of ways. If your group members are very young, you may want to plan their snack lunch for them, then discuss with the group the foods you chose while you're enjoying the lunch. If your group members are capable of planning their own meals, you may want to provide them with a list of suggestions or options from which to choose. Or you may allow them complete freedom to plan all the meals for their day trip or overnight.

Some of the meal planning process may depend on what's available. If you are planning a trip as part of a resident camp program, the camp cook may have only certain foods that are available at particular times. If you are planning a trip as part of a day-camp program or a program that generally meets after school, you may allow the group to plan their meals then select two or three members of the group to go with an adult to the grocery store.

Packaging
Packaging considerations should include space constraints, the sturdiness of both the packaging and the food item, and preparation time. You can prepare most foods by removing them from their original grocery-store containers and repackaging them in plastic bags or leftover containers. Card-

board containers contain a great deal of empty space and squash easily in packs — leave them behind.

Crackers, of course, will become cracker crumbs in plastic bags. Try putting them in neat stacks in plastic freezer leftover boxes.

Be sure to label all packaged items, including any directions for preparation. For example, suppose that you have both homemade granola and purchased hot cereal. Can you tell the difference between them if each is in a plastic bag? Will you remember how much water, salt, and cereal to combine for the right consistency and flavor?

One general food suggestion, is to put all the ingredient packets for one meal together in a large plastic bag. This way, you won't have to search for miscellaneous items.

Purchasing Food for a Trip

Some of the foods you can buy before your trip are listed in this section. By no means is this list exhaustive; you'll probably think of many more things as you wander through the grocery store.

Breakfast

Granola
Cold cereal, with or without fruit and nuts
Instant hot cereals
Bagels
English muffins
Dried fruits (maybe soaked and cooked the night before)
Compact cinnamon toast
Canned bacon
Bacon substitute made of textured protein
Hot-chocolate mix, teabags, instant coffee
Breakfast bars and drinks that require water only
Pancake mixes that require only water (no eggs)
Powdered milk
Solid or liquid margarine
Dried hash browns
Freeze-dried eggs and other breakfast foods
    (usually purchased at a backpacking outfitter)

Lunch

Rye or whole-grain bread (good for the first day on the trail)
Hard rye or other crackers
Chips (hard chips, such as corn chips are less likely to be crushed than regular potato chips)
Cheeses
Meat sticks or salami (ask the deli which will last longest without refrigeration; some are "shrink-wrapped" to keep air out)
Peanut butter (try putting it in a squeeze tube)
Honey or jelly (try putting it in a squeeze tube, perhaps mixed with peanut butter)
Powdered and other instant soups
Raisins and other dried fruits
Nuts
Beef jerky
Bouillon
Canned fish (tuna and sardines don't weigh much)
Canned meat
Oranges (peeled at home and wrapped in plastic, otherwise, you must carry the peels back home with you)
Apples (The cores will recycle naturally, and the birds and animals will relish them)
Carrots, celery, cauliflower
Hard-boiled eggs (for the first day out)
Instant drinks

Dinner

Potatoes, zucchini, corn on the cob
Fruits, fresh and/or dried
Instant potatoes
Instant or 30-minute soups
Macaroni-and-cheese dinners
Spaghetti
Rice mixes
Instant puddings
Dinners requiring water only and five to thirty minutes to cook
Instant sauces (to mix with canned meat or fish)
Dried herbs, onions, etc.
Dried ice cream (a tasty novelty and a good source of sugar)
Freeze-dried complete meals (usually purchased at a back-packing outfitter)

Choosing Utensils for a Trip

The type and sizes of cooking utensils to be used depend on the size of the group. But each person will need a plate, cup, fork, spoon, and maybe a bowl. (Some veteran campers use just a spoon and forgo the fork.) The cup may be used as a bowl, and the knife can be each camper's own folding pocketknife.

Make sure that utensils are cleaned thoroughly before and after each meal. Sturdy plastic is now available; mismatched old silverware from home, however, may work just as well. If you decide to use metal flatware, choose stainless steel instead of silverplated items from your great-aunt's collection of peeling antiques. Stainless steel will not rust or accumulate bacteria in the pitted spots common to old silverplated utensils.

The following lists describe the utensils that each individual camper and each group of campers should take along. Many people travel with groups but do their own packing and menu planning; others travel as a group, sharing everything.

Utensils for one camper

Knife, fork, spoon (same one for cooking and eating)
Plate
Plastic or metal cup and maybe a plastic bowl
Cooking pot (maybe two that nest one inside the other)
Potholder (either the metal pincer type or a hot pad)
Spatula
Stove
Matches
Fuel
Biodegradable soap
Scouring pad
Can opener

The stove can be placed in the shelter of a rock or log, and the entire meal prepared and eaten by one person sitting in one spot. This style of cooking is simple, convenient — and often lonely.

Utensils for a group

Groups usually consist of four to eight campers; larger groups are generally hard on the environment, and the meals take much more time and effort to prepare. If your group is larger than eight, try breaking it into subgroups of four to eight for cooking.

The following list is for a cooking group of four to eight people. For larger groups, adjust accordingly.

Plate, fork, spoon and knife for each camper
Cup for each camper
Bowl for each camper (optional, you can eat your cereal from the cup and then drink your hot chocolate, but if you want your liquid along with your cereal, you'll need a bowl)
One frying pan big enough for cooking four servings
Two or three nested kettles (depending on how many items are to be cooked and whether you'll want a separate pot for heating dishwater)
Two cooking spoons big enough to be used as serving spoons
Cooking fork
Spatula
Pot lifter
Plastic containers of salt, pepper, and optional spices
Backpacker's grill
Griddle (optional)
Ladle
Mixing bowl (optional, you could use one of the pots for mixing)
Can opener
Scouring pad
Biodegradable soap
Stove(s)
Matches
Fuel

In the next section, you'll find recipes for dishes that you and the members of your group may want to fix at base camp or on a trip.

Summary

Tasty food is part of the pleasure of outdoor living. Meal planning and preparation involves many decisions; what to cook, how to cook it, and what kinds of stove and fuel to use. There is no single best way to prepare camping food, so you should consider were you'll be camping, how much you want to spend, how large the group is, where the group is going, and what kinds of fuel and stove you'll be using.

RECIPES

There are literally hundreds and probably thousands of recipes you can use outdoors. The ones presented here represent only a small portion of the easy ones. They are presented to give you a variety of things you can prepare with simple ingredients, a few utensils, and a small fire or stove. Some of the items will require cooking at home; some use perishable foods and are intended for base camp cooking; others are for meals on the extended trip. In all cases, practice before deciding which will be part of your permanent collection. Then look for more recipes until you have found a wide selection of delicious items.

Beverages

Cocoa
(Per person)

1 teaspoon cocoa
2 teaspoons sugar
4 Tablespoons milk powder
1 cup water
extra water (a little)

Mix cocoa and sugar with water in kettle, cook to a smooth paste, letting it bubble vigorously. Add milk and stir thoroughly. Heat almost to a boil. Add a pinch of salt. Beating with a whip prevents any scum from forming.

Spiced hot tea
Serves: 10
Method: No cook
Approximate time: 10 minutes

2 cups orange-flavored instant breakfast drink
¾ teaspoon cinnamon
2 cups sugar (try using 1 cup)

1½ cups instant tea
¼ teaspoon nutmeg
1 4-oz. package instant lemonade

Mix above ingredients together in base camp and store in tightly sealed can. Use in camp as needed. To make one cup of spiced tea, add 1 cup boiling water to 2 tsp. mix.

Cereals

Crunch dry cereal
Serves: 8-10

3 cups rolled oats
1 cup wheat germ
1 cup sesame seeds or sunflower seeds
1 cup shredded, unsweetened coconut
¼ cup oil
¾ cup honey
1 teaspoon vanilla
dash of salt

Mix all ingredients. Spread ½-inch deep on cookie pan and bake at 250 degrees until golden brown. Stir occasionally as the sides will brown first. Let cool. Good for breakfast with milk, or for trail lunch.

Granola

4 cups rolled oats
1 cup wheat germ
1 cup sunflower seeds
¾ cup shredded coconut
½ cup sesame seeds
1 cup chopped nuts
½ cup oil
¾ cup honey
1 ½ teaspoons vanilla

Mix the dry ingredients in a large bowl. Heat oil, honey, and vanilla until combined. Pour mixture over dry ingredients and mix well. Spread on greased cookie sheet. Bake at 350 degrees for 20 to 30 minutes or until lightly browned. Stir frequently. Add 1 to 2 cups of raisins when cool. Makes 3 pounds. Good with milk for trail lunch or for snack.

Granola
Serves: 20

2 cups oatmeal
1 cup sesame seeds
1 cup rye flakes
½ cup pumpkin seeds
1 cup sunflower seed kernels
1 cup wheat germ
½ cup broken cashews
½ cup broken pecans
1 cup slivered almonds
shredded coconut (optional)
½ cup oil
¼ cup honey
¼ cup molasses

Mix all dry ingredients together, then add oil, honey, and molasses. Use hands to mix well. Spread on shallow pans not more than half an inch thick. Bake 15 minutes at 300 degrees. Stir. Bake 5-10 minutes longer, watching carefully. Sprinkle over top: raisins, chopped dried apricots, chopped dates to taste. Store in tightly closed plastic bags in refrigerator.

Homemade cereal
Serves: 10-12
Method: Home oven
Approximate time: 45 minutes

2 cups rolled oats
1 cup wheat germ
2 ½ teaspoons sesame seeds
1 cup shredded coconut
½ cup nuts
¾ cup raisins
½ cup chopped dates
¼ teaspoon cinnamon
¼ teaspoon allspice
½ teaspoon salt
¾ cup molasses
⅓ cup salad oil
½ teaspoon vanilla

Preheat oven to 300 degrees. Mix dry ingredients in large bowl. Add molasses, oil and vanilla. Mix and spread on baking sheets and heat for 30 minutes, stirring often. Cool. Store in airtight container. Serve with milk.

Mountain cereal

Serves: 24

In a large bowl, mix together:

4 ½ cups rolled oats
1 ½ cups pumpkin seeds, chopped
2 cups sunflower seeds
1 cup shredded coconut
¼ cup sesame seeds, ground in blender

In a separate bowl, blend together:

½ cup warm water
¾ cup honey
¼ cup oil
1 teaspoon salt

Mix all ingredients well and bake at 275 degrees, stirring often, till golden brown (about 10 minutes). Now add:

2 cups dried currants or raisins
½ cup dried banana flakes

Stir often as mixture cools. Store in sealed bag in refrigerator.

Oatcake

3 cups rolled oats
½ teaspoon salt
1 teaspoon cinnamon
1 cup boiling water
1 Tablespoon oil
1 teaspoon vanilla

Mix dry ingredients with oil and vanilla. Stir boiling water into mixture and let sit for 15 minutes. This will make a stiff batter. Roll batter to quarter-inch thickness and cut into cakes. Brown both sides in an unoiled skillet. Then dry cakes in a 200-degree oven for half an hour. These cakes keep well. On the trail, they are delicious when dipped into the juice from stewed fruit.

Soups

Curried vegetable soup

Serves: 4

At home: Bag together 1 package dried onion soup mix; ¼ cup each dried tomatoes, carrots, celery and onion; 2 beef bouillon cubes; ½ teaspoon curry powder, and salt and pepper to taste.

In camp: Simmer 15 minutes in 5 cups water.

Vigorous veggie soup

Serves: 4

At home: Bag together ½ cup each dried potatoes and carrots, ¼ cup each dried celery and onions, 2 chicken bouillon cubes, these seasonings to taste: marjoram, salt and pepper, paprika, caraway seed, dill seed.

In camp: Simmer 15 minutes in 5 cups water, adding ¼ cup margarine and ¼ cup dry milk.

Hearty soup pot

Serves: as many as you like

Cook several kinds of soup mix together, adding slivered cheese and crumbled meat or bacon bar. Use plenty of water so it isn't too concentrated and salty.

Cheese soup

Serves: 4

At home: Bag together ¼ cup each dried carrots, celery, peppers, onion, 2 bouillon cubes. In a second bag put 1 cup sunflower seed kernels and ¼ cup dry milk.

In camp: Simmer contents of first bag 15 minutes in 5 cups water, then add second bag plus ¼ cup margarine and 1 ½ cup grated cheese; heat till cheese is melted.

Fish chowder

Serves: 4

At home: Bag together ½ cup each dried tomatoes and potatoes, ¼ cup each dried onion and celery, salt and pepper and a little crumbled bacon bar.

In camp: Cook until tender in 4 cups water. Add 1 can minced clams (fresh fish if you've been lucky) and ½ cup dry milk. Cook 5 minutes more.

Snacks

GORP (the famous trail snack)

GORP actually stands for Good Ole Raisins and Peanuts, but any combination of mixed nuts, sunflower seeds, M & Ms, raisins, shredded coconut, butterscotch drops, is good. Some people add crumbled bacon bar.

Fruit balls

Grind together dried figs and raisins, mix in some peanut butter and flaked coconut. Roll into balls. Roll in chopped nuts if desired.

Fruit balls

In amounts to suit your taste, grind together dried apricots, raisins and dates. Shape into balls and roll in sesame seeds or chopped nuts.

Roasted pumpkin and sunflower seeds

Roast raw seeds in butter on a cookie sheet in the oven, over low heat until pumpkin seeds are slightly puffy. Season with salt, soy sauce, chili powder, etc. Stir well.

Trail fudge

Blend together the following ingredients in amounts to suit your tastes and make a stiff batter, then bake about 20 minutes at 300 degrees: honey, peanut butter, oats, coconut, soy oil, chopped peanuts, chopped pecans, soy flour, wheat germ, sesame seeds, sunflower seed kernels, and sea salt.

One-Pot Dishes

American chop suey

Serves: 8

2 16-oz. cans spaghetti with tomato sauce
2 teaspoons cooking oil
3-4 onions (small), peeled and diced
1-1 ½ lbs. ground beef

green pepper (if desired), cut small
salt and pepper

Fry onions and pepper in shortening or oil until brown. Pour off excess oil. Add ground beef and cook until well done, but not crisply brown. Add spaghetti and heat well. Season to taste. Serve hot.

Variation: Instead of canned spaghetti, use 1 package macaroni and 1 16-oz. can concentrated tomato soup. Cook macaroni in boiling water. (Takes an extra kettle.)

For variety: Use a little sausage meat with the ground beef; add some cooked celery or peas.

Scrambled potatoes

Serves: 8

8 medium-sized, cold, boiled potatoes, diced
2 small onions, peeled and diced
4 pieces bacon, chopped, or small amount bacon fat
8 eggs
salt and pepper

Fry onions with bacon pieces, or in bacon fat until light brown. Add potatoes, and fry until brown and crisp. Break eggs into mixture, stirring while it cooks; cook until eggs are set. Season well. Serve hot. Add a little cheese or tomato catsup or both, if desired.

Chili con carne

Serves: 8

4 Tablespoons cooking oil
8 Tablespoons (about) chopped onion
1 ½ to 2 lbs. ground beef or left-over meat
2 qts. canned tomatoes
2 cans kidney beans
salt

Fry onion until light brown. Add meat and cook until done. Add tomatoes and beans and cook together. Season with a little chili powder and salt. Let it all simmer. Thicken with a little flour if needed. Add 2 Tablespoons of Worcestershire sauce, if more seasoning is needed.

Campfire stew
Serves: 8

1 ½ to 2 lbs. ground beef
3 teaspoons cooking oil or shortening
1 large onion, peeled and diced
2 cans concentrated vegetable soup
salt and pepper

Make little balls of hamburger, adding seasoning. Fry with onion in frying pan, or in bottom of kettle, until onion is light brown and balls are well browned all over. Pour off excess grease. Add vegetable soup and enough water to prevent sticking. Cover and cook slowly until meat balls are cooked thoroughly. (The longer, the better.)

Master plan one-pot meals [7]
Serves: 10
Method: In a Dutch oven or kettle
Approximate time: 30 minutes

Master plan ingredients:

2 lbs. hamburger
2 Tablespoons dehydrated onions or finely chopped onion
2 cans tomato soup
2 teaspoons dehydrated sweet peppers or ½ fresh pepper
    chopped
salt and pepper to taste

To prepare master pot, brown hamburger with onions and pepper. Drain grease. Add soup, season, and add ingredients to make any of the following variations.

Macaroni beef — master plan variation one
1 twelve oz. package macaroni

Boil macaroni according to instructions on package. Drain and add to master pot. Serve.

Chili — master plan variation two
3 no. 2 cans red kidney beans
2 no. 2 cans tomatoes (broken)
chili powder to taste

Add to master pot. Simmer ten minutes and serve.

7. *The Outdoor Book*. Kansas City, MO: Camp Fire, Inc., 1980.

Sloppy joes — master plan variation three
10 hamburger buns

Cook master pot to desired consistency and serve on buns.

Hunter's stew — master plan variation four
2 no. 2 cans mixed vegetables
3 no. 2 cans of other vegetables such as potatoes, corn, green beans and tomatoes

Add to master pot. Simmer 10 minutes and serve.

Spanish rice — master plan variation five
1 small package quick-cook rice
3 cups water

Add water to master pot and bring to boil. Add rice and remove from heat. Cover with lid and let stand for five minutes. Serve.

Hungarian hot pot — master plan variation six
3 no. 2 cans pork and beans

Add pork and beans to master pot. Simmer 10 minutes and serve.

Mexican delight — master plan variation seven
1 no. 2 can Mexicorn
1 small jar pitted black olives (optional)
1 small box cornbread mix, plus ingredients noted on pkg.
1 cup water

Add water to master pot and bring to boil. Mix cornbread mix, Mexicorn, and olives. Drop by spoonfuls into master pot. Cover Do not peek! Cook 15 minutes.

One-pot spaghetti
Serves: 10
Method: In a Dutch oven or kettle
Approximate Time: 45 minutes

2 medium onions chopped
2 lbs. hamburger
2 no. 2 cans tomatoes (broken up)
2 cups water
garlic powder

16 oz. spaghetti broken in small pieces
2 Tablespoons oregano

Brown hamburger with onions until tender. Pour off grease. Add remaining ingredients. Bring to boil for 1 minute. Simmer 25 more minutes covered, stirring occasionally.

Cascade stew
Serves: 4

Cook in 4 cups water 10 minutes:

⅓ cup dried diced potato
¼ cup dried tomato and carrot chunks
1 Tablespoon each dried onion and celery
2 beef bouillon cubes

Stir in ⅓ cup instant potato. When thickened add 1 can roast beef chunks (or leftover beef from home). Heat through.

Rice and vegetable dinner mix
Serves: 4-6

Bring to a boil in 3 cups water:

½ cup dried onion
½ cup dried carrots
¼ cup dried parsley
salt and pepper to taste
3 bouillon cubes

Add 1 ¼ cups quick brown rice and simmer till tender. Top with margarine or cheese. An elegant camp dish, perhaps for a special trip.

Super-scramble
Soak dried potato shreds and crumbled meat or bacon bar in water. Drain and cook with dried onion, parsley and pepper flakes until browned, then stir in cubed cheese and heat until melted.

Spanish rice with meatballs
Serves: 4

Cook 10 minutes in 3 to 4 cups water:

1 cup dried tomato flakes or several home-dried slices
2 tablespoons dried onion flakes
salt and pepper
freeze-dried or canned meatballs

Add 1 cup quick rice and cook, covered, 8 minutes. If dried meatballs were used, add 1 package gravy mix and cook 1 minute.

Shrimp creole

Serves: 4

Cook 6 minutes in 4 cups water:

¼ cup each dried tomatoes and green pepper flakes
1 cup quick rice
salt and pepper to taste

Add:

1 can shrimp (if dried, cook with above)
1 package powdered cream of mushroom soup mix
more water if needed

Heat through. Serve.

Methods for Outdoor Cooking

There are several ways you can bake outdoors. You will need to make or buy a special oven for some things. Some things can be baked in a manner you may find unfamiliar. Dumplings are biscuits steamed on top of stews by dropping the dough onto the bubbling stew, covering the pot and leaving it alone for 10 to 15 minutes. Some biscuits and breads can be baked in a frying pan, much like pancakes. If you have a Dutch oven at your base camp, you can bake almost anything in it. It will be too heavy to carry on a pack trip but some people take one on a canoe trip (when there is ample room).

When you bake a pie or cake in a Dutch oven, it is best to put a triangle of three small stones between the bottom of the oven and the baking pan. This elevates the baking pan and permits air to circulate freely around the food that is baking — just as in the oven at home.

Ovens work by reflecting heat onto all sides of the food being cooked. Your home oven does this well. You can make an oven by covering a cardboard box with aluminum foil or shaping aluminum foil into a box shape. With care, you can re-use the foil box many times. If you throw it away after each use, you are not practicing minimum-impact skills. The foil box should be two to three inches larger than your baking pan so that reflected hot air can circulate around it. When you bake, put a grill over the coals, place the baking pan on it and cover with the box oven.

A light weight, inexpensive, folding, metal reflector oven can be purchased from many camping equipment outlets. With proper care, these ovens can last for years. They are fun to use because one side is open to the fire and you can actually watch a cake rise and brown.

The secret to baking — at home or outdoors — is correct temperature. Nearly all baked goods are cooked at 350 degrees Fahrenheit. To determine the temperature of your coals, put your open hand, palm down, above the coals where the bottom of the pan will rest. Count for five seconds (one thousand and one, one thousand and two, etc.). If your hand gets so hot you have to pull it away before you get to one thousand and five, the coals are too hot. If you can keep your hand there much longer, they are too cool. Chances are you can determine a range of temperature between 325 and 375 degrees accurately enough for successful baking with this method.

Ovens use heat — not roaring fires and dancing flames. You might try to bake over your little gas stove. It can be done. Regardless of your oven style, try brownies, corn bread and coffee cake first. Even beginners are usually successful with them. If the brownies are black on the bottom and doughy in the middle, the coals were much too hot.

For a real challenge, try cooking a chicken or pot-roast on a string. In front of the fire, (not directly over it), hang a well bound chicken or piece of pot roast from a tripod, crane, or angled stick. Use string that is strong enough to support the weight of the meat during the cooking. Place a drip pan under the meat. Make a reflector behind the fire to reflect the heat toward the meat in front. Keep the fire at 350 degrees, baste the meat occasionally with pan drippings, margarine or butter. Cooking the meat will take as long as indoors. For this reason you may decide that string-cooking takes more fuel than you wish to use. Toward the end of cooking time you might want to baste the meat with barbecue sauce. Don't use the barbecue sauce too early — the sugar in the sauce burn and the meat will become chewy. Using the string-cooking method will make the pot roast drier than if it were simmered. Chicken and beef will have the same taste and consistency if you use string-cooking or if you simmer them.

This is a type of cooking you will want to do with adequate fuel and time. Perhaps it will be on a day that you have many things to do at base camp and group members can take turns feeding the fire to keep the temperature at 350 degrees.

At many base camps, baking in a hole in the ground is popular when there is an adequate supply of wood. The hole can be used year after year. This type of cooking has lost its popularity where there is no surplus fuel to use, and it is definitely not a trip skill.

1. Dig a hole about two feet deep and two to three feet in diameter. Be sure not to disturb roots or organic materials.

2. Line it with bricks or dry, somewhat flat rocks. Do not use shale or slate — they will split apart.

3. Build a fire in the pit and keep it going for two to three hours to heat the rocks thoroughly.

4. When the rocks are hot, put your bean or stew pot into a burlap bag and lower it carefully onto the coals.

5. Cover with loose dirt or sand, tamp down, and leave for four to five hours. The hot coals will heat the sand or dirt and cook the contents of the pot. Be sure there are no roots or loose organic materials nearby that can catch on fire.

6. After four to five hours, dig up the pot and eat the contents. After the rocks and coals have cooled, cover the hole for use another time.

You may keep using the same *bean-hole* at your base camp year after year. Some times they are used only once a year and only by participants with advanced skills.

Ice cream outdoors

Have you ever thought about making ice cream outdoors? There is a way to make it without using the old-fashioned ice cream freezer many people use. To make ice cream in a hay hole:

1. Dig a hole at least one foot larger than the ice cream container you will use.

2. Put the ice cream mixture into a container with a tight cover and lower it into the hole.

3. Pack around the container with alternating layers of hay (or straw), cracked ice (or ice cubes) and ice cream salt. Use at least five layers of each.

4. Cover the container lid with more hay, ice and salt, and cover the entire project with a heavy cloth or tarp to keep the sun off the top.

5. Leave for five hours or more and return to eat milk-shake consistency ice cream.

How does it work? The salt helps the ice to melt, by releasing the cold from the ice (a temperature that is below 32 degrees). The hay swells as it soaks up the melting ice. As the hay swells, it absorbs heat from the ice cream container, making a colder and colder ice cream mixture. This is a good base camp activity that requires no fuel.

For trips, plan simple menus with little cooking and no perishable foods. At base camp, try something more elaborate and time-consuming. Outdoor cooking is fun. Outdoor eating is a treat.

7

Tying It Up

Velcro, buttons, snaps, pre-made gift bows — why learn to tie knots? If you wear shoes with velcro closures, and package gifts with transparent tape and pretied bows, you may not have to tie knots very often.

Imagine replacing a broken shoelace five miles from home, or trying to keep your tent from falling down and blowing away without any knowledge of how to tie it securely. Will your canoe drift away because you didn't secure it tightly? Can you put up a clothesline? Can you make simple repairs to your equipment if you can't tie a knot?

"It won't happen to me," is the excuse of a person who's destined for disaster. Knowing how to tie a few knots can be the difference between a successful trip and a miserable one.

Campers talk about knots and hitches but rarely know the difference between them. The difference is just this simple: **knots** (at least the ones you will learn here) are easy to tie, are permanent fastenings until they're untied, and are easy to untie. **Hitches** are temporary fastenings that can be undone easily and quickly. Sound pretty similar? Don't worry. Learn the names of a few knots and hitches, their uses and how to tie them, and it will become more clear. This chapter includes thirteen of the most popular, most useful knots and hitches.

You can tie knots and hitches with twine, cord or rope made of natural or synthetic materials. The advantage of synthetic materials, such as nylon and plastic, are that they don't rot as easily, are not affected by water, and stretch only under pressure. Some synthetics, however, are stiff and hard to tie, particularly the plastic cord used for clotheslines. Natural fibers, which are more fragile than synthetics, may shrink, stretch or rot when wet but they are generally easy to tie.

Most shoelaces are made of natural materials (although some of the new fashion-colored laces are nylon); most tent cords are made of nylon.

You may find that "parachute cord," a flexible nylon, fairly small rope, is the best for your everyday needs. If so, you may want to include twenty-five to fifty feet of it in your group gear. It can be cut into shorter lengths if necessary. Parachute cord makes a good clothesline, is strong enough to secure large items, and will last for many years.

TYING KNOTS

When learning or teaching others how to tie knots, use a standard language so that everyone knows what parts of the rope you are referring to. The following are the terms you need to know and use.

- The part of a rope that you are working with is called the *working end* or the *free end*.
- The rest of the rope — the part you are not working with, whether it is twelve inches or a hundred feet long — is called the *standing end*.
- A *bight* (rhymes with "bright") is simply a bend in the rope.
- A bight becomes a *loop* when you cross one part of the rope over another part. If the free end crosses over the standing end you have an *overhand* loop. If the free end crosses under the standing end you have an *underhand* loop.

Preparing a Rope

When you buy a rope, bind the ends so that no unraveling occurs. Nylon rope can be melted so that it won't unravel. Simply touch a burning object, such as a match, to the end of the rope. As soon as the strands are melted together, dip the end into water. Be sure to do this outdoors and be careful that you don't inhale the fumes which are poisonous. Also, take care not to drip melted nylon on anyone or anything. It is very hot and will burn skin or fabrics.

To bind natural materials (and nylon that you don't want to melt) you can use heavy metal staples or tape on the ends. This method, however, is not very permanent. A better method is to tie a knot in each end. These knots are called *stopper knots*.

Stopper Knots

There are two kinds of stopper knots: the *overhand knot* and the *figure eight*.

Overhand knot

To prevent the end of a rope from unraveling, tie an overhand knot. To tie an overhand knot follow these steps:

1. Make a loop in the end of the rope, and push the free end in and out of the loop.

2. Pull the rope tight and you will have an overhand knot.

Practice tying the knot close to the end of your rope. If you can pull the knot out by tugging on it, you tied it too close to the end.

Figure 7.1 Overhand knot, steps 1 and 2.

Figure eight knot

Tying a figure eight involves one more step than the overhand knot, but this knot holds tighter and prevents the rope from unraveling longer. To tie a figure eight, follow these steps:

1. Make a loop in the end of the rope, just as you did for the overhand knot.

2. Pass the free end of the rope once around the standing end and back on top of itself before you push it through the loop. You'll see a figure eight. Pull free end tight to secure knot.

Figure 7.2 Figure eight knot.

Whipping a rope

You can also prevent unraveling by *whipping a rope*. The term "whipping" means wrapping a piece of twine or smaller rope around the end of the rope. The twine must be wrapped neatly and tightly and must not slip off the rope when you pull on it.

Whipping is a good activity to practice as you sit around talking about camping. It takes time and patience to master.

To whip a rope, follow these steps:

1. Make a bight in a piece of twine or twine that is about twelve inches long. Lay the bight on the rope so that both ends (free and standing) are toward the end of the rope to be whipped. The free end of the twine should be hanging off the end of the rope.

2. Holding the bight with your finger, start wrapping the standing end around both the twine and the rope, toward the bight itself. Be sure to leave the free end of the twine hanging out. Make the wrapping neat; don't let any wrap

cross a previous wrap. Be sure to keep winding the twine tightly against the previous turn. Whippings must be precise, even, and smooth so they won't catch on anything.

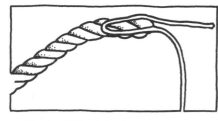

Figure 7.3 Whipping, step 1.

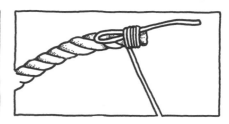

Figure 7.4 Whipping, step 2.

3. After you have whipped about one inch around the rope, slip the end of the twine through the bight (which should still be sticking out) and, holding tight, pull on the free end. Pull the twine until the bight disappears into, and goes about halfway down inside, the length of the wrapping. Cut off the dangling ends. The length of a whipping is usually the same as the diameter of the rope being whipped.

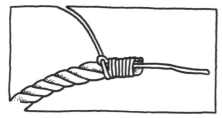

Figure 7.5 Whipping, step 3.

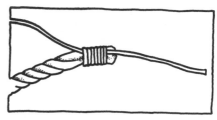

Figure 7.6 Whipping, step 3 cont.

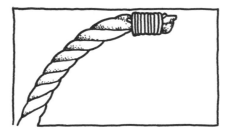

Figure 7.7 Whipping, step 3 cont.

You may see references to *splicing* or *back splicing* and may want to learn these techniques for advanced sailing activities. They aren't necessary, however, for camping purposes.

Joiner Knots

As the name suggests, *joiner knots* are used to join two pieces of rope, cord or twine. Joiner knots include the square knot, and the sheet bend and double sheet bend, the bow knot, the granny, the slip knot, the fisherman's knot, the surgeon's knot, and the carrick bend. You probably know how to tie a bow knot (the knot you use to tie your shoe laces); the granny has little use to campers; and the others are knots you can learn on your own from books or leaders who have advanced knot-tying skills. The square knot and the sheet bend are the ones you must know how to tie for basic outdoor-living skills.

Square knot

The most useful knot of all may well be the *square knot*. It is used to join two pieces of rope, twine, or cord, each of equal thickness. It is the knot used to hold a bandage in place.

You can practice tying square knots, with two pieces of rope or cord of equal thickness, with one piece of rope that you want to tie around something such as a package or branch, or with a bandage that you want to tie around an arm, leg, or finger. To tie a square knot, follow these steps:

1. Hold one end in each hand. Cross one end over the other, then around behind, underneath, and back up in front of the other.

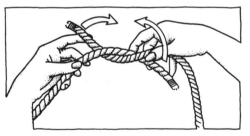

Figure 7.8 Square knot, step 1.

2. Using the same end (it is now in the other hand), cross it over the other, around behind, underneath, and back up in front of the other. Essentially, you are doing the same thing that you did in step one, only backwards. Pull tight and you have a square knot.

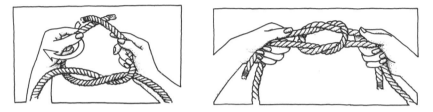

Figure 7.9 Square knot, step 2.

An old rule says, "Right over left and under; left over right and under." Try left over right and then right over left; it doesn't make any difference. Make something up that helps you and your group remember. Practice tying square knots with your shoelaces, parachute cord, and one-inch ropes. Can you tie a square knot with your eyes closed? Can you tie one behind your back?

Sheet bend

If the two pieces to be tied together are of different thickness, a modified square knot called the *sheet bend* is used. This knot prevents the smaller rope from sliding out. Follow these steps:

1. Make a square knot, but don't pull it tight.

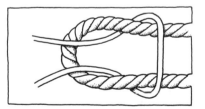

Figure 7.10 Sheet bend, step 1.

2. Cross the working end of the thinner rope over its standing end, and tuck it down through the loop of the thicker rope.

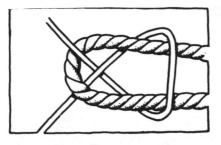

Figure 7.11 Sheet bend, step 2.

3. Pull the rope tight. The extra turn of the thinner rope will hold the knot in place.

Figure 7.12 Sheet bend, step 3.

TYING HITCHES

There are many different kinds of hitches, including the slippery, timber, rolling, chain, marlin spike, midshipman's and tiller's hitch. This book is concerned only with the most common hitches; the clove hitch, the half hitch, the bowline hitch, and the tautline hitch.

Clove hitch

A *clove hitch* is used to fasten a rope to a tree, post, or similar object when there will be a steady pull on the rope (i.e. a clothes line). It is used to start lashings. Because a clove hitch will slip unless kept taut, it is not used to secure moving objects, such as a boat or an animal (for example, a horse). To tie a clove hitch, follow these steps:

1. Pass the free end of the rope behind the post.

2. Bring the free end around to the front of the post and cross the standing end, making an X.

3. Pass the free end behind the post again, below the X.

4. As you bring the free end around to the front of the post again, pass the it under the X so that it comes out between the previous two turns around the post.

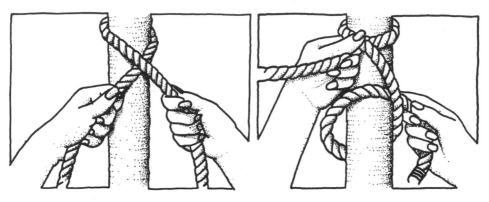

Figure 7.13 Clove hitch, step 4.   Figure 7.14 Clove hitch, step 2.

5. Pull both ends tight. Be sure to pull the free end directly opposite the standing end — if you pull one part out at a right angle to the other, the hitch won't hold.

Figure 7.15 Clove hitch, step 5.

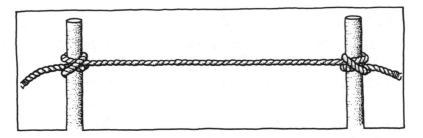

Figure 7.16 Two clove hitches to make a clothesline.

Half hitch

Half hitches are tied at the ends of ropes holding boats or horses to rings or poles. A couple of half hitches tied in the ends of a cord used for tying square knots adds security. To tie a half hitch, follow these steps:

1. Pass the free end of the rope behind a pole or through a ring and around to the front again, then under the standing end.

Figure 7.17 Half hitch, step 1.

2. Bring the free end up and in front of the standing end, then tuck it into the bend.

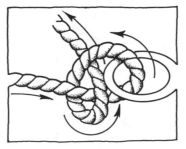

Figure 7.18 Half hitch, step 2.

3. Make another half hitch on the standing end of the rope, away from the ring or post. Now, you have two half hitches, which make a sliding knot. The two half hitches can be moved up and down the standing part of the rope. They will not hold firmly unless they're snugly against the pole or ring.

Figure 7.19 Half hitch, step 3.

Bowline hitch

At times you'll need a loop that won't slip into a smaller or larger size. The *bowline* (pronounced bowl'n) is the knot to use. To tie a bowline hitch, follow these steps:

1. Holding the rope in one hand, make a small (four-inch-diameter) overhand loop about twelve inches or more from the free end. The length of rope from the overhand loop to the free end should be a little longer than the circumference of the loop that you want to create. (see figure 7.20)

2. Now, pass the end of the rope around something like a log, pole or metal ring to make this larger loop. (Be sure that the small loop you made is an overhand loop.) (see figure 7.21)

3. Hold the overhand loop with one hand and, with the other hand slip the free end of the rope through the overhand loop from behind. Pass it around behind the standing end, and back down into the original overhand loop. (see figures 7.21 and 7.22)

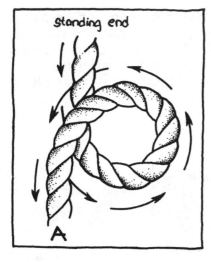

Figure 7.20 Bowline, step 1.

Figure 7.21 Bowline, step 2 and 3.

Figure 7.22 Bowline, step 3.

4. Hold the free end against the large loop with one hand. With the other hand, hold the standing end above the knot, and pull. The knot will tighten but will not slip.

Figure 7.24 Bowline, step 4.

To teach the bowline to beginners, you could call the free end of the rope the "rabbit" and tell the campers to make a hole (loop) for the rabbit. The rabbit comes out of the hole, runs around behind the tree (standing end), and goes back down into the hole.

Or use a variation. Call the loop something else, such as a lake, subway or drain. Have a "dragon", a turtle, or a person (the free end of the rope), come out of whatever you call the loop and go around the standing end, which you may call by some other name. Then have the dragon, turtle, or person return to the loop and pull on both ends to stop your imaginary tale. You can use many different scenarios. Each time you name the loop, the free end and the standing end, demonstrate by making the bowline as you go along.

The keys to making bowlines are as follows:

- Be sure that the first loop is an overhand loop.
- Be sure that the free end goes into the overhand loop from behind and comes toward you.
- The free end then goes around behind the standing end and back down into the original overhand loop.
- Be sure to practice and practice.

Can you tie a bowline with your eyes closed? Behind your back? Behind your back while swimming or taking a shower?

Tautline hitch

Everyone using a tent should learn the *tautline hitch*, which regulates the tension (tightness) of the lines that hold the tent and/or rain-fly to the tent stakes. Sometimes, tent lines come with a preformed loop and metal fastener already in place. The loop and metal fastener may not be included in your tent, may be missing or you may need to use a longer line. In such a case you will need to tie a tautline hitch. It's easiest to tie a tautline hitch if you tie it *to* something. To tie a tautline hitch, follow these steps:

1. Tie one end of a piece of rope two or three feet long to a fixed object (a tree, your partner's leg, etc.) with two half hitches. Push a tent stake or a stick into the ground about two-thirds of the length of the rope away. Make sure the tent stake or stick is angled slightly away from the fixed object as you push it into the ground.

2. Pass the end of the rope around the tent stake, and pull it fairly tight (so that it won't slip off while you finish the hitch).

3. Make two or three overhand knots around the standing end and toward the tent stake.

4. Make another overhand knot around the standing end *toward the fixed object.* Pull this knot tight.

You can pull on the taut line hitch and slide it up toward the fixed object. If you use this hitch on a tent or tent-fly, you'll be able to hold the tent tight, because the hitch won't slip back until you pull it back.

> A generous loop and two little coils
> And a half hitch down below;
> Then push them tight
> And you'll be all right
> With a tautline hitch to show! [8]

LASHING

In the past, when people set up base camps, and even when they were setting up sites for just one night, they often made elaborate tables and cooking apparatus out of neatly cut branches. Twine was lashed around the branches to keep the

8. *The Outdoor Book.* Kansas City, MO: Camp Fire, Inc., 1980.

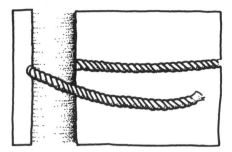

Figure 7.25 Tautline hitch, step 2.   *Figure 7.26 Tautline hitch, step 3.*

Figure 7.27 Tautline, step 3 cont.   *Figure 7.28 Tautline hitch, step 4.*

wood even, straight, and in semipermanent position. Campers rarely engage in lashing today, for this skill usually requires cutting branches — definitely *not* an environmentally sensitive activity. Should you need to lash something, however, always use fallen branches, and return them to their natural setting when you are finished using the object that you made.

If you carry *binders' twine* with you for lashing, it can also be used for tinder (if you are in a place where a fire is environmentally acceptable), or disposed of when you get home. Binders' twine doesn't decompose very well outdoors because it has been treated with a preservative.

There are some uses for lashing that don't impact the environment greatly. Among them are repairing broken ski poles, making stretchers, joining two sticks together to lengthen or strengthen them, and making a cross or a diagonal. All require simple lashing skills, fallen branches or sticks and a minimal amount of twine. The following are the uses of four types of lashing.

Square Lashing is used to tie two sticks or poles at right angles. This type of lashing can be used for joining table legs together.

Diagonal Lashing is used to tie two sticks or poles in the shape of an X. This type of lashing can be used to make a temporary tent pole or shelter frame.

Sheer Lashing is used to tie two sticks or poles parallel to each other. This type of lashing can be used to lengthen sticks for cooking, or strengthen them so you can hang objects on them. You can lash one stick to each end of a broken ski pole, a splint; or you can make a tripod for a temporary wash basin stand.

Continuous Lashing is used to join several sticks, laid parallel to one another, and a long pole crossing them, at a right angle. This type of lashing may be used for making a bridge over a swampy spot (so as to avoid disturbing the swamp life), or making a simple tabletop.

Each kind of lashing involves the following four steps:

1. Start with the sticks or poles as close as possible to their final positions. Make a clove hitch on the bottom pole close to the pole to be lashed. Leave enough free end to tie a square knot when you finish the lashing.

2. Wrap the poles or sticks.

3. Tighten the wrapping by *frapping.* Frapping means winding the cord several times around the wrapping and then several times between the sticks you just wrapped. Pull the cord tight at each stage. Always *frap* at least three times around and between the sticks.

4. Finish the lashing by tying the ends of the cord (the clove-hitch end and the frapping end) in a square knot. Snip off the long ends to make the lashing neat.

Square lashing

To perform *square lashing*, follow these steps: Tie a clove hitch on one pole and lay the other pole on top of the first so they are at right angles. Pass the cord over the top pole, behind the bottom pole, up and around the top pole, behind the bottom pole again, and up to the front of the top pole. Repeat this pattern until you feel the lashing is strong enough then frap.

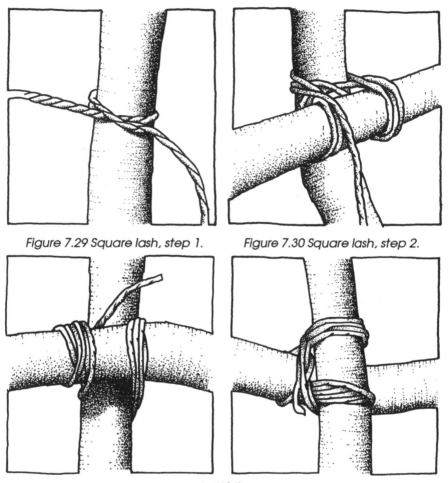

Figure 7.29 Square lash, step 1.

Figure 7.30 Square lash, step 2.

Figure 7.31 Square lash, step 3.

Figure 7.32 Square lash, step 4.

Diagonal lashing

Diagonal lashing is even easier. To practice diagonal lashing, follow these steps:

1. Lay the sticks diagonally, as they will be in the final product. Tie a clove hitch around both sticks at the point where they cross.

2. Wrap the twine several times around the crossed sticks in the same direction as the clove hitch.

3. Wrap the twine several times around the crossed sticks, at a right angle to the first wrapping. The wrapping will look like an X.

Figure 7.33 Diagonal lash, step 2.

Figure 7.34 Diagonal lash, step 3.

4. Frap, by wrapping the twine several times between the sticks and over the wrapping from step 2.

5. Finish by tying a square knot.

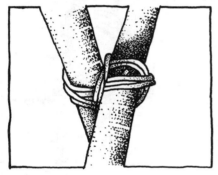

Figure 7.35 Diagonal lash, step 4.

Figure 7.36 Diagonal lash, step 5.

Sheer lashing

Sheer lashing is also easy. To practice sheer lashing, follow these steps:

1. Lay the sticks parallel to one another.

2. Tie a clove hitch on the end of one stick, then wrap the twine around two or three sticks about eight times, and frap.

3. Frap around the wrapping and between each stick.

4. If you have lashed three sticks, you can make a tripod. Twist the sticks into tripod form.

Figure 7.37 Sheer lash, step 1.

Figure 7.38 Sheer lash, step 2.

Figure 7.39 Sheer lash, step 3.

Figure 7.40 Sheer lash, step 4.

Caring for ropes

- All ropes, no matter what size, should be kept clean.
- To clean ropes, soak in water and air-dry. Don't twist or wring the rope. Simply, lay flat to dry.
- Never step on rope. Even little bits of soil ground into the rope will break down the fibers (natural or synthetic) and weaken the rope considerably.
- Ropes should always be coiled neatly when not in use. They will last longer and be much easier to use.

If you want to lash two sticks together to lengthen them (or make a splint), follow these steps:

1. Lay the sticks so that a few inches of each are side-by-side.

2. Tie a clove hitch on the end of one of the sticks.

3. Wrap the twine around both sticks about eight times.

4. Frap between the two sticks.

5. End with a square knot.

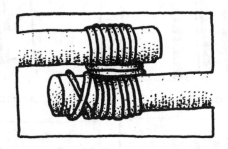

Figure 7.41 Sheer lashing to make a splint.

Continuous lashing

For *continuous lashing*, it's best to start with a piece of twine about three feet long. To practice continuous lashing, follow these steps:

1. Tie a clove hitch onto one end of the base pole. Make sure the hitch is at *the midpoint* of the twine so that each end is of equal length.

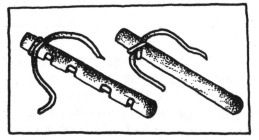

Figure 7.42 Continuous lashing, step 1.

2. Lay the crosspieces over the base pole and start lashing, using both long ends of the twine. Bring the twine up over the first crosspiece. One strand will go on each side of the base pole.

3. Pull each strand of the twine tight and as each strand goes behind the base pole. Cross the twine underneath.

4. Pull the twine tight again and go over the next cross piece.

5. Alternate going over the crosspieces and making an X underneath them.

6. If you run out of twine, tie new strands onto the ends with square knots.

7. Finish by tying the two ends of the twine in a square knot under the long base pole.

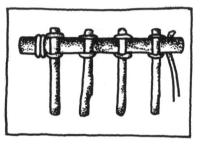

Figure 7.43 Continuous lashing.
(front side)

Figure 7.44 Continuous lashing.
(back side)

You have just learned about knots, hitches, whipping, and simple lashing. These are basic outdoor living skills. If you wish to learn more knots — and there's a lot more to learn — you have a choice of about 75 simple knots and hitches and up to 8,000 intricate ones. If you decide to study new knots, keep practicing the basic ones explained in this chapter. Always remember the simple ones.

8

Toolcraft

When most of us need to have something repaired or built, we call a service person or go to a store to purchase parts or tools. But when you're practicing outdoor-living skills, you won't be able to do this, because you probably won't be near service providers or stores. Furthermore, when you're taking a prolonged trip on foot, canoe, bicycle, or horseback, you can't carry a large tool chest. Actually, the only times outdoor-living skills participants need tools are when they need to cut something to make it shorter or smaller or to dig a hole for some specific purpose. Ropes, strong cords, and a good selection of knots can take care of most repairs. This chapter is devoted to the tools you'll need to make outdoor living, cooking, and eating enjoyable, safe, and environmentally sound.

In selecting tools for outdoor use, consider the following: use, location (base camp, or on backpacking, canoe, or horseback trip), safety, and environmental impact. Tools used in outdoor living are usually for cutting or digging.

USING A POCKETKNIFE

The most common tool — one that every camper should learn to use carefully and safely — is the pocketknife or jackknife. Many types of knives are available; many of them are too small or too large for your needs. Pocketknives, however, are compact, yet big enough and strong enough for tasks requiring sturdy blades. Experienced outdoors people use two kinds of pocketknives: a knife with one or two blades, and a knife with four blades (one cutting blade, a combination bottle opener and screwdriver, a can opener, and an awl, or two cutting blades and no awl). Other tools that may be part of a pocketknife include a corkscrew, a saw, a Phillips screwdriver, a toothpick, tweezers, scissors, and even a magnifying lens.

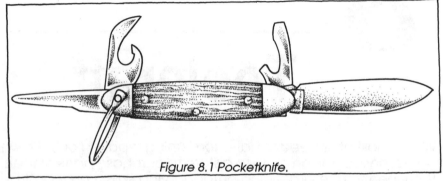

Figure 8.1 Pocketknife.

The main reason for selecting a relatively small knife is ease of use. If the knife doesn't fit comfortably in your hand, it's too big. Your camping knife should fit into your pocket securely and in your hand comfortably. It should be made of good-quality steel, fashioned so that the cutting blades stay sharp. Look for a knife that has a textured handle (such as bone or staghorn, or textured plastic) or a strong plastic handle (such as the well-known Swiss Army knife).

To open a pocketknife, hold it in one hand, pinching it between the thumb and fingers or the base of the thumb and the tips of the fingers, and insert the thumbnail of your free hand into the slot in the knife blade. Don't move the hand you're holding the knife in until the blade is all the way open.

To close the knife, reverse the process. Be sure to hold the handle between the base of the thumb and the tips of the fingers so that no part of your hand is near the slot into which the blade will fit. A good knife closes with a snap caused by a fairly tight spring, and if your fingers are in the way, the knife will cut them as it snaps shut.

Practice opening and closing several pocket knives to find one that feels comfortable and is easy use. Then practice opening and closing the other tools on the knife. If you're using a knife that has a screwdriver, can opener, and awl, practice with the screwdriver first, because it's the tool that's least likely to cut you if you close it incorrectly.

Of course, only youngsters who are capable of following directions — and of understanding the importance of keeping their fingers away from the slot in the handle — should be taught how to use a pocketknife. Also, young children probably won't have the fine motor skills it takes to open and close a pocketknife.

Although the pocketknife is the most common camp tool, it's also the one that causes the most cuts. Why be one of the statistics? You can use a pocketknife for years without ever having a cut, if you always open and close the knife correctly; never take chances, trying to be fancy or to find new and different ways to do it. Close the knife and put it away when you are not using it; *never* run or walk around with an open knife.

Using a pocketknife is relatively safe if you follow one simple, never-to-be-broken rule. *Keep your thumb off the back of the blade.* Pressure on the back of the blade causes it to close, so putting any pressure on the back of the blade is dangerous. A skilled knife user holds a knife with his/her fingers around the handle so that the thumb is on the index finger.

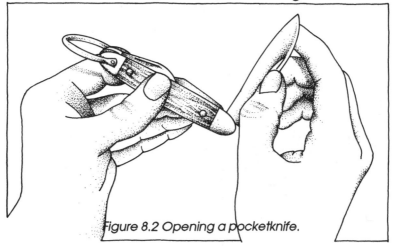

Figure 8.2 Opening a pocketknife.

When you use a knife, hold your elbows against your sides to keep the knife from moving farther from your body than the hand and wrist can move. You'll get better leverage, strength, and control if you regulate the distance in which the blade travels by hold your arms snugly against your sides.

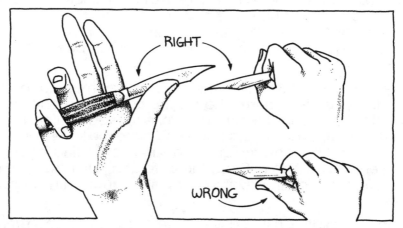

Figure 8.3 Holding a pocketknife.

Practice this by pretending that a short stick is your knife and a long stick is what you are cutting. Let your arms go as far as they can reach when you sharpen an imaginary point on the long stick. Your "knife" will travel as far as your arm can reach. Now keep your elbows in. This time, the "knife" can travel only as far as the length of your forearm. If you keep your wrists against your body, the knife travels only as far as the length of your hand. Do you see how the position of your arms regulates the distance that the knife travels?

Now, practice using a real knife to cut the loop of a doubled-over piece of string. Hold the string in one hand so that a small loop hangs in front of you; hold the knife in your other hand. Cut the string by pushing the sharp edge of the blade against the string, pushing the blade away from your body. Next, try cutting some rope. Cut a piece of meat or vegetable. Sharpen the end of a small stick to use for toasting marshmallows or hot dogs. Cut up some vegetables, such as carrots and celery. Always push the blade away from your body. Be sure to keep your elbows in so that the knife won't make a large arc and cut someone standing nearby.

A knife is a small tool for use in small areas. A good whittler rarely moves the knife farther than the length of his/her closed fist and keeps his/her elbows in, watching carefully what he/she is doing. Not only is this procedure safer, but it also takes far less energy.

Figure 8.4 Whittling.

Before you pass a knife to a friend, it's best to close it first. You can, however, pass it opened if you hold the back of the blade between the base of your thumb and fingertips, cutting edge facing the ground, so that the receiver can grasp the handle. Always pass a knife slowly, making sure that the receiver has a good grip on it before you let go. Never put your fingers under the blade, or they could be cut as the receiver pulls the knife from your hand.

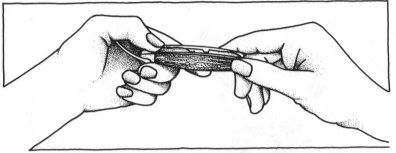

Figure 8.5 Passing a pocketknife.

If you need to put a knife down so that you can do something else, either leave it open on a cutting board, or close it. Never leave an open knife where someone might sit on it, stumble on it, or run into it.

When you finish using the knife, be sure it is clean and dry before you put it away. Your knife may occasionally need a drop of lightweight machine oil to keep the hinge free of dirt and rust.

Some knives have a cord or metal loop on the handle that prevents the knife from dropping out of your pocket. Use some lightweight rope, such as parachute cord, and tie the cord onto the knife with two or three half-hitches; then tie the rope to your belt. (It's better to tie a knife to your belt than to your belt loops because the loops often tear.) A good way to tie a knife to your belt is to make a bowline in the end of the cord and slip it over the belt, and then slip the other end of the rope through the bowline and pull it light. If the bowline is bigger than the pocketknife itself, you can keep the knife tied to the other end and simply slip the knife in and out of the bowline when you want to remove it. But be sure that the cord that's still attached to the knife is wrapped around your hand — not dangling in the air or wrapped around the knife, where it could be severed when you close the knife. Also, be sure that the cord is long enough that the knife will fit easily into your pocket while it's attached to your belt.

You may prefer to fasten a hook to the loop of the knife and attach the cord to that hook with two half-hitches. When you use the knife, remove it from the cord by undoing the hook and slipping the knife off. Of course, in this case you must remember to fasten the knife to the hook again so that it won't fall out of your pocket. Because the knife is one of your 10 essential items, keep it in a safe place and in good condition.

USING OTHER CUTTING TOOLS

Other cutting tools include saws, axes, and hatchets. These tools are used to cut wood, usually for a fire.

Saws

Saws for use at base camp usually can be larger than those for use on a trip because you won't have to store and carry them in small spaces. One of the best base-camp saws is the *bow saw* because it is sturdy. Another kind is the *trail saw*, usually a folding type that resembles and works like a large pocketknife. When open, a trail saw is about twelve to eighteen inches long, including the handle.

Saws are made so that they cut on the *forward move*, or the move away from the cutter. The *backward move* returns the saw to another cutting position and removes sawdust. A saw has two kinds of teeth: cutting teeth and sawdust-removing teeth.

As was noted in chapter 6, "Putting It On Your Plate," you need not cut large pieces of wood for a cooking fire. And, it's safer and easier to use a saw to cut small logs than it is to use an ax. When you use a saw, follow these three safety rules:

- Keep your fingers away from the saw blade.
- Keep your eyes on the what you're cutting.
- Brace the log securely.

Many times, people using saws try to guide the first cut by running the saw against the thumb or fingers of their free hand. The first cut, however, is hard to start, so the saw may jump a bit, cutting the guiding fingers. It's better to make several attempts at the first cut than to be in a hurry and saw off your fingers as you attempt to guide a blade. You may also want to have someone hold the end of the log that you're cutting so that you'll have an immobile piece of wood to cut.

Figure 8.6 Trail saw.

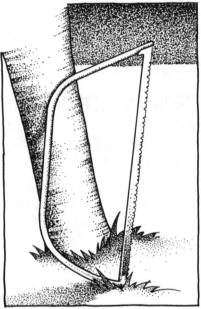

Figure 8.7 Bow saw.

Most bow saws can be used by one person, but two people can easily use a bow saw if each remembers only to pull. This is the opposite procedure from using the folding saw; the *sawyer* (the person who saws) has to push a folding saw to make the cut. With the bow saw, both sawyers pull, each person serving as the cutter for the other one. The saw still cuts on the stroke away from you, but your partner is the one who applies the force. The teeth of the bow saw are designed to cut and to remove sawdust both directions.

Using a bow saw with a partner is easy because it's easier to pull than it is to push. As a matter of fact, if both partners try to push, the saw will buckle, progress will stop, and the partners will get very frustrated. To have a good time sawing with a partner, let your partner pull on alternating strokes. Try to set up a rhythm; sing a song with an even cadence so that one of you can pull on each major beat.

Saws can also be used to trim tree branches and to cut sticks evenly. But before you trim any branches, always ask why you need to cut them. If you're going to be making a temporary trail, why destroy part of the forest in the process? Also ask why sticks or poles need to be cut evenly. if the only pieces of dead wood available for the fire are too long to use safely or conveniently, cutting them with a saw is appropriate.

Keep in mind that both at base camp and on the trail, it's rarely necessary to use a saw. Try getting by without one to see what a good minimum-impact camper you really are.

Axes and Hatchets

The importance of axes has changed over the past fifty years. At one time, all campers were taught how to use a hatchet and an ax, but today, they rarely need to use either. If you are at a base camp, for example, your wood may be delivered in precut lengths of eighteen inches or so, and all you'll need to do is split the bigger pieces into smaller ones for your fire. If you're on the trail, carrying a gas stove, you may find enough small pieces of dry wood on the ground to use for cooking, so you won't need big logs for a campfire. (See chapter 6, "Putting It On Your Plate" for information about campfire ethics.)

At base camp, you should confine use of an ax to splitting wood to make it fit the fireplace, to make a fire smaller and more useful, or to make kindling to start the fire. Depending on the size of the wood, you can use either a hatchet, or an ax. A hatchet is a small ax-like instrument with a handle not longer than two feet. The head of a hatchet is smaller than that of an ax, and because of the shorter handle, hatchets are used to split small pieces of wood that don't take much strength or energy to split. The ax, which is heavier, has a bigger head and a handle three feet long or longer. You can use a hatchet with one hand; using an ax takes both hands.

Between the ax and the hatchet is the Hudson's Bay ax, which many canoeists use. The head has a broad cutting edge and a narrow back edge, reducing the weight, and the handle is eighteen to thirty-six inches long. This ax is lightweight, making it easy to take along on canoe trips. Because it usually has a very sharp cutting edge, the Hudson's Bay ax is used to clear branches for portages, to cut logs for a fire, and to make poles for the campsite. Few people, however, canoe where there are no trails already cut and no campsites already designated, so most people have little or no need for a Hudson's Bay ax.

Axes are tools of the past. Only experienced hunters, trappers, explorers, and other people who may need to clear trees, make poles, or develop sites need them today. Still, it's good to know how to handle an ax, especially for splitting firewood at the family vacation cottage or at base camp.

Safe use of an ax or hatchet depends on the position of your body and the stability of the piece of wood you want to cut. Regardless of the size of the ax, you should stand so that your weight is evenly distributed with your feet comfortably astride. The wood to be cut should be directly in front of you so that when the ax falls, it swings between your legs.

To split wood, first put it on a chopping block upright, with one end firmly positioned on the block. A chopping block may be a firm board on the ground, a sturdy stump, or an evenly cut log. Whatever you use as a chopping block, make sure that it's firmly positioned in or on the ground. The block should be low enough so that your waist is above the top of it — ideally, about two to four inches above it. But because it's almost impossible to find a group of campers who are all the same size, you may have to adjust to the height of the available splitting block, which probably was cut by an adult.

Next, lift the ax above your head and bring it down to slice through the wood; the blade should go partway into the chopping block. Always hit the wood so that the ax cuts it lengthwise, top to bottom, not across the top. Remember to split wood with the grain not against it. If you drive the axe at an angle across the top, part or all the wood usually flies into the air, landing who knows where — perhaps on your head. Also, always stand with your feet apart, and the wood in front you.

When you use an ax to sever a large branch or to cut a log in two, cut at an angle of forty-five degrees to the piece you want to cut. If you cut at forty-five degrees, you'll take out a chip. But a cut made at a right angle (ninety degrees), makes only a slight dent, and a cut at a larger angle just slides over the surface — a rather dangerous stroke. Always cut at an angle of about forty-five degrees, first in one direction and then in the opposite direction, so that you take out one chip of wood at a time: you can make the cut increasingly deep and wide until the log or branch is severed. Be sure to cut on the side of the log opposite you, and always make sure that nothing is in your way as you raise the ax over your head to get a good swing.

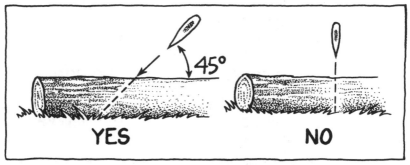

Figure 8.8 Proper angle to chop wood.

Before cutting anything, a practiced woodsperson holds an ax out at arm's length and moves it slowly all around him/her in a wide arc to make sure it won't catch on anything as the swing carries it up and down again. Do this before you begin to split wood. Also, keep your eye on the spot where you hope to make the cut. If you look away, the ax will stray, too.

Follow these steps when you cut wood with an ax:

1. Place the wood in front of you on a chopping block.

2. Stand with your weight evenly distributed and feet apart.

3. Swing the ax around slowly to make sure nothing will be in the way of the upward or downward stroke.

4. Hold the ax in both hands and raise it over your head.

5. Look at the spot you want to cut.

6. Make a cut at a forty-five degree angle to the log. Then do it from the other direction.

Figure 8.9 Passing an ax.

When you pass an ax to another person, it's best to pass it head first, with the blade pointing down. The receiver should grasp the handle close to the head. Passing an ax handle first could be dangerous for the receiver if he or she isn't prepared for the weight of the head.

To carry an ax safely, hold it by the handle as close to the head as possible, with the rest of the handle behind you. Then, if you should trip or fall, the ax head will go into the ground — not into you.

USING DIGGING TOOLS

Digging tools are needed for making a toilet, and for certain types of fire pits. During a trip away from existing toilet facilities, every environmentally concerned group takes along a trowel. At base camp, a shovel is used to dig holes for baking beans, making ice cream in a "hay hole," and for other kinds of fancy meals (explained in chapter 6, "Putting It On Your Plate." Shovels are also useful on horseback trips, mainly for firefighting; people who are guiding horseback trips into remote areas are often required to carry shovels.

Trowels and shovels should be kept clean and relatively sharp. To keep them rust-free, wipe them with a rag bearing lightweight machine oil after cleaning.

Figure 8.10 Carrying an ax.

The type of trowel used by many backpackers is made of Cycrolac, a hard, lightweight plastic that withstands rugged use. Cycrolac is lighter than metal and doesn't bend the way inexpensive lightweight metal does. Furthermore, it doesn't get rusty.

Before you use a trowel to dig a cathole or a latrine, review the material on minimum-impact practices in chapter 4, "Being Safe."

Shovels are available with handles of various lengths. The ones used in camping activities are rather pointed at the end so that they can cut into hard soil.

USING COOKING TOOLS

Two cutting tools — The paring knife and the peeler — are especially useful at base camp and perhaps on a trip a can opener also comes in handy.

Paring knife

A paring knife is used to pare, or peel, potatoes, apples, and other fruits and vegetables, and to cut them into small pieces. You use a paring knife just as you do a pocketknife, with one other skill added.

Usually, people pare toward themselves, rather than away. Because the skin of most fruits and vegetables is thin and the objects themselves are small, you'll be most successful if you learn to pare apples, potatoes, carrots, and other foods by carefully moving the knife toward you.

Hold the knife in the hand you use for cutting and the object to be pared in the other hand. Holding your elbows close to your body, lay the knife handle across the base of the fingers of the knife hand, with the blade extending beside your thumb. Close your fingers around the handle. Then flex all your fingers at once, and you'll be able to move the knife toward and away from your palm. Learn to move the knife, using only the fingers and palm of the knife hand, so that the blade passes beside the thumb.

Now hold the knife against an apple or potato and push against the apple or potato with your thumb while you move the blade across the peel and above the side of your thumb. The lower part of the fingers holds the knife handle and moves it toward the palm. Push the apple or potato with the thumb, and move the knife with your fingers and palm. This process is tricky at first, but once you learn it, paring will be as easy as riding a bicycle. Always exercise good judgement and caution when using any knife.

Peeler

The peeler, which is used in the same way as a paring knife, is really easier to use because the guide on the back of the peeler prevents you from cutting off too much of the apple or potato.

Many peelers are made to go forward *or* backward. When peeling something long, such as a carrot, you have the choice of pushing the peeler away from you or pulling it toward you, or alternating.

As you do with a knife, be sure to keep the fingers that are holding the object below the object so that only *it* will be peeled.

Can Opener

Because many types of can openers are available, the only kind explained here is the pocketknife can opener, which is often a curved blade resembling a hook. To use it, place the curved part (the bottom of the hook) outside the rim on the top of a can and the sharp blade part (the top of the hook) inside the rim, running parallel to it. Using the hook, press against the outside of the can while lifting the knife handle. The blade inside the rim will move into the can top and make a small cut in it. Move the hook forward and lift the handle again, and keep repeating this movement until you've gone all around the can. This will take some time.

A pocketknife can opener works just as well as an electric one, but because it operates on your power, it's slower, so using one may be a bit tiring if you aren't skilled at it. Keep practicing. You'll soon be able to open those cans in much less time. Just remember to keep the bottom part of the opener blade tight against the outside of the rim of the can and to lift slowly at first. Be aware of the sharp edge of the lid and the can — either can cut fingers very easily.

SHARPENING KNIVES AND AXES

A sharp knife or ax cuts better than a dull one does. And if either cuts you, it's better to get a clean cut from a sharp knife than a rough, tearing cut from a dull tool. Sharp tools cut people less than dull ones do because they're less likely to slip off the surface that's being cut. Used correctly, a sharp blade cuts cleanly into wood. (Of course, you'll never use your ax on anything but wood.)

Practice sharpening a knife first. You will need a sharpening stone, called a *whet stone.* ("Whet" means to sharpen. We whet our appetites, whet our curiosity, and use a whetstone.) A whetstone must be moistened with either water or oil to keep the knife moving freely and to prevent the blade from becoming too warm.

A whetstone usually has a rough side and a smooth side. The rough side removes nicks and very dull edges; the smooth side hones the blade to a truly keen edge.

Hold the moistened or oiled whetstone in one hand, being sure to keep your fingers *below the top edge* so the knife won't cut them. Place the knife, blade down flat on the top of the stone, and then raise the back of the blade at a slight angle (about fifteen to twenty degrees). Pull the blade across the stone, leading with the sharp edge. The back edge should never touch the stone. Stroke the blade across the stone, and after a few strokes, make circular strokes as you pull the blade across. After a few more strokes, turn the knife over and sharpen the other side. Keep this up, alternating sides, until you think that the blade is smooth. Be sure to sharpen the entire blade, from base to tip.

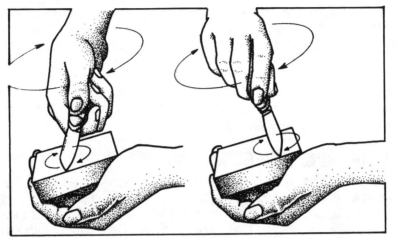

Figure 8.11 Sharpening a knife.

To test the blade, cut some wood or rope. If the knife seems sharp, finish the job by stroking the blade across the stone a few more times to remove any rough edges, or *feathers*.

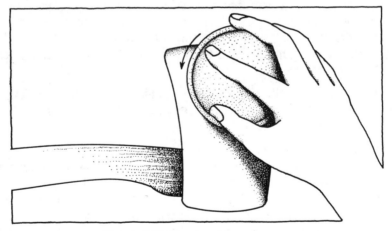

Figure 8.12 Sharpening an ax.

An ax is sharpened the same way; the whetstone, however, is usually larger. Sometimes a grinding stone, a small vertically mounted grinding wheel, is used; if so, the sharpening procedure is quite different. You may have the opportunity to watch someone grind an ax on a wheel at state fairs and rural festivals, but you may never use the skill yourself. This may be just one more indication that the ax is rarely used today.

SUMMARY

The most important camp tool is the pocketknife; you may find the saw useful, too. Trowels are also needed on trips. Beyond that, you'll have limited need for tools.

Two things to keep in mind: use tools safely, and make sure that cutting or digging is really necessary. Ask the question "Is this act going to be environmentally sound?" Follow that question with "Do I really know how to do this safely?" Correct practice will perfect your use of camping tools.

9

Finding Your Way

To get a rough idea of direction, you don't always need a compass — nature offers some wonderful, easy-to-remember direction indicators. For example, if you face the rising sun, you are facing east, and north is on your left side. Where are south and west?

At noon, though, the sun is pretty much overhead but a little to the south, so to determine direction, drive a stick into the ground and examine its shadow. Generally, in the Northern Hemisphere, north is the direction of the shadow. However, in the Southern Hemisphere, south is the direction of the shadow. You can use your body instead of a stick, but the shadow cast by a stick is much sharper.

On a starry night, you can find north by locating the Big Dipper and the two stars that make up the end of its bowl. These two stars are *pointer stars.* If you draw an imaginary line from the bottom of the bowl to the top and extend it, the first star your extended line will touch is the North Star, or Polaris. (Polaris is also the last star in the handle of the Little Dipper.) As the earth rotates, the Big and Little Dippers rotate around the North Star. So whenever you walk in the direction of the North Star, you will always be walking north.

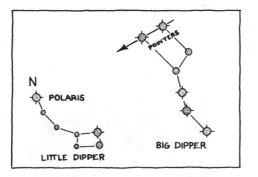

Figure 9.1 Stars.

Do you know any other ways to find direction? Maybe you can devise some while using your map and compass.

MAPS

Maps are wonderful tools for finding buried treasure, locating lost mines, and traveling to strange places without getting lost. People have been using them for centuries, you've probably been using them for years yourself.

In its simplest from, a map is a picture of something seen from above. If you draw a picture of the top of your desk, with all the items on it in their proper places, you have drawn a map. Try drawing a map of your own. Pretend that you're a fly in the center of the ceiling of a living room, dining hall, bedroom, or auditorium, and draw what you would see if you looked down. Then pretend that you're in a helicopter, and draw what you would see when you look down at a playground, a church-yard, your school, the unit you live in at camp, or any other small area. You could even draw a map of the entire village, town, or camp as you'd see it from an imaginary airplane. And if your imagination is especially vivid, you might pretend that you're soaring above the earth on a magic carpet, drawing what you see through a hole in the carpet.

A map of any land area serves two basic purposes:

1. It helps you establish your *bearings* or directions of travel, in the area represented by the map.

2. It helps you orient yourself through *triangulation.* Triangulation means finding two visible landmarks, noting your relative position to them (you and the two landmarks make the three points of a triangle), and then locating that same relative position (the same triangle) on the map.

The following sections describe the two major types of maps you'll probably use.

Planimetric Maps

Planimetric means plain, or flat place, and *metric* means measurement. So a planimetric map is a drawing of the land as if it would appear if it were as flat as the top of a table, that indicates in some way the measurements between the places on the map. The highway map you use to find your way to another city or across the country is a planimetric map because the roads, highways, and cities are drawn as though they were flat. You know that the area represented by the map has hills and valleys, but you don't care; all you need is a drawing of the roads and highways, showing their names or numbers and where they go.

Figure 9.2 is a planimetric map of roads and highways near the Hoosier National Forest in Indiana. You can use this map to learn how to get there, but you can't tell whether there are hills around or in the forest. For that, you'd need another kind of map.

Topographical Maps

Topography is the study of the land and the natural and man-made objects on it. *Topo* means place, and *graphic* refers to writing; therefore, *topographical maps* are written records of the land and the man-made objects on it. Most hikers and canoeists call these maps "topo" maps, for short.

Topo maps contain *contour lines* that show the locations of hills and valleys, as well as how steep, high, and low they are. This information is especially useful to hikers who want to know how

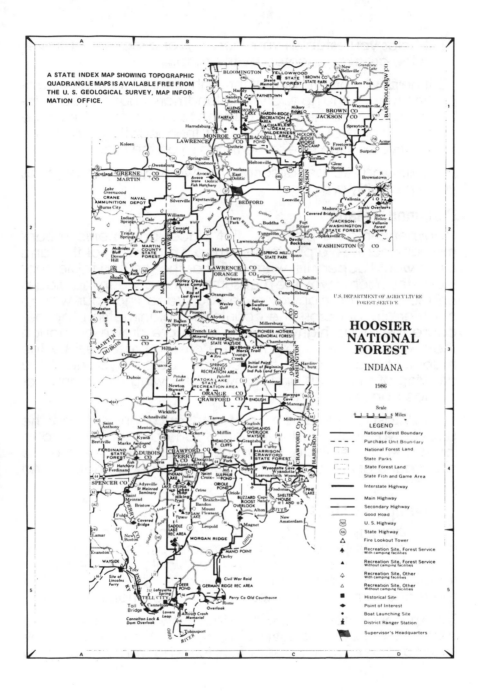

Figure 9.2 Planimetric Map.

steep the hills along a certain route are; if the hills are too rugged, they might want to select an easier route.

Highway maps don't have contour lines because there's no need for them; the steepness of highways is limited by legally approved standards. But hiking trails aren't built according to the standards for car or truck traffic. As a matter of fact, some hiking trails follow deer or elk routes, and those routes can be *very* steep! That's where a topo map comes in handy.

How to get a topo map

Topographical maps of nearly all of the United States are available from the Office of the United States Geological Survey (often referred to as USGS). To get a map of an area in which you plan to practice your outdoor-living skills, write to the USGS and ask for the following items: a map index of the state you're interested in, a topographic map symbols sheet, and an order form. When the index comes, you'll see that each state is divided into rectangles called *quadrangles.* Select the quadrangles you want maps of, and fill out your order form accordingly.

If you live east of the Mississippi River, use this address:

> Branch of Distribution
> U.S. Geological Survey
> 1200 Eads Street
> Arlington, VA 22202

If you live west of the Mississippi River, use this address:

> Branch of Distribution
> U.S. Geological Survey
> P.O. Box 25286   Federal Center
> Denver, CO 80225

You may also be able to find topo maps in map stores, college bookstores, specialty bookstores in areas known for hiking and boating trails, and outdoor equipment stores. Two other sources are the U.S. Forest Service and the National Park Service, which have developed both planimetric and topographical maps of many of the areas that they administer. You may want to supplement your collection with some of these agencies' maps.

Reading Contour Lines on a Topo Map

Topo maps are very easy to read, particularly if you like to look at pictures; the symbols on the map represent the things that they look like. Contour lines are drawn to represent how the land or water changes elevation, so quite logically, contour lines representing land are brown, and those representing water are blue.

Usually, contour lines for land are drawn to show elevation changes of twenty, forty, or eighty feet, with every fifth line drawn heavier than the others. You can easily determine the elevations by reading the numbers listed on the heavy lines and adding or subtracting twenty, forty, or eighty feet for each of the lighter lines in between them. On maps with twenty-foot contour intervals, the elevation difference between dark lines is 100 feet; on maps with forty-foot contours, the difference is 200 feet; and on maps with eighty-foot contours, the difference is 400 feet. Contour intervals are listed at the bottom of USGS topographical maps.

Figure 9.3 shows the difference between a topographical map with forty-foot contours and one with eighty-foot contours. A map with the twenty-foot contour intervals would be more detailed. Figure 9.4 shows the shapes of various hills as depicted by contour lines.

When you learn to read contour lines, you can look at a topo map and see how the land rises or descends and how steep it is. The closer together the contour lines are, the steeper the land is. Look at figure 9.5. You can see that the land rises to more than 12,000 feet here; this map obviously came from a state that has elevations above that height. In the example, the contour lines are forty feet apart, and there is a difference of 200 feet of elevation from one dark line to the next. The highest point is 12,212 feet. Can you find it?

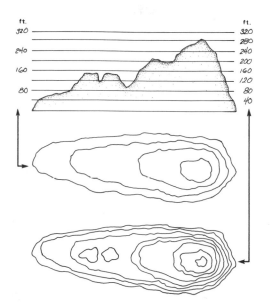

Figure 9.3 Contour Intervals.

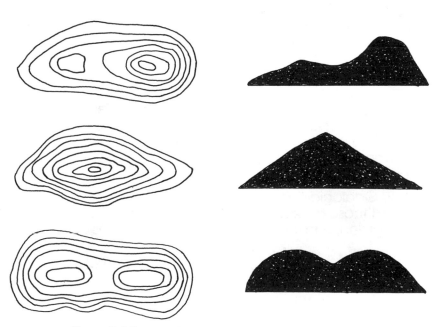

Figure 9.4 Comparison of Contour Lines and Landscape.

Figure 9.5 Topo Map.

Reading Symbols on a Topo Map

The fun part of map reading is describing an area you've never seen just by looking at a topo. Such a map can help you identify man-made structures (*cultural features*), water (*hydrographic features*), plant life (*vegetation features*), and elevation (*hypsographic features*). Some examples of the symbols for these features are shown below. These examples are taken from the USGS Topographic Map Symbol sheet. Look at the examples and locate the symbols for trail, footbridge, school, buildings, and spring. Do these symbols look like the things they represent?

On a U.S. Geologic Survey map, contour lines for land are brown, and those for water are blue; areas covered by vegetation are green; and rocks, glaciers, and snowfields are white.

At this point, you should be able to look at a topographic map and describe what you would find if you were walking around in that area. Try it.

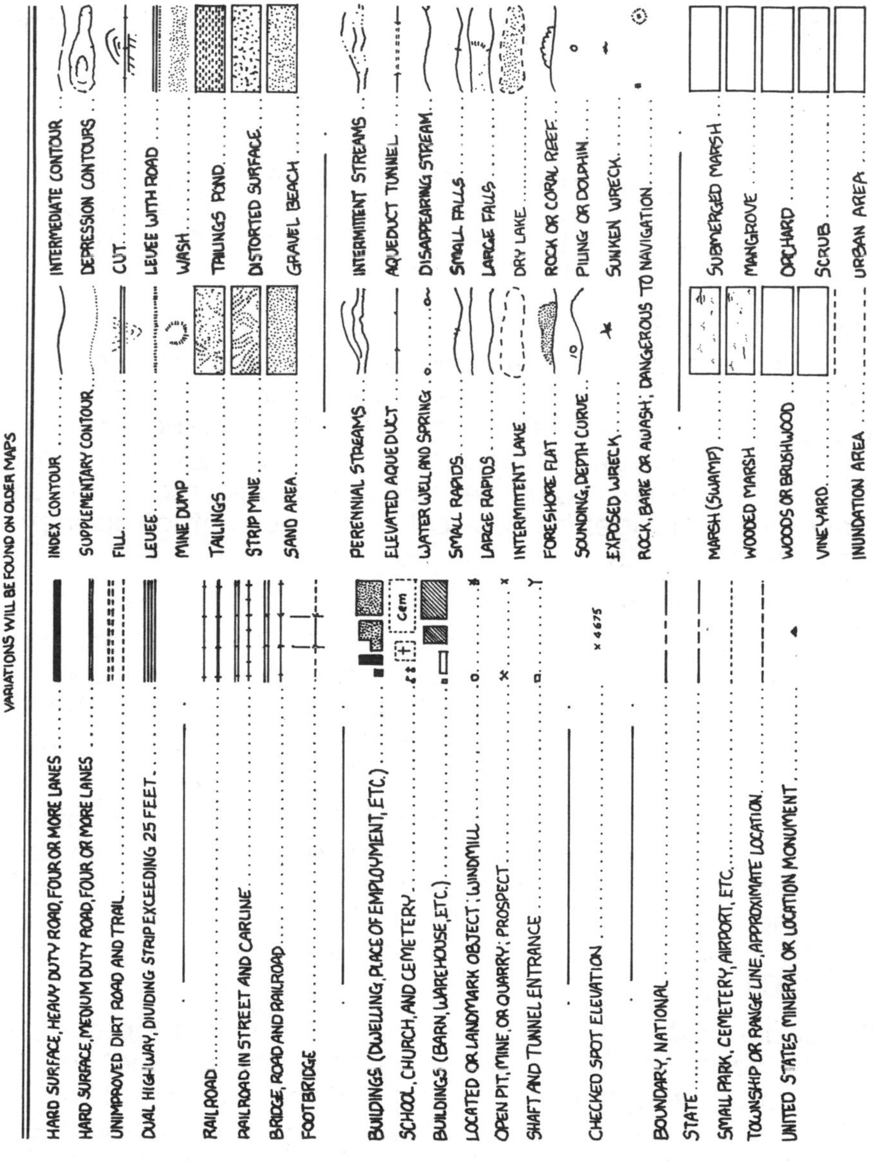

VARIATIONS WILL BE FOUND ON OLDER MAPS

HARD SURFACE, HEAVY DUTY ROAD, FOUR OR MORE LANES . . . .
HARD SURFACE, MEDIUM DUTY ROAD, FOUR OR MORE LANES . . . .
UNIMPROVED DIRT ROAD AND TRAIL . . . .
DUAL HIGHWAY, DIVIDING STRIP EXCEEDING 25 FEET . . . . .

RAILROAD . . . .
RAILROAD IN STREET AND CARLINE .
BRIDGE, ROAD AND RAILROAD . . . .
FOOTBRIDGE . . . .

BUILDINGS (DWELLING, PLACE OF EMPLOYMENT, ETC.) .
SCHOOL, CHURCH, AND CEMETERY . . . .
BUILDINGS (BARN, WAREHOUSE, ETC.) . . . . . .
LOCATED OR LANDMARK OBJECT; WINDMILL . . . .
OPEN PIT, MINE, OR QUARRY; PROSPECT . . . . . .
SHAFT AND TUNNEL ENTRANCE . . . .

CHECKED SPOT ELEVATION . . . .   x 4675

BOUNDARY, NATIONAL . . . .
STATE . . . .
SMALL PARK, CEMETERY, AIRPORT, ETC. . . . . . .
TOWNSHIP OR RANGE LINE, APPROXIMATE LOCATION . . . . . .
UNITED STATES MINERAL OR LOCATION MONUMENT . . . . . .

INDEX CONTOUR . . . .
SUPPLEMENTARY CONTOUR . . . .
FILL . . . .
LEVEE . . . .
MINE DUMP . . . .
TAILINGS . . . .
STRIP MINE . . . .
SAND AREA . . . .

PERENNIAL STREAMS . . . .
ELEVATED AQUEDUCT . . . .
WATER WELL AND SPRING . . . . . .
SMALL RAPIDS . . . .
LARGE RAPIDS . . . .
INTERMITTENT LAKE . . . .
FORESHORE FLAT . . . .
SOUNDING, DEPTH CURVE . . . . . .
EXPOSED WRECK . . . .
ROCK, BARE OR AWASH; DANGEROUS TO NAVIGATION . . . . . .

MARSH (SWAMP) . . . .
WOODED MARSH . . . .
WOODS OR BRUSHWOOD . . . .
VINEYARD . . . .
INUNDATION AREA . . . .

INTERMEDIATE CONTOUR . . . .
DEPRESSION CONTOURS . . . .
CUT . . . .
LEVEE WITH ROAD . . . .
WASH . . . .
TAILINGS POND . . . .
DISTORTED SURFACE . . . .
GRAVEL BEACH . . . .

INTERMITTENT STREAMS . . . .
AQUEDUCT TUNNEL . . . .
DISAPPEARING STREAM . . . .
SMALL FALLS . . . .
LARGE FALLS . . . .
DRY LAKE . . . .
ROCK OR CORAL REEF . . . .
PILING OR DOLPHIN . . . .
SUNKEN WRECK . . . .

SUBMERGED MARSH . . . .
MANGROVE . . . .
ORCHARD . . . .
SCRUB . . . .
URBAN AREA . . . .

Figure 9.6 Map Symbols.

Reading Other Information on a Topo Map

Now that you're familiar with the features of a topo map, it's time to look at the material printed in the margins. This material is described in the following sections.

The name of the map

The name of a topo map is printed in the top right corner and the bottom right corner of each map. Many people fold their topo maps so that these corners are on the outside. This way, they can pull the maps they want out of a file without having to unfold them to see their names.

The age of the map

The date when the map was made is printed under the map name in the bottom right corner. If your map is old, it may not show recent changes in man-made structures, such as trails and roads, and you'll need supplementary maps that show the new structures. Forest Service planimetric maps, which show these changes in areas administered by that agency, are often available.

The scale of the map

When you drew your practice maps earlier you may not have drawn things according to their relative sizes. If your bunk is three times the length of your suitcase, your map should have shown a bunk three times as long as a suitcase. Such a map would be drawn to scale.

The *scale* (the actual distance represented by an inch or other measurement) is written somewhere on every map. A highway map may list the scale in a box titled "Map Explanation" or "Legend." On a USGS topo map, the scale is listed at the bottom of the map. This scale will be 1:24,000, 1:62,500, or 1:250,000.

The scale *1:24,000* means that one inch on the map equals 24,000 inches, or 2,000 feet in the field (the ground, snow, water, or other surfaces shown on the map). Such a map might be useful to you if you're going to practice general orienteering or to travel in an area limited to about four miles radius. This scale is used for the most-detailed topo maps.

Maps drawn to the scale of *1:62,500* are the ones most commonly used by hikers and canoeists. This scale is very close to being one inch to one mile. (There are 63,360 inches in a mile, but that figure is cumbersome; 62,500 is close enough for most purposes.) Today, this scale is used for almost all topo maps in the United States.

You'll probably enjoy using a 1:62,500 map to figure how far you'd have to hike to reach a certain lake. To do so, just measure the inches on the map from your starting point to the lake, remembering that one inch on the map equals one mile in the field. If you measure two and a half inches on the map, your hike would be two and a half miles.

The scale *1:250,000* is equal to about one inch for every four miles. Maps drawn to this scale are generally not detailed enough for outdoor-living skills use and are good mainly for locating points of interest within 100 miles, because one inch equals four miles. Think how difficult it would be to put detailed information of a four-mile square into one square inch on a map.

Right now, you may wonder just how long a mile *is*, in terms of everyday walking. In school, you learned that there are 5,280 feet in a mile. Did you ever wonder why we use such an odd number? During the days of the Roman Empire, someone determined that the average pace (two steps) of a Roman soldier was 5.28 feet, and that when a soldier had taken 1,000 paces (double steps), he had traveled *milia passuum* — Latin for one thousand paces (or 1,000 times 5.28). In English, that phrase was shortened to mile. So, if you walk 1,000 paces, you have walked close to one mile.

You can measure your pace by the distance from the back of one foot to the back of the same foot after you have taken two steps. Your pace may be about five feet long (a fairly accurate measure for most adults). Because a pace is two steps, count your paces by counting only each time you put your left (or right) foot down, or by saying, "One-and-two-and-three-and," each time you put a foot down. ("Number" for one foot, "And" for the other foot.) When you count 1,000 paces, you'll have walked close to one mile. Try it. The mile may seem to be shorter or longer than you guessed.

Have each member of your group count 1,000 paces and see where each of them end up. They won't all end up in the same place, but they should be fairly close to one another.

How long will it take you to travel one mile? On a well-worn, path, a strong walker may cover one mile every 15 minutes. In a field, it may take him/her 25 minutes to go a mile; in open woods, 30 minutes; in deep woods or very steep terrain, 40 minutes. On a hiking trip, however, you may average only two miles per hour; your pace will be shorter, depending on the weight you're carrying. When traveling in a mountainous area, remember that for every 1,000 feet of elevation gain, you should add an hour of travel time. Plan carefully!

The declination of the map
At the bottom of the topo map and to the left of the contour data, you will find an angle. One line points to true north. The other will be pointing to magnetic north. If you are east of a line drawn roughly from Chicago to Florida, the line pointing to magnetic north will be the left of the true north line. If you are west of the Chicago-Florida line, the magnetic line will be on the right of the true north line. (The line from Chicago to Florida is called the *agonic* line. Agonic means "without angle.") This angle shows you how far magnetic north is from true north. If you had a huge map, you could follow each line of the angle and end up at the two different poles.

The longitude and latitude of the map
The numbers in the corners of topo maps represent the longitude and latitude. *Longitude lines* (long lines, to help you remember) run up and down (north and south) on the map. *Latitude* lines (lines like the rungs of a ladder) run side to side (east and west). These lines are not especially useful for outdoor-living skills activities unless you're traveling a great distance or perhaps sailing in the ocean.

Many topo maps also feature smaller grids drawn throughout the map and numbers in the margins relating to these lines that indicate townships and ranges. If you do much hiking, you may want to know more about townships and ranges, but it is not necessary for basic map and compass activities.

Figure 9.7 shows the bottom margin of a topo map of an area in Idaho and a little of the map itself. Can you locate the name

227

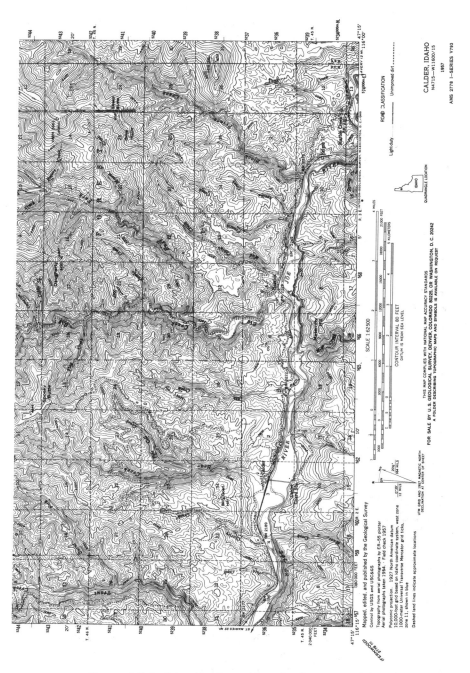

Figure 9.7 Calder, ID., Topo Map (bottom margin).

of the map, the location it represents, the date of printing, the scale, and the contour intervals? Can you describe the area, too? Imagine a group of campers traveling in this area. Should they travel by foot or by canoe?

COMPASSES

A *compass* is a simple but amazing instrument that was developed by the Chinese around 2500 B.C. It works because the earth's magnetic force causes the needle (a piece of magnetized steel) to swing around and point to a particular place in that magnetic field. This place is called *magnetic north.*

If you have a picture of the area where you are traveling (a map), you know which part of the map is the north, know where you are on the map, and if you have a compass, you can find your way to other places on that map.

Selecting a Compass

You'll probably want an orienteering or camping compass, and you'll be able to find one that's quite inexpensive, yet quite accurate. But before you buy a compass, you should know a little bit about the parts of the instrument.

Most compasses today have plastic base plates on which the compass housing is mounted. The compass housing should be filled with liquid — either water or oil — so that the magnetic needle inside will quickly stop swinging around when you hold the compass still; compasses that are not liquid-filled permit the needle to swing for a long time. A liquid-filled compass may be a little more expensive, but it's well worth the extra cost.

The floating needle, housing, and base plate are the mechanical parts of the compass. Each needle has a north end and a south end; the north end may be red or white, or may have a broader end. Learn which end of the needle of your compass points north. Otherwise, you could be going the opposite way from everyone else.

Every compass has lines, numbers, and letters. The *direction-of-travel arrow* is the most important line; one that you'll use each time you use the compass. The direction-of-travel arrow, which does not move the way the needle does, is printed on the base plate, outside the compass housing.

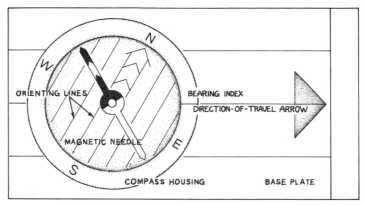

Figure 9.8 Parts of an Orienteering Compass.

The compass housing usually bears letters or numbers indicating north, east, south, and west. Each compass is divided into 360 degrees, or *points*. North is both 0 and 360; east is 90; south is 180; west is 270; and north is, again, 360 or 0. (0 and 360 overlap at north). Other degrees are marked accordingly. These degrees are called *bearings.*

The place where the direction-of-travel arrow and the degrees on the compass housing meet is called the *bearing index.* This index is where you read bearings.

The compass housing also features a set of parallel lines that run north to south. These lines are called *north-south lines* or *orienting lines.* They help to orient the compass to the map.

How to Use a Compass

The best way to hold a compass is to hold your elbows against your sides as though you were holding up your pants. Then cross your hands in front of you, palms up, in a straight line with your arms, and place the compass on top of your crossed palms. The base plate should be parallel to your waist, and the direction-of-travel arrow should point away from you. Practice this position until you can put the compass on your palm easily.

This position keeps the compass squarely in front of you. If you maintain this position every time you use the compass, you'll consistently travel straight ahead, not veering from the direction you have selected.

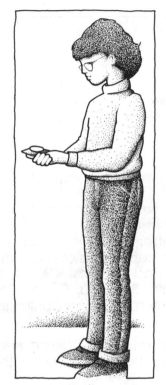

Fig. 9.9 Holding a Compass.

A few warnings about using a compass

- Be sure that your belt buckle isn't metal. If it is, the buckle might affect the magnetic end of the needle, making it point to you instead of to north!

- A knife in your pocket, metal snaps on your clothing, a whistle hanging on a lanyard around your neck, or any other nearby metal object will also disturb the magnetic end of the needle.

- If your compass is sitting on a hardwood floor, the nails holding the floor together may affect the needle as well.

To practice using a compass, try facing north first. Turn the compass housing until north is lined up with the direction-of-travel arrow. Holding the compass correctly, turn your body until the floating needle is aligned with north and the direction-of-travel arrow. You are now facing magnetic north.

Now try facing east. Turn the compass housing so that east (or 90 degrees) is lined up with the direction-of-travel arrow. Holding the compass correctly, turn your body until the needle points to the N, for north (not to the direction-of-travel arrow). You are now facing east, and you have taken a 90-degree bearing. Do the same for south (a 180-degree bearing) and west (a 270-degree bearing). You are not paying any attention to declination yet.

Practice with other degrees, or bearings. Have a friend give you a bearing to face, and turn that way. Or have a contest with several friends; see who can face the correct way first. Remember: Turn the housing so that the direction in which you want to travel is lined up with the direction-of-travel arrow, then

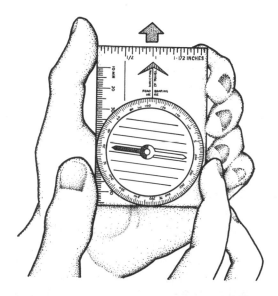

Figure 9.10 Taking A 105-Degree Bearing.

turn your body until the needle points north, and you will be facing in the proper direction.

You know that you have not been facing a true direction because of the magnetic field that forces your compass needle to veer to the east or the west. Let's get the direction just right. If you don't, you could be on a compass trail and be off the route a quarter of a mile after only one mile of travel!

To use declination, just look at the angle at the bottom of the topo map. *Your compass needle should point to the angle instead of true north.* If you wish to travel true north, set the direction-of-travel arrow on N (because that is the direction in which you want to travel.) If declination is 15 degrees east (to the right) of true north, turn your body until the needle comes to rest at 15 degrees. You will then be traveling *true north.*

If the declination angle is 15 degrees west (to the left) of true north, turn your body until the needle comes to rest at 345 degrees (360 minus 15). You will then be traveling *true north* for that part of the country.

The illustration shows that the direction of travel is to be 105 degrees. The compass is set so that the north end of the needle points to the magnetic declination of 20 degrees. The hiker will be going 105 degrees.

If you put a little piece of masking tape with a line on it on your compass housing at the degrees of declination for the part of the country in which you are traveling, you can set your compass without adding or subtracting. Just set the housing at the direction you wish to travel and turn your body around until the needle points to the line on the tape next to the declination angle. Practice facing different bearings using the declination angle.

Geographic and Magnetic North

Unfortunately for those who like things to be simple, the geographic north pole and the magnetic north pole are not the same place, as you learned earlier in this chapter. The geographic, or true north pole is at the geographic top of the earth, so this is the north pole indicated by maps. Magnetic north is a different place — the place to which your compass points. Because of mineral deposits in the earth, the earth is like a giant magnet, with one positive, or magnetic pole. Magnetic north is about 1,200 to 1,400 miles south and west of the true north pole — somewhere north of Hudson Bay and the northern coast of Canada.

Why aren't maps made with magnetic north in mind? Mapmakers start from the equator, which runs true east and west. Because they draw maps from the equator to true (or geographic) north, all map lines run in even lines of longitude and converge at the north pole. If mapmakers made maps go from the equator to magnetic north, however, the lines would go in different directions.

To illustrate this principle, draw an equator around the middle of a ball or balloon, and then mark the north pole precisely at the top. Next, draw a spot southwest of the north pole to represent the magnetic pole. Now divide the equator into eight or sixteen even parts, and draw a line from each of the marks on the equator to your magnetic north pole. You'll find that the lines are different lengths and that they go in slightly different directions. How confusing that would be for a mapmaker or a map user.

Because of this discrepancy, when you face magnetic north (the north that your compass tells you to face), you are not necessarily facing the same north that your map shows.

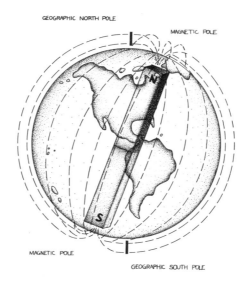

Figure 9.11 Magnetic North.

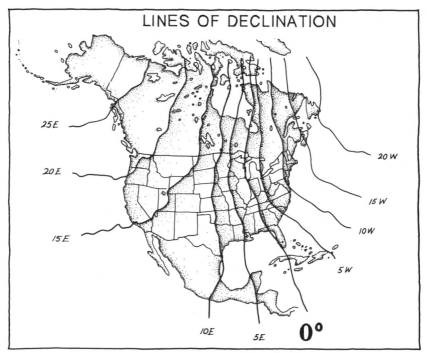

Figure 9.12 Lines of Declination.

difference between the two norths is called *declination,* or variation. When you are using both a map and a compass at the same time, you must be aware of and compensate for, declination. If you don't, you could follow a compass trail and go a quarter-mile off the route after only one mile of travel!

To orient the map to true north, place it on a flat surface, set the direction of travel arrow on N, place the compass parallel to one of the side margins of the map, hold the map and compass steady and rotate both until the needle comes to stop on the masking-tape declination mark. Your map is now lined up with true north. You may have a more expensive compass that has a device for setting the declination angle on the housing so you won't need the little piece of masking tape. Be sure that each time you go to a new area you check the declination and reset the marker if necessary. You don't want to follow the wrong declination — that could be worse than not following it at all.

It is always necessary to locate your starting point on the map *before* you start the trip. Then you can orient the map and read what lies ahead. You can plan on a route, estimate your travel time and anticipate any difficult spots such as steep ravines and streams to cross or places you want to use as rest stops such as springs, meadows, or the shelter of trees.

To use the map and compass together:

1. Using your compass, orient the map so it lies north and south as explained above. (The needle will point to magnetic north.) Keep the map in that position.

2. Locate the spot where you are now, and the spot to which you wish to travel.

3. Using the side of your compass or something else with a straight edge, make a line between where you are and where you want to go (your direction of travel.)

4. Lay the compass along the straight line, and rotate the housing until the needle points to the direction of travel.

5. You can now read the bearing at the direction-of-travel arrow and head in that direction toward your goal.

6. Line up a couple of trees (or other recognizable objects) ahead of you and head for the first one. Then line up

a third object with your second object and head for the second object. Keep doing this until you reach your destination.

In time, you'll be able to line up objects that are farther and farther apart. You'll spend less time taking bearings, and you'll hike more rapidly toward each object and toward your destination. You'll be able to navigate ravines, rivers, and other land formations.

Reading from land to map

You may want to make a record of your travels for backtracking on your return trip, or so that someone else can follow the same trail. To plot your direction of travel on a map as you are hiking, follow these steps:

1. Prepare your map for declination, as you did before.

2. Next, make a dot on the map at your current position.

3. Observe the landscape and decide which way you wish to travel. Choose some easily recognizable land formation, bend in the river, or building in the direction that you want to walk. When you are just beginning, choose something that is only 100 yards or less away.

4. Take a compass bearing in that direction.

5. Place your compass on the oriented map so that its north-south orienting lines are parallel to the true north lines, and so the center of the floating needle is exactly on your current position. The direction-of-travel arrow should be pointing to the land formation on the map that you sighted in the field.

6. Draw a line on the map from your current position to the easily recognizable destination, by extending the direction-of-travel arrow with your pencil. Read your bearing on the compass.

7. Walk to your chosen destination.

8. Observe the landscape again and choose another easily recognizable destination.

9. Repeat steps 4, 5, 6, and 7.

10. Continue these steps the entire time you are walking. You will then be able to retrace your steps to return to your original position by reading from the map to the landscape on the way back, or share your course with others.

11. When you arrive at each new destination, be sure to turn around for a moment and look back at where you were. If you do this, things won't look so unfamiliar on the return trip.

Compass courses

To create a compass course for someone else to follow, follow these steps:

1. Orient your map.

2. Locate your starting point on the map.

3. Write down a description of the starting point on a piece of paper. "Begin at the camp director's cabin door."

4. Observe the landscape and choose an easily recognizable land formation, bend in the river, or building as a destination.

5. Take a compass bearing in that direction.

6. Write down that compass bearing on your paper. "Take a 90-degree bearing."

7. Plot that path from your current position to your first destination on the map.

8. Walk to the first destination, counting the paces as you go.

9. Write down the number of paces on your piece of paper. "Go 30 paces to the flag pole."

10. Observe the landscape and choose another destination.

11. Take a compass bearing in that direction.

12. Write down that compass bearing on your paper. "Take a 27-degree bearing."

13. Plot that bearing and direction-of-travel line on your map.

14. Walk to that destination, counting the paces as you go.

15. Write down the number of paces on your paper. "Go 62 paces to the infirmary."

16. Continue doing this until your course is as long as you like. If you are in an area where there is no chance of you getting lost you need not plot your directions on the map (steps 1, 2, 7 and 13).

When you finish, your compass course directions might look like this:

1. Start at the camp director's cabin door.

2. Take a 90-degree bearing and go 30 paces to the flag pole.

3. Next, take a 27-degree bearing and go 62 paces to the infirmary.

Or they might look like this:

To begin your adventure,
at the director's front door you'll need to be,
then follow these directions,
and you'll arrive at the treasure, one, two, three.

1. Your first set of directions are,
   30 paces at 90 degrees,
   where you'll the find stars and stripes,
   forever blowing in the breeze.

2. Walk for 62 paces,
   from a 27-degree bearing,
   find a place where you'd go,
   if its a bandage you need to be wearing.

3. You'll get a blue ribbon,
   you found this place in record time,
   now it's your turn to make for someone,
   another compass course rhyme.

Make your compass course as easy or difficult as you like, but always make it as fun as possible. If you are in an area where campers are sure not to get lost, hide the clues along the way so that the participant must find them before continuing. Hide a treasure at the end. Work in groups of two or more. Have each group make a compass course, then follow the course the other group made. Make sure that an adult works with or checks the work of the group making the course, so that the other group isn't off on a wild-goose chase.

For More Information

When you want to learn more about maps and compasses, you'll find many easy-to-understand, inexpensive books on the subject. At the end of this book is a list of suggested references.

Finding your way is lots of fun. Many people read maps as though they were stories, imagining, as they travel, all the things they'd find along the way. But maps are really just ways to keep us going in a straight line, and as long as we know what direction to face, that isn't hard to do. Reading map language and compensating for declination take a little practice, though. You can practice finding directions as you travel in a car, on a sidewalk, on an airplane, or on your bike. If you travel by subway, read the map and imagine how the train travels beneath the city streets. Finding your way is something you can do everywhere, every day.

May you step carefully and travel gently,
finding friendship and beauty in your natural world. The end.

Outdoor Living Skills Level One — Earth

1. Plan a half-day hike. Show your group what you will wear and what you will take with you in order to be prepared for thirst, hunger and changes in the weather. Talk with your group about what to wear and what to take, how the weather affects your clothing and liquid needed while hiking.

2. Pack a day pack with the essentials for a half-day hike.

3. Go on a hike. While hiking, look for birds, signs of the seasons and special natural treasures.

4. Talk about when you need shelter and extra water. Find the closest shelter.

5. Plan and pack a sack lunch made up of foods that will not spoil before you eat. When you eat the lunch, take care of the trash correctly.

6. Make some fire starters for charcoal. Light a match and keep it burning for 10 seconds. Use it to light a wood or charcoal fire.

7. Use a trowel, rake, paring knife and peeler safely and show how to put each away.

8. With your group, list safety rules for outdoors and hikes. Write these rules in the back of your *OLS Tracker.* Talk about why rules are important. Give each member of your group one or more of these safety rules to monitor. Put a check mark by the one you are responsible for. Decide what to do if someone breaks the rules.

9. Find out where to go when you get sick or get hurt while on a walking or boating trip. Practice what to do if someone gets hurt in three different types of outdoor areas while on a hike.

10. Tour your outdoor area and identify natural hazards such as cliffs, water, slides or holes. Explain what you can do to avoid these dangers.

11. Find an appropriate place to use as a toilet, a place to wash your hands, and safe water to drink. Explain why you selected these places.

12. Name three things that might require first aid on a hike. Explain what you can do to prevent these problems. Talk about what you would need in a first aid kit. Explain why you chose those items.

13. Draw a picture in the back of your *OLS Tracker* of a plant in your area that is a nuisance to humans — either poisonous or harmful in some way. Tell what part that plant plays in its natural setting.

14. Show where and what kind of knots a camper uses most often. Tie a square knot and a granny. Explain why the square knot is better. Tie a stopper knot and explain why it is used.

15. Find east by using the sun and knowing the time of day. Show where north, south, and west are.

16. Count the number of double steps (paces) between two points about 100 feet apart and compare with others in your group. Do it for 50 yards, 100 yards. Find the average length of your pace.

17. Locate where you are on a highway map of your area.

18. Discuss how to stay found. Practice "Hug-A-Tree."

19. With your group, play one nature game that helps you understand ecology.

20. Using your sense of sight, touch, smell, and hearing, explore what is around your outdoor or camping area. Describe 10 things you observed by using those four senses.

21. Show that you can take care of your outdoor area by cleaning up after lunch on your day hike.

22. Explain what you eat and where it comes from. Look for wildlife or birds in your outdoor area. What does the wildlife around you eat?

Outdoor Living Skills Level Two — Sun

1. Plan an all-day hike or overnight trip, where you will cook at least one meal. Talk with your group about personal and group equipment needs. Pack and carry the equipment you need. Be sure to consider the effects of the weather and pack appropriately.

2. As a group, plan and make a snack that requires cooking outside. Tell how you will cook your snack, the kind of heat you will use and the safety rules to prevent you and the environment from being hurt.

3. Go on an all-day hike or overnight trip and cook at least one meal. Show how you have prepared to keep warm and dry from rain or dew.

4. Explain what a balanced meal is and what foods can be cooked outside. With your group, plan a meal and the food and equipment items needed to cook and clean up.

5. With your group, discuss the heat sources you can use for cooking outside in your camping area.

6. Practice the skills you need to provide heat for cooking.

7. Practice the safety and conservation rules you are following.

8. List the uses of a pocket knife. Demonstrate your ability to use a pocketknife for cutting, paring, and whittling. Discuss the selection and care of a pocketknife.

9. Identify possible needs for a saw. Demonstrate your ability to use and care for a saw appropriately. Explain where the saw should NOT be used.

10. With your group, list safety rules in the back of your *OLS Tracker* for your hike or overnight trip. Plan and practice what to do if a stranger approaches and how to protect group and personal equipment from damage or theft by humans and animals.

11. Make a poster or draw a picture in the back of your *OLS Tracker* that shows why a buddy system is important. Use the buddy system on a hike.

12. Name three problems that plants, animals, or insects in your area cause humans. Tell how to avoid these dangers.

13. Draw a picture or make a poster of an animal in its natural environment and demonstrate how to watch animals and respect them.

14. Find out where there is water that is safe to drink and if there is water that is unsafe for drinking.

15. Discuss importance of good health practices and personal cleanliness in camp and/or on an overnight.

16. Tie a joiner knot and demonstrate its uses. Show how to tie one other knot you might use on an overnight trip.

17. Estimate heights and distance without using manufactured measuring tools. Measure 100 yards by pacing.

18. Explain the difference between a highway map and a topographical map and how each is used.

19. Show that you know how to hold a compass correctly. Use your compass to face north, east, south and west. Identify what is nearby that could prevent the compass from working correctly.

20. Discuss procedures for staying found.

21. With your group, play two nature games that help teach ecology.

22. Explain what the word "pollute" means and identify three places you know are polluted and why.

23. Explain "minimum-impact camping."

24. While hiking or camping, look for camouflaged animals including birds. Discuss what camouflage does for these animals.

25. What evidence proves people have been in your area? Do a project that will reduce the impact of people on the environment. Make a list of things you can do on a camping trip that will reduce the impact of your group.

26. Learn the Outdoor Living Skills Pledge in the front of your *OLS Tracker* and recite it.

Outdoor Living Skills Level Three — Water

1. Plan an overnight trip needing four meals. Plan to cook at least two of them. Make a list of personal and group equipment needed. Pack and carry the equipment for at least two hours. Be sure to pack for changes in weather.

2. With your group, plan a balanced menu for at least three meals away from base camp. Consider how much and what type of food you need for the activity you will be doing.

3. Select, use, and care for two different kinds of cooking fuels for your overnight trip (charcoal, wood, butane, kerosene, etc.) Before you leave on the trip, use cooking methods that include charcoal, wood, and backpack stoves. Prepare food at least three ways: baking, boiling, grilling, frying, roasting.

4. Go on an overnight trip, cooking at least two meals. Build and use a temporary shelter.

5. On your overnight, make and carry out a plan for washing and sanitizing your dishes and cooking utensils, and disposing of trash, garbage, dish water, foil, cans, plastic, paper, etc.

6. Demonstrate methods for care, storage, and protection of food from insects, animals, and spoilage.

7. Name three things that might require first-aid on a hike. Explain what you can do to prevent these problems. Identify the contents of the group first-aid kit and explain what each item is used for.

8. Demonstrate the proper care and storage of the rope you are using.

9. Explain different kinds and sizes of rope and give examples of how each is used in camp.

10. Demonstrate how to prevent a rope from becoming unraveled.

11. Tie two kinds of hitches and use them on your overnight trip. Show the difference between a knot and a hitch.

12. Demonstrate proper use, care, and storage of a pocket-knife.

13. Find the North Star by using the Big Dipper. How many stars are included in the Big Dipper? In the Little Dipper?

14. Use a compass to take a bearing from a cardinal point. Follow this bearing for 100 feet. Play a compass game.

15. Discuss the use and appropriateness of road or trail signs that do not harm the environment but give direction. Draw three appropriate trial signs in the back of your *OLS Tracker.*

16. Use a compass to make a simple map of an outdoor area.

17. Explain how to read a map related to your locality. Identify north, the legend and at least three landmarks on your map.

18. Identify plants, animals, and/or insects in your area that are harmful to some or all people. Make up a skit to tell others about these problems and how they harm you.

19. Name at least three problems campers might have to face in your area that are caused by weather conditions, altitude change, or land or water movement. Identify warning signs of these environmental forces. Demonstrate how you can be prepared for them — no matter where you are.

20. Make a poster that shows at least two different kinds of cloud formations and the type of weather conditions that usually accompany these formations. Or, make a poster that shows at least two different weather conditions.

21. Discuss what "ecosystem" means. Explore the ecosystem in which your camp site is located, and with your group, make a list of what you saw. Write this list in the back of your *OLS Tracker.*

22. Discuss the meaning of air and water pollution and other damage done by wind, water, or fire. With your group, take responsibility for improving an area by cleaning paths, checking erosion, reforesting, or some other project.

23. Explain what the Outdoor Living Skills Pledge means to you.

Outdoor Living Skills Level Four — Weather

1. Plan a two-night overnight with at least five meals (2 dinners, 2 breakfasts, 1 lunch). Make a list of personal and group equipment needed. Plan how to pack and carry the equipment. Consider the possible weather conditions and plan appropriately.

2. Go on a two-night overnight with at least five meals.

3. With at least one other person, pitch a tent or a tarp shelter.

4. With a group, plan a complete menu for a two-night overnight. Consider nutritional needs, demands of the activity, amount of food safe for consumption and minimum impact on the environment.

5. Demonstrate how to care for and cook on a camp stove for at least one meal. Prepare one meal using dehydrated foods and one other meal without cooking.

6. While on your camping trip, carry out a plan for washing and sanitizing your dishes and cooking utensils. If trash and garbage receptacles are not provided, discuss what garbage and trash may be disposed of at your site and what needs to be brought back for proper disposal. Minimum-impact camping should be discussed as part of this plan.

7. Discuss and demonstrate appropriate toilet practices for your area.

8. Discuss the kind of tools needed for your environment. Learn the use, care, safety, and storage of the tools you need. Consider their impact on the environment. Discuss when these tools are not appropriate for the environment.

9. As a group, write and sign an agreement about what each member has agreed to do to take responsibility for their own health and safety. Write this in the back of your *OLS Tracker.*

10. Explain how to treat insect bites, contact with poisonous plants, injuries from animals or snake bites, or other hazards common to your area. Practice any skills needed.

11. Plan first-aid procedures and individual and group supplies needed for an overnight trip. Identify items needed for a group first-aid kit and pack it.

12. Tie five basic knots and three hitches, and explain what they are used for. Discuss the type, size, use, and care of ropes used in your camp.

13. Learn three different kinds of lashing and their purpose. Dismantle and properly dispose of wood and twine when use is over. Discuss need, use, and impact on the environment.

14. Using a topographic or similar map, select a starting point and with a compass, orient the map, figure the bearing and distance to at least three points.

15. With a group, lay a compass course using five changes of direction. Identify bearings and distance at each change of direction.

16. Follow a compass course that another group has laid.

17. Identify the rules or steps you need to take to keep from getting lost and what to do if you are lost and cannot contact an adult. Develop and put on a skit for a younger group to help them from getting lost.

18. Discuss the relationship of plants and animals to each other in your ecosystem.

19. Discuss the food chain and how humans fit into the chain. Find examples of the parts of the food chain in your outdoor area.

20. Observing clouds, wind, and temperature, predict the weather daily for at least a week. Keep a chart of the cloud types, your predictions, and the actual weather in the back of your *OLS Tracker.*

Outdoor Living Skills Level Five — Stars

1. Plan a trip that has at least three nights of non-motorized travel. Make a list of personal and group equipment appropriate for the type of trip you are planning. Plan how to pack and carry the equipment. Consider the possible weather conditions and plan appropriately.

2. Go on a trip for at least three nights of non-motorized travel. Use shelter appropriate to terrain, weather and type of trip. Demonstrate the level of skill needed for the type of trip you're going on.

3. With a group, plan complete menus for your trip. Consider nutritional needs, demands of the activity, availability of water, the type of food needed for safe consumption and minimum impact on the environment.

4. Plan the fuel and/or cooking gear needed for the trip. Demonstrate how to use different cooking fuels safely.

5. While on your trip, carry out a sanitation plan that will have minimum impact on the environment. Include washing and sanitizing your cooking and eating utensils, personal hygiene, human and food-waste disposal.

6. Demonstrate proper toilet practices for your area.

7. Plan the tools needed for your trip. Demonstrate the use, care, safety, and storage of the tools you need. Explain their impact on the environment.

8. Review or write safety rules needed for your trip. Write out directions for getting emergency medical help while on the trip. Write this information in the back of your *OLS Tracker.*

9. Learn handling and care of a person with injury from an animal, poisonous plant, snake, and/or insect bite or sting when medical help is not readily available.

10. Explain the affects of heat, cold, and wetness on the body and explain how to recognize signs of problems in your own body and in those around you. Discuss when to alert an adult and what you can do.

11. Explain the common health or allergy problems and/or emergencies you may encounter on a trip, the first-aid skills needed to handle these, and plan and pack the first-aid supplies needed.

12. Explain the handling and care of a person with head or back injuries, broken bones, burns, sprains, or lacerations when medical help is not readily available.

13. Demonstrate a method of purifying a water supply for drinking and for cooking. Include ways that will make water safe from Giardia. Discuss and plan for appropriate trail sanitation.

14. Plan the type of ropes and knots you will need to use on the trip. Show you can tie the knots without any assistance.

15. Demonstrate use of compass, maps, charts, and/or navigational or trail markers used on your trip.

16. Explain how you would use emergency signaling to indicate you are lost, injured, or in need of food.

17. Discuss and practice minimum-impact camping skills while on your trip.

18. Discuss the ecosystem and food chain you see on your trip.

19. Practice weather forecasting while on your trip.

20. Evaluate what you have gained in completing these requirements and how your feelings toward the outdoor world have changed or intensified.

SKILLS	PROGRAM	
	Level 1 — Earth	Level 2 — Sun
On Your Way (planning an outing)	• Plan a ½-day hike. • Pack a day pack. • Go on a ½-hike. • Describe different kinds of shelters.	• Plan an all-day hike or overnight. • Go on an all-day hike. • Discuss clothing for your hike.
Being Safe (first aid, safety, environmental hazards)	• List safety rules for outdoors and hike and practice. • Identify where to go if sick or injured and practice. • Identify natural outdoor hazards and ways to avoid them. • Identify safe water and personal sanitation practices. • Identify and draw pictures of poisonous or harmful plants. • Identify bathroom.	• List safety rules for outdoors and practice while on hike. • Make poster showing buddy system, use system on hike. • Identify 3 problems caused to humans by plants, animals, and insects and how to avoid. • Draw picture or make poster showing animals, birds, insects in their natural environment and explain how to watch, protect and respect them. • Find sources of safe and unsafe water. • Discuss personal health practices in camp.
Being Prepared (use of tools and equipment)	• Demonstrate safe use of trowel, rake, paring knife, and peeler.	• List uses of pocket knife. • Demonstrate use and care of pocket knife. • Identify possible needs for saw. • Demonstrate use and care of saw.
Putting it on your plate (selection, storage, preparation of food)	• Plan a snack. • Pack a sack lunch. • Plan a snack that requires cooking outside. • Make a fire.	• Describe balanced meals. • Plan, prepare, and cook 1 meal. • Identify different heat sources for cooking. • Discuss safety. • Make fire and show different ways to provide heat for cooking.

PROGRAM		
Level 3 — Water	**Level 4 — Weather**	**Level 5 — Stars**
• Plan overnight trip needing 4 meals. Cook 2 of them. • Go on overnight using temporary shelters.	• Plan a 2-night overnight needing 5 meals. • Go on 2-night overnight trip with 1 other person using tent or tarp shelter.	• Plan a 3-night overnight trip. • Go on a 3-night overnight trip.
• Develop first aid kit. • Identify 3 things that might require first aid and how to prevent. • Identify contents of first aid kit and what contents are used for. • Discuss proper toilet practices for your area.	• Develop and sign individual/buddy health and safety agreement. • Learn how to treat insect, animal, snake bite and contact with poisonous plants. • Practice where applicable. • Plan first aid procedures and supplies needed for overnight. • Demonstrate proper toilet practices for your area.	• Review and write safety rules for overnight trip. • Learn affects of heat, cold, wetness on body; how to recognize problems; and what to do. • Learn common health or allergy problems, supplies and skills needed to treat in an emergency. • Learn handling and care of persons with head or back injuries, broken bones, burns, sprains, and lacerations. • Learn methods for purifying water and trail sanitization. • Demonstrate proper toilet practices for your area.
• Demonstrate use and care of pocket knife. • Demonstrate proper use and care of camp stoves.	• Identify tools needed for overnight. • Demonstrate use and care of tools. • Discuss when saws, axes and other tools are/are not appropriate.	• Identify tools needed for overnight. • Demonstrate use and care of tools. • Explain when saws and axes are/are not appropriate.
• Plan 4 meals. • Cook minimum of 3 meals with at least 1 on overnight. • Use 2 kinds of cooking fuel. • Plan and carryout sanitization of cooking utensils, dishes, trash, etc. • Demonstrate methods of care, storage, and protection of food from insects, animals, and spoilage.	• Plan complete menu for 5 meals. • Cook 1 meal on camp stove. • Cook 1 meal using dehydrated food. • Prepare 1 meal without cooking. • Plan and carry out sanitization of cooking utensils, dishes, and trash disposal.	• Plan complete menu for 8 meals. • Prepare appropriate meals for terrain, weather, and type of trip. • Plan and carry out sanitization of cooking utensils, dishes, trash, etc.

SKILLS	PROGRAM	
	Level 1 — Earth	**Level 2 — Sun**
Tying It Up (knots)	• Learn knots campers use most. • Demonstrate square, granny, and stopper knots.	• Learn and demonstrate joiner knot and 1 knot of choice.
Finding Your Way (map and compass)	• Demonstrate directions north, south, east, west. • Determine average length of a step and measure distances by pacing. • Locate a specific place on a map. • Discuss procedures for staying found. • Practice hug-a-tree.	• Demonstrate how to estimate heights without use of manufactured measuring tool. • Learn and demonstrate difference between highway map and topographical map. • Learn how to use a compass and demonstrate proper handling, direction finding. Identify things that can prevent compass from working right. • Discuss staying found.
Exploring Your World (understanding basic ecology, minimum impact camping, outdoor hazards, weather, etc.)	• Play a nature game that helps you understand ecology. • Clean up the site after lunch. • Using your senses of sight, touch, smell, and hearing, describe 10 things in your outdoor or camping area. • Describe what you eat and where it comes from. • Discuss what wildlife eats.	• Play 2 nature games that help you learn about ecology. • Describe what the word pollute means and identify 3 places that are polluted and why. • Describe what minimum impact camping means. • While camping or hiking, identify camouflaged animals and birds and describe how camouflage affects them. • Identify evidence of people in the area and make a list of things people can do to reduce impact on the environment. • Learn and recite the OLS Pledge.

PROGRAM

Level 3 — Water	Level 4 — Weather	Level 5 — Stars
Learn different kinds of rope and show how each is used in camp. Demonstrate proper care and storage of rope. Demonstrate how to prevent rope from unraveling. Tie 2 kinds of hitches and explain difference between knot and hitch.	• Tie 5 basic knots, 3 hitches, explain what they are used for and discuss. • Learn 3 different kinds of lashing and their purpose.	• Identify type of ropes needed for 3-night overnight. • Demonstrate tying knots and hitches without assistance.
Learn about the Big Dipper and use it to find the North Star. Learn about Cardinal Points, use to take a bearing and follow the bearing for 100 ft. Use a compass to make a simple map of an outdoor area. Learn how to read a map, identify north, the legend and 3 land marks.	• Using a topographical or similar map, select a starting point and identify at least 3 points. • With a group, lay a compass course using 5 changes of direction, identifying bearings and distance at each change. • Successfully follow a course another group has made. • Demonstrate rules for not getting lost and what to do if you get lost.	• Demonstrate use of compass, maps, charts and/or other navigational or trail markers. • Learn and demonstrate emergency signaling.
• Identify plants, animals, and insects that are harmful to people. • Design a skit to tell others about these problems. • Name 3 problems and identify warning signs of problems caused by weather, altitude, land or water movement. • Demonstrate how to be prepared for them. • Learn what ecosystem means and make a list of what you see at the campsite that is part of the ecosystem. • Learn the meaning of air, water and soil pollution. • Improve the campsite by cleaning paths, reforestation or similar projects. • Explain what the OLS Pledge means to you.	• Learn relationship of plants and animals in the ecosystem. • Learn the food chain and how you fit into the chain. • Find and describe examples of the food chain in the camp area. • Observe clouds, wind, and temperature and predict daily weather for 7 days. • Keep chart of observations and predictions.	• Record practices of minimum impact camping while on a trip. • Record observations of food chains, ecosystems and what you can do to preserve the environment. • Record weather forecasting while on trip. • Record feelings and knowledge about the outdoors.

Where to Go for More Information

There are many books, pamphlets, magazine articles and videos that can help you learn more about any outdoor topic you can think of. It would take much too much space to list them all so the following list represents only what seems to be the most well-known and easily available books concerning the outdoor living skills covered in this program. Most of these books are available from the Publications Department of the American Camping Association or from the youth agencies that produce them. In addition, most bookstores carry nature identification books.

Some of the books can be used for reference to several topics so be sure to look at the list carefully.

Chapters 1, 3, 4, and 5

American Camping Association. 1991. *Take a new bearing: Skills and sensitive strategies for sharing spiders, stars, shelters, safety, and solitude.* Martinsville, IN: American Camping Association.

Boy Scouts of America. 1990. *Fieldbook.* Irving, TX: Boy Scouts of America.

Cagle, Bob. 1989. *Youth ministry camping: A start to finish guide for helping teenagers experience the greatness of God's creation.* Loveland, CO: Group Books.

Coutellier, Connie (Compiler). 1980. *The Outdoor book.* Kansas City, MO: Camp Fire, Inc.

Ford, Phyllis and Blanchard, James. 1985. *Leadership and administration of outdoor pursuits.* State College, PA: Venture Publishing Company.

Girl Scouts of the USA. 1984. *Outdoor education in Girl Scouting.* New York, NY: Girl Scouts of the USA.

Hampton, Bruce and Cole, David. 1988. *Soft paths.* Harrisburg, PA: Stackpole Books.

Hart, John. 1977. *Walking softly in the wilderness.* San Francisco, CA: Sierra Club Books.

Johnstone, D. Bruce. 1986. *Guide to canoe camping.* Martinsville, IN: American Camping Association.

Mitchell, Dick. 1985. *Mountaineering first aid book.* Seattle, WA: The Mountaineers.

Narvey, Alex. 1989. *The Canadian canoeing companion.* Winnipeg, Manitoba, CN: Thunder Enlightening Press.

National Wildlife Federation. 1988. *Ranger Rick's wild about weather.* Washington, DC: National Wildlife Federation.

McNair, Robert; McNair, Mattie L.; and Landry, Paul A. 1985. *Basic river canoeing.* Martinsville, IN: American Camping Association.

Reifsnyder, William F. 1980. *Weathering the wilderness.* San Francisco, CA: Sierra Club.

Silva Compass Co. *Your way with map and compass, Map symbol relay game,* and *Beginner's compass game.*

Sumner, Louise. 1988. *Sew and repair your outdoor gear.* Seattle, WA: Mountaineers.

Vogel, Stephen and Manhoff, David. 1984. *Emergency medical treatment.* Oshkosh, WI: Recreational Products Marketing International.

Watters, Ron. 1982. *The white-water river book.* Seattle, WA: Pacific Search Press.

Wood, Robert S. 1982. *The 2 oz. backpacker.* Berkeley, CA: Ten Speed Press.

Chapter 5

Brown, Vinson. 1987. *The amateur naturalist's handbook.* New York, NY: Prentice-Hall.

Brown, Vinson. 1982. *Reading the outdoors at night.* Harrisburg, PA: Stackpole Books.

Brown, Vinson. 1983. *Investigating nature through outdoor projects.* Harrisburg, PA: Stackpole Books.

Cooperative Extension Service. 1985. *Birds, beasts, bugs, and us.* Ames, IA: Iowa State University.

Cornell, Joseph. 1989. *Sharing the joy of nature.* Nevada City, CA: Dawn Publications.

Cornell, Joseph. 1979. *Sharing nature with children.* Nevada City, CA: Dawn Publications.

Fadala, Sam. 1989. *Basic projects in wildlife watching.* Harrisburg, PA: Stackpole Books.

Hoessle, Kirk, and Van Matre, Steve. 1980. *Earthwalks.* Warrenville, IL: Institute for Earth Education.

Katz, Adrienne. 1986. *Naturewatch: Exploring nature with your children.* Reading, MA: Addison-Wesley Publishing.

Kennedy, Carolyn. 1981. *Exploring wildlife communities with children.* New York, NY: Girl Scouts of the USA.

Lawrence, Gale. 1984. *A fieldguide to the familiar.* Englewood Cliffs, NJ: Prentice-Hall.

Linglebach, Jenepher. 1986. *Hands-on-nature.* Woodstock, VT: Vermont Institute of Natural Science.

Miller, Lenore Hendler. 1986. *The nature specialist: A complete guide to program and activities.* Martinsville, IN: American Camping Association.

National Wildlife Federation. 1990. *Ranger Rick's Answer Book.* Washington, DC: National Wildlife Federation.

National Wildlife Federation. 1989. *The unhuggables: The truth about snakes, slugs, skunks, spiders, and other animals that are hard to love.* Washington, DC: National Wildlife Federation.

Rockwell, Robert E.; Sherwood, Elizabeth A.; and Williams, Robert A. 1986. *Hug a tree: Other things to do outdoors with young children.* Mt. Rainier, MD: Gryphon House.

Storer YMCA Camps. 1989. *Nature's classroom: A program guide for camps and schools.* Martinsville, IN: American Camping Association.

Van Matre, Steve. 1972. *Acclimatization.* Martinsville, IN: American Camping Association.

Van Matre, Steve. 1979. *Sunship earth: Getting to know your place in space.* Martinsville, IN: American Camping Association.

Van Matre, Steve; Johnson, Bruce; Soloway, Eddie; and Bires, Fran. 1989 *Conceptual encounters.* Warrenville, IL: Institute for Earth Education.

Chapter 6

Barker, Harriet. 1982. *Supermarket backpacker.* Chicago, IL: Contemporary Books.

Hefferon, Lauren. 1983. *Cycle food: A guide to satisfying your inner tube.* Berkeley, CA: Ten Speed Press.

McSherry ed.. 1987. *Pocket stew.* New Orleans, LA: Southeast Louisiana Girl Scout Council.

Perry, Rick. 1988. *Hurricane Kitchen.* Camden, ME: Yankee Books.

Prater, Yvonne and Mendenhall, Ruth D. 1982. *Gorp, glop and glue stew.* Seattle, WA: Mountaineers.

Reid, Chris. 1981. *AYH outdoor food book.* Pittsburgh, PA: Pittsburgh Council AYH.

Yaffe, Linda Frederick. 1989. *High trail cookery: All-natural, home-dried, palate-pleasing meals for the backpacker.* Chicago, IL: Chicago Review Press.

Chapter 7

Budworth, Geoffrey. 1985. *The knot book.* New York, NY: Sterling Publishing.

Cassidy, John. 1985. *The klutz book of knots.* Palo Alto, CA: Klutz Press.

Day, Cyrus L. 1953. *Knots and spices.* Camden, ME: International Marine Publishing Company.

Chapter 9

Brower, David Editor. 1971. *The Sierra Club wilderness handbook.* New York, NY: Ballantine Books.

Disley, John. 1967. *Orienteering.* Harrisburg, PA: Stackpole Books.

Hart, John. 1977. *Walking softly in the wilderness.* San Francisco, CA: Sierra Club Books.

Kjellstrom, Bjorn. 1955. *Be expert with map and compass.* New York, NY: American Orienteering Service.

Kjellstrom, Bjorn. 1976. *Be expert with map and compass.* 4th edition. New York, NY: Charles Scribner's Sons.

Merrill, W. K. 1965. *Getting out of outdoor trouble.* Harrisburg, PA: Stackpole Books.

The Mountaineers. 1960. *Mountaineering the freedom of the hills.* Seattle, WA: The Mountaineers.

Owendoff, Robert. 1964. *Better ways of pathfinding.* Harrisburg, PA: Stackpole Books.

Province of British Columbia. 1976. *Outdoor safety and survival.* Victoria, BC: Information Branch, Ministry of Forests.

About the Author

Phyllis Ford has been teaching outdoor-living skills for a lot of years. She has shared these skills with students at five universities: University of Iowa, Indiana University, University of Oregon, Michigan State University, and Washington State University. She has worked with practitioners at the Bradford Institute in Indiana, the American Camping Association National Conference, and National Parks and Recreation Association. She has trained staff and worked with campers in private camps, agency camps, and camps for special populations. Her work has touched the lives of children involved in the Girl Scouts of the USA, the YMCA, and the YWCA, in at least four states. Phyllis is the author of *Informal Recreational Activities: A Leader's Guide, Principles and Practices of Outdoor Environmental Education,* and the coauthor of *Camp Administration,* and *Leadership and Administration of Outdoor Pursuits.* She has contributed many times to *Camping Magazine,* the journal of the American Camping Association, and to other works on camping.